THE HOLOCAUST–
Final Judgment

THE HOLOCAUST–

Final Judgment

by
VICTOR H. BERNSTEIN

with an introduction by
MAX LERNER

The Bobbs-Merrill Company, Inc.
Indianapolis/New York

Author's Preface copyright © 1980 by Victor H. Bernstein
Published by the Bobbs-Merrill Company, Inc.
Indianapolis / New York
Manufactured in the United States of America

Library of Congress Cataloging in Publication Data
Bernstein, Victor Heine, 1904–
    The Holocaust—final judgment.
    Originally published in 1947 under title: Final
judgment.
    1. Nuremberg Trial of Major German War Criminals,
1945–1946. 2. Holocaust, Jewish (1939–1945) I. Title.
D804.G42B4 1980   940.54'05'0943   79-55440
ISBN 0-672-52624-7

This is Selma's book.

Acknowledgments

.... to John P. Lewis and Ralph Ingersoll, who made it possible for me to stay away from New York to write this book; to my hosts at the Nuremberg Press Camp and the Nuremberg Palace of Justice, who made it possible for me to work at Nuremberg; to the Charles Stubings, in whose friendly house this book was begun; to Edith Simon, Research Analyst on the U.S. Prosecution Staff, who found time above and beyond her own manifold duties to research and analyse nearly every word I wrote; to William Stricker, chief of DANA in Nuremberg for help in times of need; to Tom Dodd, U.S. Chief Trial Counsel and many good friends on Justice Jackson's staff and in the Subsequent Proceedings Division, whose brains I picked with shameless greed; to Max Lerner, who thought I should do this book in the first place; and to my wife, with whom and for whom I did.

Author's Preface

The last few years have witnessed a remarkable renewal of interest in Hitler's Germany. The media abound in dramas, documentaries, books, and magazine articles on the horrors of the camps, the rise of the party, psychological studies of torturer and victim, psychoanalyses of the Nazi leadership, the peculiarities of the German "soul" and *weltanschauung* that predisposed the Germans to the blessings of authoritarianism.

Does this reflect merely a heightened public morbidity induced by the violence of the times in which we live? Or a fresh and welcome stirring of the world's conscience? Perhaps a little of both. But perhaps there are also more mundane explanations. The Third Reich ended in 1945; a gestation period of thirty-odd years is not unusually long for the serious scholar producing serious work. Moreover, many hitherto classified documents (held secret for stipulated periods which vary from country to country) are now being opened to public scrutiny. Many camp survivors who needed years to regain some sanity have now reached a time when they can grope for the past, and record it, without unbearable pain. And even some of an older, guilt-laden German generation now find it profitable to recall their pasts—even if, like Albert Speer, they manage to find every German guilty but themselves.

Yet, in all this literary outpouring, a remarkable omission is to be noted. Not for years, to my knowledge, has there been produced a major work in which the Nuremberg trial itself has been a central factor. Yet it was the evidence produced at Nuremberg—the documents made available from German archives, the transcript itself—which is the ultimate fount of knowledge for almost all who have written about Nazism and the holocaust that was World War II (the best estimate indicates that 30 million were killed, including

v

battle and civilian casualties). For, what was unique about Nuremberg was that the defense itself provided the chief witnesses for the
prosecution. The defendants at Nuremberg were found guilty not by
the testimony of third parties, but by their own words, their own
documents, their own records signed, sealed and delivered to posterity with characteristic German meticulousness.

I think it fair to say that there is not a single serious work on
World War II and German guilt, with the exception of some purely
personal memoirs, that does not owe a debt directly or indirectly to
the evidence produced at Nuremberg. I think this alone justifies a
retelling of the Nuremberg story. And there are other equally cogent
reasons.

Time has given us the perspective necessary for a fair judgment of
the trial's successes—and failures. Surely, in terms of its immediate
purpose—the judging of the war-makers—Nuremberg was an indisputable success. Of the twenty-two major Nazis in the dock,
twenty—more than ninety percent—were convicted. And theoretically, at least, the trial established two important international legal
concepts: (1) the waging of aggressive war was affirmed as a criminal
act; (2) the principle of "superior order," i.e., that a subordinate
cannot be found guilty of criminality if he was simply following
military orders, was declared to be invalid as a defense.

The trial's failures? "Nuremberg was a promise for the future,"
Dr. Richard Falk of Princeton University wrote in the fall of 1979.
"Now, some 125 wars and many trillions of dollars' worth of arms
later, we realize that the Nuremberg promise has not been kept."
What he is saying is that the international legal concepts affirmed at
Nuremberg remain theoretical. In not a single instance of international conflict since 1945 has the world moved to hold anyone
juridically accountable. Nor has the world brought anything but
rhetoric to bear upon "subordinates" who have repeatedly, whether
under military orders or no, violated the conventions of war. "It is
obvious," notes Dr. Falk, "that the leaders of the main countries of
the world don't want to be reminded of the Nuremberg promise."
Nor will they want to be reminded as long as they continue to play at
deadly nuclear gamesmanship and wage or support "proxy" wars by
"clients" in Africa, Indochina, the Middle East, and elsewhere.

Do the Germans want to remember Nuremberg? The evidence is
ambiguous. German leaders are well aware that if more than ninety
percent of the ruling Nazi cadre put on trial at Nuremberg were
found guilty, more than ninety percent of subordinate Nazis—the
SA and SS and military men who actually did the shooting and
hanging and gassing in camps and in the countryside when hostages
were taken—have never even been brought to trial. Ostensibly, the
Bonn government is still searching for these criminals. Repeatedly,
the Reichstag has prolonged the statute of limitations with regard to
Nazi crimes; German archives are fat with criminal records; German
prosecutors are still at work preparing cases. But actual trials are few
and far between, and as time goes on—and witnesses die or
disappear—they become fewer. How many murderers walk as free
men along German streets today? The German people have flocked
to see the stage play, *Anne Frank;* they have watched *Holocaust* on their
TV by the millions. But apparently they cannot, or will not,
generate the public pressure necessary to cleanse their country, once
and for all, of the Nazi killers.

*   *   *

Max Lerner's introduction, which appeared in the original edition
of this book, is here reprinted without change. It is a tribute to
Max's talents as journalist, teacher and social historian that his views
of Nuremberg sound as fresh and relevant today as when he first put
them to paper.

The reader may ask: You wrote this book more than a generation
ago; is there not much that you want to change? My answer: no. The
text sticks closely to documentary evidence that only a handful of
unregenerate fascists (some of them, by the way, financed by American groups) has even attempted to challenge. Of the few editorial
comments I permitted myself, there are some that need altering, I
think. In places I have been too bland about the Russians *(Babi Yar*
and the *Gulag Archipelago* were then unsubstantiated by hard fact); in
some respects too hard on the Americans (the guilt of the Coughlin-
ites and the America Firsters weighed heavily upon me as an American); and not hard enough on some of our allies, notably the French
and British (movies like *The Sorrow and the Pity* and books like
Wasserstein's recent *The British and the Jews of Europe* were still far in

the future). Without in the least diminishing the guilt of the Nazis, Nuremberg also dramatized the guilt of a world and its peoples who, in ignorance, apathy or malice let tragedy overtake others before they found that they themselves could not escape.

A few years ago, journalists who had covered the Nuremberg trial were invited to a reunion in Warsaw. We met and reminisced, closing our assembly with a communique that read in part: "It was the conviction of the meeting that a full understanding of Nuremberg will assist in the struggle against trends in international policy which threaten world peace in the nuclear age."

Each of us who attended the meeting agreed, as individuals, that we would try to keep the promise of Nuremberg alive. I am indeed grateful to Bobbs-Merrill, and in particular to James Fisher, publisher, that they have made possible another edition of this book. It makes me feel that I have done what I could to fulfill the pledge I made to my own conscience and, at Warsaw, to my journalistic colleagues.

Victor H. Bernstein

New Milford, Conn.
1979

Table of Contents

Introduction

Using documents from German sources that have become available only in the past year, this book is a revealing X-ray of the whole political, economic, and moral system that the Nazis built up. It uses the Nuremberg trials as its starting point. But it peels away, one after another, the layers of meaning behind Nuremberg. Anyone who followed the reports of the trials in the American press must have been dismayed by their fragmentary and superficial character. All we got were bits and pieces of the Nazi story. Millions of words were, of course, cabled from Nuremberg by correspondents to the twelve corners of the world—especially in the first few days. But mainly they were color stuff, portraying the trial as a spectacle. There were pictures of the defendants and detailed accounts of their behavior in jail. There were excerpts from United States Prosecutor Robert H. Jackson's opening indictment, and some scattered debate on the international law at the basis of the trial. And at the end there was a sensational flare-up of think-pieces about how Goering managed to cheat the gallows by concealing his lethal poison. It is some kind of commentary on our press and our ways of thought that the most important trial of our era should have ended on the cheap note of a mystery thriller entitled *The Case of the Hidden Poison*. Nuremberg is still the Trial Nobody Knows.

In contrast with this surface stuff, Victor Bernstein has written an attack-in-depth on what the Nazis did, and the techniques they used, and what Nazism did to them. The book is a scalpel-dissection of the whole Nazi disease of which the Nuremberg criminals were only the more ulcerous outcroppings. As a good newspaperman—and he is one of the best I have ever encountered—the author does not omit the elements of personal drama. But he is also

—as every first-class newspaperman must be—a student of ideas
and social systems, and a human being sensitive to moral values.
That is why he has written not only a gallery of portraits of the
Nuremberg criminals, but an analysis of the outer predations and
inner impulsions of the Nazi system. He lays bare the meaning
of what the German nation did—a nation led by scoundrels and
sadists (but also ready for such leadership, terrorized by them)
but with hysterical undertones in its history that seemed to exult
in terrorism, indoctrinated by them but ripe for such indoctrination.

We have recently had a spate of now-it-can-be-told stories about
the Second World War. But the biggest story of all has up to now
been neglected — the story of how seventy million minds were
poisoned and seventy million hearts were hardened beyond human
recognition, and the deeds that the poisoned minds and the dehu-
manized hearts found it possible to do. Now is the time to tell
the Fascist story—the story of the men and the forces which turned
Europe into a cemetery and the human heart into a petrified forest.

Victor Bernstein is the right man to tell it. He was *PM's* correspondent at Nuremberg all through the weary months of the
trials. He came to his assignment wonderfully prepared for it.
He had covered Berlin during the years when Hitler was building
his power. He knew Germany—its language, its history, its politics, its people. He had followed closely the whole tragic course
of the diplomacy which failed to stop Hitler's aggressions and
prevent the war. As a war correspondent in Germany, he witnessed
the final collapse of Hitler's power, and saw the concentration
camps and the human furnaces which were its ghastly memorial.

And so, when the hidden Nazi documents began to turn up—
in Nazi headquarters overrun by American troops, or in the vaults
and salt mines in which they had been hidden—Bernstein knew
how to read them, what they meant, how they furnished the final
cement to the damning structure of evidence that had been built
up for over a decade. He has pieced it all together in this book:
how Germany rearmed for war even during the Weimar days, and
how Hitler and Goering and the Nazi generals speeded it up as
soon as they came to power; how Austria was betrayed from within
and conquered from without while Goering directed the psychological terror by telephone; the inner story of how the blow was
prepared for Poland and fell on it; the Nazi documents relating

to the assault on Norway to the north and Yugoslavia to the south; the top-secret *Case Barbarossa*, or military operational plan for the invasion of Russia, conceived even before the Nazi-Soviet Pact and prepared during it; the frantic Nazi efforts to draw Japan into the war and divert American attention from the European front.

But the diplomatic and military revelations are not nearly as important as the light that the captured documents shed on the Nazi treatment of its human victims. Here for the first time the material has been put together on how the Nazis planned and carried out the mass extermination of Poles and Russians through their *Einsatsgruppen*, or military-occupation genocide squads, and how (in the author's words) "Germany, seeking *Lebensraum*, created . . . the Death Space that is today's Europe"; how the Nazis planned and carried through, by assembly-line methods, the work of the extermination camps at Auschwitz, Treblinka, Buchenwald, Mauthausen, which turned millions of human beings into corpses, ashes, and their by-products; how German industrialists competed eagerly for the jobs of supplying the furnaces, and how German businessmen and officials grew rich on the "ghoul's gold" that was torn from the victims; how the Nazi idea for ridding Europe of all its Jewish humanity was conceived and matured and almost completely executed; how foreign slave labor was recruited for the German war machines, and how the Nazi officials carried on their Great Debate between the extermination plans and the needs of war industry for labor; how deeply the German generals were involved in the Nazi guilt, despite their later protestations of being merely neutral professional craftsmen; how the Nazi doctors and the "pure" scientists experimented on the living bodies of their victims.

These things are no longer a matter of guesswork. We have now the secret memoranda which the German generals kept with a German thoroughness—memoranda giving the General Staff discussions and Hitler's speeches to his lieutenants; we have transcripts of Goering's long telephone conversations; we have the Nazi military operational plans; we have memoranda that passed between the Gestapo leaders, the bureaucratic orders to the commanders of concentration camps, the business invoices and correspondence of the German corporations, the scientific write-ups of human experiments by Nazi professors. What is needed is no longer any supporting evidence; there is plenty of that. It is rather the will and intelligence to grasp the full meaning of a powerful evil and an evil power which beggar all historical parallels.

Many of the documents which the author cites were put into evidence at the Nuremberg trials. Some of them were not. It is to the author's great credit that he does not restrict himself, as the trials largely did, to the inhumanities of the political leaders of the Nazis. He brings the military in. He brings the men of science in. And, above all, he pays his full respects to the role played by men like Schacht, who got off free, and by other industrialists.

It is so terribly easy to forget what the Nazis did and were—and still are. I hope this book will jog our memory by laying bare the anatomy of Nazi evil, an evil which still exists in Germany today. For while the Nazi military power has been shattered, there has been no real effort to root out the Nazi ideas, or to destroy the power of the cartels, or to smash the potential rebuilding of the war machine. There has been no real effort to re-educate the German mind and heart. Such an effort would have to be a concerted one by the four Great Powers which today share the occupation of Germany. Yet they are too busy to make it—too busy wooing the Germans while jockeying for position in the struggle between East and West which darkens the horizons of the future.

The great result of Nuremberg was the creation of a new base for international law: the proposition that mass murder is no less murder because it is done on a vast scale; that when a state undertakes aggressive warfare, the men who conspire to that end and who carry it out and who commit the crimes against humanity involved in it will be punished as individuals. This is a vast stride forward—pitiable, perhaps, when compared with the human cost preceding it, but still a decisive step toward a body of world law.

We have now the machinery in the United Nations to prevent a repetition of the crimes portrayed in this book. We have the beginnings of a world law ready to punish them. What is lacking is the collective and cohesive will to use both—world law and the machinery for its execution. The author will have performed an immense service if this book can help to cement that will. He has written as a soldier of peace. I hope he will be read by many other soldiers of peace—in the schools, the colleges, the churches, the trade unions, the homes of America.

                                                    MAX LERNER

Part I

NOT PEACE
BUT THE WORD

Chapter I   November, 1945

1.

Justice Robert Jackson, chief of counsel for the United States, reads his opening speech quietly, almost without emphasis. He stands in the middle of the business end of the courtroom, his back to the press section and visitors' gallery. To his right, at their high bench, sit the members of the Tribunal—the four justices and their alternates. To his left is the dock, built like a jury box with tiered seats. Defense counsel sit at tables in front of the dock; the prosecution, at tables immediately behind Justice Jackson; court stenographers and clerks are ranged in front of the Tribunal bench.

"In the prisoners' dock sit twenty-odd broken men . . ."

Goering, in the dock's number one seat, shakes his massive head, his pale eyes fixed on Jackson's slight figure. The ex-Reich Marshal does not consider himself broken. He shows, indeed, immense vitality, and his expressive moon face is by turns defiant, cynical, appreciative. He is by far the most photogenic of the defendants, an extrovert and a skilled actor with a high IQ and the morals of a Renaissance prince. I am not surprised when, some weeks later, women correspondents attending the trial hold private caucus and vote him their overwhelming choice as bedmate among all in the dock.

3

The competition is not great, it is true. Hess, sitting in the number two spot, is really frightening to look at, the skin drawn drumtight around the skull bones, eyes under bushy black brows so deepset they are indeterminate shadows at the distance of a few feet. What goes on behind those eyes, no one knows. The claim is, almost nothing. He is supposed to be suffering from amnesia and in repose his face is that of a sleepwalker lifting himself from the cabinet of Dr. Caligari. But there is a flicker of consciousness somewhere within; occasionally he draws back his upper lip, showing large even-spaced teeth, and you suddenly realize he is smiling.

Ribbentrop, sitting next to Hess, looks indeed a broken man. Sparse gray hair crowns a thin face with sharp nose and small chin. There is about him an air of fright and of immense weariness; he walks as if he had been Hitler's foreign minister for a thousand years.

Farther along in the front row are Funk and Streicher, both short, chunky, and gross-featured, a pair of caricatures sprung full-blown from Streicher's own Jew-baiting newspaper, *Der Stuermer*. Schacht is in the first row, too; it is an honor he does not seem to enjoy very much. There is something of the catfish in the inverted U of his mouth and his goggly eyes. He wears an air of complete aloofness; he cannot understand what has happened that he, ex-president of the great Reichsbank, intimate of honored American and British and French figures in the banking world, should now find himself in the dock with criminals.

The rest of the faces are hardly worth recalling. Meet Jodl, Keitel, Doenitz, Rosenberg, Frank, Speer, Fritzsche under other circumstances, and you might be meeting a salesman, a physician, a lawyer, a real estate broker. Kaltenbrunner of the lantern jaw and Sauckel of the Hitler mustache, stand out a little; I've seen their type on "Wanted" posters in American post offices. But truthfully I've also seen it behind delicatessen counters and the small barred windows of a bank teller's cubicle.

"What makes this inquest significant," Jackson's quiet voice goes on, *"is that these prisoners represent sinister influences that will lurk in the world long after their bodies have returned to dust."*

Yes, of course. I look at the dock and think that it would easily be justifiable to populate hundreds like it with Americans alone, gangster Americans who might look like Kaltenbrunner, say, and very respectable Americans who might resemble the immaculate diplomat, von Neurath, or that other defendant, the solid citizen and respectable engineer, Speer. The charges against them would not be the same in fact, but they would be in principle; for, after all, what other difference is there between the German Fascist and the American, except that the former had the chance for a while to practice untrammeled what he preached?

"The United States does not desire to enter into discussion of the complicated pre-war currents of European politics, and it hopes this trial will not be protracted by their consideration. . . ."

That disembarrasses, so to speak, a lot of people. I look at Sir Geoffrey Lawrence, British Chief Justice of the Tribunal, owlish and Pickwickian behind glasses perched well down on his nose. Is he remembering, I wonder, that in 1935 his country entered into a naval agreement with Hitler and that three years later a handful of his countrymen were the leading spirits at Munich? I look at the American Justice Biddle, slim and beak-nosed, a miniature bald eagle hovering over the courtroom in search of some unwary fact or laggard legal point. Is *he* thinking that *his* countrymen—and yours and mine—raised not a hand to help the Spanish Loyalists who, long before anyone thought in terms of World War II, were trying to beat down that same *Luftwaffe* which Goering later hurled against London? I look at the professorial French Justice de Vabres; is he thinking back to the fascist rot and corruption within his own country that led naturally from putridity at Munich to dissolution at the Armistice of Compiègne? And I look at blond, impassive General Nikichenko, the Soviet justice, and I wonder what he is thinking. Is it, perhaps, that those who inveighed loudest against the Nazi-Soviet Pact of 1939 were precisely those who least supported Soviet pleas, during the preceding decade, for collective international action against fascism?

"Our position is that whatever grievance a nation may have, however objectionable it finds the status quo, aggressive war is

not a legal means for settling those grievances or for altering those conditions."

That's better, much better. A legalism, but also a magnificent and daring vision. A legalism, but also something revolutionary. For this time the guilty will not merely be pilloried in speeches and reviled in history books; this time the guilty will be punished like common criminals; someone armed with a gun, or a hangman's noose, or at the very least with a jail key, will *do* something with them. Strange how obvious it sounds now, how unheard of it was but a few years back!

A revolutionary trial, but a world not yet revolutionary enough to put itself in the dock alongside the accused. That is why there are only Germans in the dock, of course. And I see no reason, as I listen to Jackson's calm recital of the truly monstrous crimes he intends to prove against these Germans and this Germany, to beat my breast with a perfectionist's despair. We can at least learn the *what,* if not altogether the *why,* of fascism. And I have the feeling that if this trial is put carefully into proper light, as one adjusts a mirror, there will be more to see in it than Justice Jackson says he is putting in, including a few shadowy and unpleasant figures with more than a remote resemblance to ourselves.

"Unfortunately, the nature of these crimes is such that both prosecution and judgment must be by victor nations over vanquished foes. The world-wide scope of the aggressions carried out by these men has left few real neutrals. Either the victors must judge the vanquished or we must leave the defeated to judge themselves. After the First World War, we learned the futility of the latter course."

Futility is a mild word. After World War I, the Allies turned over a list of nine hundred Germans to the new Weimar Republic for trial as war criminals. The German courts at Leipzig called to trial twelve of these, found guilty six who were given light sentences which they never served in full. The rest got off scot free, some of them to fight again, for Hitler, in World War II.

The Allies warned the Nazis as early as 1943 that this time they would not have the chance to put on another such Leipzig fair. The Moscow Declaration of that year, signed by Roosevelt,

Churchill and Stalin, told the Germans that this time the victors would be the judges, that the lesser Nazi criminals would be tried in the countries in which their crimes had been committed, and that those whose crimes had no "geographic boundaries" would be tried by an International Military Tribunal.

But in 1943 the Nazis looked at their war map, which showed Europe still firmly in their grasp, and they laughed and laughed and shot another couple of hundred thousand Poles, Russians, and Jews. The victors would judge the vanquished indeed!

But of course there was nothing really funny about it, and the Allies went ahead steadily with their plans, both military and legal, and in accordance with agreements reached at the Yalta Conference and instructions issued by the late President Roosevelt, the U. S. A. formulated a proposed International Agreement on the trial of war criminals which was submitted during the San Francisco Conference to the foreign ministers of the United Kingdom, the Soviet Union and what was then the Provisional Government of France.

Subsequently, and after many modifications, this proposal became the Charter, or basic law, for the Tribunal which Jackson was now addressing.

"Less than eight months ago today the courtroom in which you sit was an enemy fortress in the hands of German SS troops. The law had not been codified, no procedures had been established, no Tribunal was in existence, no usable courthouse stood here, none of the hundreds of tons of official German documents had been examined, no prosecuting staff had been assembled, nearly all the present defendants were at large, and the four prosecuting powers had not yet joined in common cause to try them."

I had myself visited Nuremberg, city of the annual Nazi Party Congress, five months before. The courtroom was then a recreation center for an American anti-aircraft unit. The bench—not the new one now in use, but the original one ranged along the far wall—was a bar; a keg of beer and a pump stood upon it, and some GI canteens. Behind it were posted some *Esquire* and *Yank* pin-up girls, and there was a sign which read "Rupperts—One Mark." On the floor were small tables and folding chairs and in the corners the debris of a wartime army—spent shells, rags, K-ration remains, rusty cans, torn copies of *Stars and Stripes*. And over all the white powder-dust which rose, each time the wind blew, from the bomb-smashed center of the huge courthouse building and settled gently like a mantle upon everything within hundreds of yards.

In the intervening months this ramshackle, attic-like space has become the brilliantly-lit, magnificently equipped courtroom of today: the center, as Jackson intones his speech, of much of the civilized world. From my seat I can see the world's eyes peering down from glass-enclosed cubicles set into the walls and reserved for still and movie photographers; I can see the world's ears in the shining microphones set up in the radio cubicles; I can see the world's couriers seated all around me, scribbling busily—four hundred members of the press who would, for the first few weeks at any rate, flood the air and the cables with half a million words a day.

It is a complicated business from beginning to end. Everything that is read in open court—documents, affidavits, arguments—must be simultaneously translated into four languages. At each seat in the courtroom—including the bench, the dock, the press and visitors' gallery—there's a telephone headset and a small black dial numbered one to five. You turn the dial to No. 1, and you hear the speaker directly, in whatever language he is speaking. On No. 2 you hear, not the speaker directly, but a translation in English of what he is saying as he says it.

In similar fashion, you can follow proceedings in French on No. 3, in Russian on No. 4, in German on No. 5. Twelve interpreters are gathered behind a glass partition at a far corner of the room. I don't envy them. People always talk faster than they realize, and the yellow bulb before Chief Justice Lawrence keeps flashing on to indicate that proceedings are a little too fast, the interpreters can't keep up.

"We know [the Nazi party] *came to power by an evil alliance between the most extreme of the Nazi revolutionists, the most unrestrained of the German reactionaries and the most aggressive of the German militarists."*

That is a very neat summary, I think, and I reflect also that it is too bad there is not at least one additional pair of ears in the courtroom to hear it. Krupp von Bohlen, the only industrialist indicted before the Tribunal, is the perfect sample of the "most unrestrained of the German reactionaries." But old age and a paralytic stroke have saved him from the dock, and the Tribunal has ruled that it is too late, at this stage, to substitute another industrialist in his place. But Bohlen or no Bohlen, German Big Business is going to obtrude itself into the courtroom for months to come, sometimes with sensational results.

And, while speaking of Big Business, it is natural for one to think of labor. I glance towards the dock and regret for the first of many times that I do not see there the swaggering, bull-necked *schnapps*-sodden Robert Ley, who destroyed the German trade unions and impressed millions of workers into a gigantic scab outfit called the Labor Front. I used to see Ley in Berlin in 1938; he wore his bemedaled SA uniform with great swank and liked to tap a light wooden baton, which he always carried, against his glittering brown boots. A few weeks before trial opening, a prison guard glanced through the peephole of Ley's cell and saw the shiny boots hanging in midair, so to speak. The champion goon squad leader of all time had hanged himself from a toilet flush pipe with the edging of a GI towel.

"I should be the last to deny that the case may well suffer from incomplete researches and quite likely will not be the example of professional work which any of the prosecuting nations would normally wish to sponsor."

I know what you mean, Mr. Justice Jackson. This trial is going to produce some most peculiar phenomena. It is going to produce supposedly competent interpreters who think that the phrase *Freimachung des Rheins* refers to early Nazi plans for reoccupation of the Rhineland, whereas it really means nothing more sinister than the clearing of the Rhine for navigational purposes. It is going to produce translators who translate total misconceptions of the original German into a gibberish with only the remotest relation to English. It is going to produce some interrogators who never know what questions to ask, and some lawyers who never know what to do with the answers. It is going to produce any number of prosecution workers who will soon learn to prefer the bar of the Grand Hotel to the bar of justice; or, maybe, on the part of some sensitive souls, this will be less a matter of preference than of dire necessity.

And it has already produced, and will produce, more serious charges than that. People are saying, and will continue to say, that there should be neutral judges on the bench as well as victors; or that they should all be German judges; or that the defendants should never have been charged with conspiracy but only with murder, or not with murder but only with conspiracy, and certainly not with aggressive war; or that the trial is taking too long and lapses too often into almost unbearable dullness; or that, Charter or no Charter, there is no legal basis for the Tribunal and therefore for the whole trial, and that we should consequently shoot the defendants out of hand; or, perhaps, that we should set them free as an example of Christian magnanimity.

I leave all these questions to the critics. God knows there are enough of them. There is not a file clerk, a stenographer, a secretary who ever worked in the Nuremberg Court House, not to speak of the lawyers and newspapermen and visiting firemen from the Army and State Department and Military Government, who isn't convinced that whatever was done there could have been done better, and is ready to tell you how. Quite often they may be right, too.

"Above all personalities there are anonymous and impersonal forces whose conflict makes up much of human history. . . . No charity can disguise the fact that the forces which these Defendants represent, the forces that would advantage and delight in their acquittal, are the darkest and most sinister forces in society—dictatorship and oppression, malevolence and passion, militarism and lawlessness. By their fruits we best know them. Their acts have bathed the world in blood and set civilization back a century."

I think the disclosure of such forces, the revelation of the acts committed by them, are more important than the question of whether there should or should not have been a trial, or if so, of what kind. Justice Jackson does not use the word "fascist" in con-

nection with these forces: I think it would have been the right
word in the right place. In any case what is important is that we
know and understand what this Germany of Hitler's, which so
many people in our own country and in other lands so much ad-
mired and continue to admire and would attempt to emulate even
today, was really like.

So this book is neither an attack on the Nuremberg trial, nor
is it a defense. It is surely what is more important than either: an
attempt to tell the story of what the trial revealed.

2.

Justice Jackson delivered his opening speech on the second day
of the trial. The opening session, November 20, 1945, was devoted
to the reading of the indictment. It took four hours to read the
particulars of the four counts: crimes against peace (the waging
of aggressive wars which were also in violation of international
peace treaties and agreements); crimes against humanity, war
crimes, and conspiracy to commit the other three.

The indictment names twenty-four defendants and six organizations, but Krupp has been dropped at the last moment, Ley has
found his own way to judgment, Bormann has not yet been captured (it is not even certain that he is still living) and Kaltenbrunner, ill in his cell, will not put in an appearance for some
weeks.

So only twenty defendants respond when their names are called
to enter pleas of guilty or not guilty. They rise in succession from
their seats and slide past the knees of their co-defendants to reach
the microphone placed in front of the dock.

There is a brief exchange, first, between defense counsel and the
Tribunal; defense counsel wants to know whether the defendants
can make speeches in connection with their pleas. That's how it
is in German law, it appears. But Chief Justice Lawrence rules
that that isn't the law here, and counsel demand and get a brief
recess to confer with their clients. Then:

The Chief Justice: "I will now call upon the defendants to plead guilty or not guilty to the charges against them.

"Hermann Goering!"

Goering: "Before I answer the question of the High Court whether or not I am guilty—"

The Chief Justice: "I informed the Court that defendants were not entitled to make a statement. You must plead guilty or not guilty."

Goering: "I declare myself in the sense of the indictment not guilty."

The Chief Justice: "Rudolf Hess!"

Hess (with a great shout): "No!"

The Chief Justice: "That will be entered as a plea of not guilty. Joachim von Ribbentrop!"

Ribbentrop: "I declare myself in the sense of the indictment not guilty."

"Wilhelm Keitel!"

"I declare myself not guilty."

"Alfred Rosenberg!"

"I declare myself in the sense of the indictment not guilty."

"Hans Frank!"

"I declare myself not guilty."

"Wilhelm Frick!"

"Not guilty."

"Julius Streicher!"

"Not guilty."

"Walter Funk!"

"I declare myself not guilty."

"Hjalmar Schacht!"

"I am guilty in no respect."

"Karl Doenitz!"

"Not guilty."

"Erich Raeder!"

"I declare myself not guilty."

"Baldur von Schirach!"

"I declare myself in the sense of the indictment not guilty."

"Fritz Sauckel!"

"I declare myself in the sense of the indictment, before God and the world and my people, not guilty."

"Alfred Jodl!"

"Not guilty. For what I have done, or had to do, I have a pure conscience, before God, my conscience and my people."

"Franz von Papen!"

"I declare myself not guilty at all."

"Arthur Seyss-Inquart!"

"I declare myself not guilty."

"Albert Speer!"

"Not guilty."

"Konstantin von Neurath!"

"I answer the question in the negative."

"Hans Fritzsche!"

"As regards this indictment, not guilty."

At this point the irrepressible Goering rises again at his seat in the dock. He still wants to make his speech. We learn later he wants to say that he is perfectly willing to stand trial before a German court, but not before this International Military Tribunal, never, never. But the court rules again that speeches are out of order at this point and Goering sits down, grinning. He thinks he has succeeded in making a martyr of himself. Hasn't he proved the Tribunal's unfairness in not permitting him to talk?

In point of fact, when it is his turn to speak, he gets nine days in the witness stand to present his case—twice as long as any other co-defendant, and twenty times as long as any opponent ever got from *him*.

I am thinking of that as, at the end of the session, we all rise and the justices file out of the courtroom. I watch Goering rise and see his pale eyes follow the blackrobed masters of his fate. And I wonder if he is thinking of that other trial twelve years ago, the Reichstag fire trial, when he was over on the other side of the room and everybody rose for *him*.

Whatever he is thinking, his face shows nothing. His hands smooth out the wrinkles in the loose front of his mauve military-type tunic—his girth has shrunk with his reputation—and he turns and follows little Raeder out through the door at the back of the dock which leads to prison and his low iron cot..

"Not guilty in the sense of the indictment." Then in what sense are they admitting their guilt? Nobody knows, for certain, and no one bothers to ask. Perhaps it's just as well. The phrase, it appears, was invented by Goering or Rosenberg out of some obscure feeling that if they *were* guilty, it wasn't for this Tribunal to find them so, because this Tribunal was illegal; and, anyway, it was ridiculous for the indictment to charge them with conspiracy, because whatever they did that may have been naughty was done on the spur of the moment or on orders from above, and if they were indeed bad boys, they never really *meant* to be.

In any case, before this Tribunal, the defendants plead not guilty.

Down the corridor from the courtroom is the huge multigraph room. I swear I can hear the machines revolving with laughter. They are turning out copies of original documents, orders; minutes of meetings, memoranda, diaries, all captured on German soil by invading Allied armies, many of them marked "top secret," most of them signed by one or another of the defendants—and all of them damning.

The story the trial tells, and essentially the story I tell, is the story told by these documents.

Chapter II   October, 1946

1.

The documents hanged ten, drove another to suicide, led seven more to prison terms ranging from ten years to life. Three others went free.

It took two days for the Tribunal to deliver its lengthy final judgment. The first day was devoted to the legal opinion and the verdicts on the indicted organizations. On the second day, in the morning, the defendants heard the verdicts: "... the Tribunal declares Hermann Goering guilty on all four counts of the Indictment."

And on the second day, in the concluding afternoon session, the sentences: "Hermann Goering . . . death by hanging."

To those of us who had watched the trial from the beginning, the Day of Judgment was more than melodrama, more than a headline for the day. As stirring as it was emotionally, it was also a triumph—by no means complete, but nevertheless a triumph—of man-made justice operating in hitherto uncharted legal spheres.

From now on, aggressive war is not only a crime, but a crime punishable upon the flesh and blood of its instigators. It is no longer an excuse for a criminal that he has killed not one man, nor two, but millions. It is no longer the warmaker's privilege that his sole judge shall be the historian who, coming upon the scene ten, twenty, fifty years too late, can but beat a dead dog. From now on the warmaker can be punished *today*, like any other common murderer.

We think of this as we watch the defendants emerge one by one, on the afternoon of that second day, from the door at the back of the dock, and listen singly to their doom. We see how the earphones go dead on Goering, first to appear, and the minutes seem to crawl around the courtroom with small, rustling sounds until the apparatus is fixed and Chief Justice Lawrence, after one false start, begins again: "The International Military Tribunal sentences you . . ."

We watch the living skull that is Hess shake violently from side to side as he spurns the earphones; he stands unhearing and uncomprehending while his sentence is read and no one knows whether those dark eyes are burning with memories of a distant and glorious past or with the wild fire of the insane. We watch Ribbentrop, so unutterably weary he cannot even fully lift his eyelids, but must observe the Tribunal with head thrown back and resting against the wall behind him. We watch Keitel and Jodl, the soldiers turned murderers; we watch the pale Rosenberg, the leering Sauckel, the half-grinning Frank (greatest actor of them all), and the small round figure of Funk, the ugly little gnome whose lower lip droops sadly as with the taste of perpetual but invisible tears.

And we note how each, in his turn before the Tribunal, finds somewhere the strength to throw back his shoulders and make rigid his spine, as if in desperate effort to stand erect before the ultimate judgment of history. But to those of us to whom this day is only the climax of many, the effort is not impressive. Because we see also, as we watch the defendants, the mounds of the dead and maimed upon which they had once climbed to eminence, and we cannot find it in our hearts to weep now that they must climb just a little higher to reach the gallows.

A fortnight later the Reich that was to last a thousand years ends, in its thirteenth year, with a series of brief tableaux upon two modest stages, each thirteen steps high and eight feet square, erected in a corner of Nuremberg prison. But Goering cheats the noose. Just before the hangings begin, he is found on his cot, his huge body jerking in death spasms, bits of glass clinging to his teeth and on his breath the smell of bitter almonds.

To millions of Germans, the smell of bitter almonds was as the fragrance of laurel, ancient symbol of victory. *"Unser Hermann,"* they whispered, "he has won again."

2.

Eleven months elapsed between the opening of the trial and the opening of the trap doors. No one can charge that the Tribunal was precipitate. The defendants had their day in court, even as they had had in life. Indeed, one could say that with the exception of the annual Party Day, held in this same city in the not-so-long ago, rarely did so many illustrious Nazis have the time to gather in one place to make so many Nazi speeches.

The prosecution knew that the defense was using the witness box as a soapbox, but could do nothing about it. I want to cite from the minutes (which I obtained from private sources) of one of the regular Chief Prosecutors' meeting at which procedures and united strategy were agreed upon. This meeting took place April 5, 1946, and in attendance were Chief Prosecutors Robert Jackson for the U.S.A., Sir Hartley Shawcross for the United Kingdom, M. Champetier de Ribes for France and General R. H. Rudenko for the U.S.S.R. I quote verbatim:

Shawcross: "According to the present estimate, the trial will last until the end of August. The Prosecution has tried to expedite this, but the Tribunal has not cooperated."

Jackson: "The Court has not adopted one of our suggestions to expedite this trial, although we have made many. The strange thing is that the Judges have privately and individually commended these suggestions but collectively they have rejected them."

Rudenko: "I agree with Shawcross that another application to the Court should be made. The examinations by Defense Counsel are too long. Keitel, for instance, spent a long time on the stand and then offered an affidavit covering very briefly all the points

he had taken so long to discuss orally. Rosenberg wishes to submit
800 pages of documents, more than 300 of which are on philo-
sophic matters. . . ."

De Ribes: "I agree with everything that has been said. We must
do all possible to shorten the trial, but it is up to the Court."

Jackson: "If the Court knew what the defendants say among
themselves—and it will be printed some day—it would feel differently. For instance, Goering told Ribbentrop that if he wanted
to get away with a long spiel the way he (Goering) had, he should
make his story *interesting*. The fault, as Rudenko says, is lack of
decisiveness in the Court. Lord Lawrence admitted that Goering
had been permitted to make speeches for three days. . . ."

On the whole, Defense Counsel did not help to speed matters.
Partly this was because the court procedure was unfamiliar to
them, but also because many among them had no wish to speed up
anything, most particularly the course of justice. Of the more than
thirty counsel and their assistants, nearly a score were acknowl-
edged Nazis. The surprise is that there were not more, for before
ever the trial began, Jackson had said defendants would have a
free hand to choose their lawyers. "We'll take them out of prison,
if it's necessary," he had said.

And indeed, on the very day that the defendant von Papen
went free, his son, who had been assisting in his father's defense,
was returned under guard to a prisoner of war camp.

Yet even among Defense Counsel, there were a few who clearly
had no stomach for their jobs. It was quite obvious that Dr. Hans
Marx, counsel for Streicher, detested his client; but, then, almost
everyone else in the courtroom did, too, including Streicher's colleagues in the dock. And even Dr. Thoma, counsel for that fuzzy
philosopher Rosenberg (of whom Jackson said that his writings,
in addition to other sins, had the supreme one of boredom) at
one point revolted. "Stop," he whispered (audibly because his
mouth was near the microphone) to his assistant, who had been
handing him excerpts from Rosenberg's *Myth of the Twentieth
Century* for reading into the record. "Stop handing me that philosophical crap!" The German word used was *Dreck*.

Defense Counsel on the whole was thoroughly enamored of

oratory, philosophical or otherwise, and there were few who could not best even their clients in getting wordage into the record. Poor Dr. Stahmer, however, tall and distinguished with his silver hair and black robe, was up against stern competition indeed— his client was the formidable Goering. I once clocked a rambling Stahmer question at eight minutes, but Goering easily maintained supremacy by taking ten to answer.

Now, when I look back upon the trial, it is difficult for me to recapture whole months of memory. During this period the voice of prosecution and defense, of witness and defendant, merge into a low murmur, meaningful as the sound of the sea is meaningful, but equally as impossible to divide into its component parts. But two vivid impressions remain against this background of indeterminate sound.

The first is fixed in its setting, bounded by space and time. On a November afternoon the courtroom goes dark, and now there are only the security footlights, attached to the inner base of the breast-high partition behind which the defendants sit, shining upwards into their faces. We in the press gallery see only profiles, because the faces are turned towards the small moving picture screen at one end of the room; all the faces, that is, except the round and pouting Schacht's, which stares back at us unblinking. Schacht has deliberately turned his back towards what everyone else is watching.

The film begins with affidavits showing that what we are to see is an authentic documentary of German concentration camps. The camp at Leipzig is first; and then we see Penig and Nordhausen and Hadamar and Dachau and Belsen and Mauthausen and Buchenwald and half a dozen more. And they are all alike, for the impression we get is an endless river of white bodies flowing across the screen, bodies with ribs sticking out through chests, with pipestem legs and battered skulls and eyeless faces and grotesque thin arms reaching for the sky.

To many of us in the press gallery, these bodies are no strangers. We have seen them before and also smelled them, and it is queer how many of us imagine we smell them again, though they are only two-dimensional now, a trick of light and shadow.

I look at the prisoners' dock and Schacht seems to be staring back at me, his back still to the screen. I can almost see him washing his hands, like Pilate, before his small paunch. Streicher is leaning forward, drinking avidly of murder and torture. I see Keitel with handkerchief to his face; is he crying, or has it made him uncomfortably warm, this reminder of his Germany when it —and he—were strong?

And now on the screen we see German civilians prodded by American soldiers through the doorway of a charnel house, and we see them come out again with handkerchiefs pressed close to their noses, their heads down and their shoulders hunched as if they would make themselves so small no one could ever see them again. And here a woman comes out, crying and beating her palms together, and behind her comes a man shaking his head and beating his breast.

I think back on the evidence presented during the morning session of the trial and I remember what Goering had said to Ribbentrop by phone on the day following the Nazi rape of Austria:

"We have a clear conscience," Goering had said, "and that is the decisive factor. Before world history we have a free conscience."

I look swiftly at Goering and Ribbentrop, who sits next but one to him, and the men with the "free conscience" look at the bodies on the screen, and one cannot tell anything from Hermann's fat face, but Ribbentrop looks more pale and drawn than ever and his small chin has disappeared altogether.

On the screen there is no end to the bodies, tumbling bodies and bodies in mounds, and single bodies with holes between the eyes, and bodies being shoved over cliffs into common graves, and bodies pushed like dirt by giant bulldozers, and bodies that are not bodies at all, but charred bits of bones and flesh lying upon a crematory grate made of bits of steel rail laid upon blackened wooden ties.

Now another body is shoved over a cliff into an open ditch by a bulldozer which the British called into use because there were so many dead lying around they were a menace to the living. And this body is not quite buried by the dirt, and it shines white here and there, a bony leg sticking out and one arm outstretched.

The film fades and the lights go on for recess and we sit quietly for a moment, and so do the defendants, which is unusual, because ordinarily they begin talking at once to each other and to their attorneys. But this has been a hard day for them. In the morning they won an ignoble war against Austria, won it by deceit and threat and the ignobility of certain Austrians and certain people in other lands. But in the afternoon they were reminded of the ultimate fruit of their victories.

Only Schacht, his back still to the screen, seemed unaffected. He had seen nothing, heard nothing, said nothing. How wise of him! Today he is a free man.

3.

My other impression is less concrete, more dynamic, a sense of movement in time rather than in space . . . a sense of a river traversing time, broadening, deepening, rushing swifter and swifter until all at once it breaks its banks and with calamitous force plunges upon the civilized world.

Thus did the Brown River threaten us all. And as I look back upon the trial, I can recognize its headwaters in the past; I see the small, sinister streams flowing through the Weimar Republic; I see them joining as Hitler came out upon the balcony of the Reich Chancellery on that memorable night of January 30, 1933, the new master of Germany; I see the subsequent course of the terrible waters, flooding first the homeland and then breaking out upon the Continent.

The prosecution did better than it knew. It sought to indict twenty-one men and six organizations; it succeeded in convicting, if not legally then historically, a system, a way of life, the great evil of our time: fascism.

This is the picture that the incredible documents which were presented at Nuremberg—many among them seen previously by no more than a dozen men in the world, and some by no more than three—slowly built up for me in the course of nine months. It is the picture which, in the following pages, I am going to try to rebuild for you.

Chapter III   Weimar

1.

First, a bit of history.

The German revolution died aborning in 1918. The victorious Allies never gave it a chance. So it was Friedrich Ebert instead of Karl Liebknecht and Rosa Luxembourg, the Weimar Republic instead of a German Soviet; and units of the German Army, which the day before had been the bitter enemy, were permitted to kick our former ally, the Russian Army, out of the Baltics.

Everyone breathed easier, especially the victorious Allies. The Weimar Constitution was a noble document, in the finest traditions of Western democracy. Its administration was in the hands of sound men, liberal enough to seem the antithesis of that Kaiserism and Junkerism which we had learned to hate and fear, conservative enough to secure Germany from bolshevism. The German Navy and its dread U-boats were gone, sunk at Scapa Flow. A uniquely underseas navy, indeed! Certainly there was nothing more to fear from the German Army, reduced to 100,000 men and only enough armament for internal policing duties. And as for the ex-Kaiser's Imperial General Staff, there was nothing left of it but a handful of *déclassé* aristocrats wandering aimlessly around their Berlin ministries, clad in splendid uniforms and with nothing more deadly in their hands than briefcases.

Yes, of course, there was trouble now and then. When the Germans failed to deliver their pledged quantity of coal, the Allies had to occupy the Ruhr; for the French, that was a pleasure. Allied inspection teams, commissioned to see that German factories did not violate the disarmament terms of Versailles, sometimes reported that funny things were going on, but no one took these vague reports seriously. There were rumors of a "Black Reichswehr," an illegal army, in training; but the function of this army seemed restricted to knocking Communists on the head. It would be silly to discourage such activity, wouldn't it?

Then, of course, there were speeches by many Germans against the harshness of Versailles. Fellow named Schacht, for instance, way back in the twenties, was demanding return of Germany's colonies. But Schacht was a good fellow, sound, conservative, with lots of friends in the City and in Wall Street. Maybe he had something, at that. Or maybe it was just home consumption stuff, or a bargaining point. Anyway, no need to worry.

Fellow named Hitler? In Hyde Park or Union Square you could hear 'em louder and crazier any day in the week.

These small unpleasantnesses did not make the Allies wary. Quite the contrary, they created sympathy. After all, Germany was too big to be kept down permanently. Europe needed her industry; Britain and America needed her trade, and all the Western World needed her friendship against the growing Communist Colossus of the East.

So there were debt moratoria and further loans to the sound Schacht and growing talk of the wrongs of Versailles and growing sympathy for the hard-pressed people of this lovely Germany, Europe's bastion against bolshevism, land of Goethe and I. G. Farben, of Beethoven and Blohm-Voss Shipyards, of Kant and Krupp, of culture and cartels.

2.

Harmless fuddy-duddies, briefcases in hand, wandering aimlessly through the corridors of the War and Navy Ministries, playing at being admirals and generals of a sunken navy and a stripped army. One could almost feel sorry for them.

What was in their briefcases?

I have before me one of the first documents presented at Nuremberg, comprising extracts from a book titled *The Fight of the Navy Against Versailles*, published by the High Command of the German Navy in 1937 for circulation among restricted military and government circles only. I quote from its page of contents:

"1. First defensive action against the execution of the Treaty of Versailles (from the end of the war to the occupation of the Ruhr in 1923); saving of coastal guns from destruction; removal of artillery equipment and ammunition; limitation of demolitions in Heligoland Naval Base.

"2. Independent armament measures behind the back of the Reich Cabinet and of the Legislature (1923-1927); attempt to increase the personnel strength of the Navy; contribution to strengthening of patriotism among the people; building up of the Air Force; preparation for the resurrection of the German U-boat arm; economic rearmament.

"3. Planned armament works tolerated by the Reich Cabinet, but behind the back of the Legislature (1928 to the seizure of power in 1933).

"4. Rearmament under the leadership of the Reich Cabinet in camouflaged form (1933 to the freedom from restrictions in 1935)."

The old fuddy-duddies in the Navy Ministry were, among other things, secretly building one U-boat for Spain and another, a 250-ton specimen, for Finland. They were perfecting techniques for the rapid assembly of U-boat parts. They were developing a new electric torpedo and training U-boat personnel both in Finland and in Spain. And in Germany itself they organized a U-boat school which was blandly disguised as an *anti*-U-boat school.

I skip to another document, this one marked "Top Secret": an order issued by the Chief of the Naval High Command in 1932 which illustrates the high-class technique applied by the Germans to the important business of breaking treaties invisibly:

"*Subject*: Torpedo-Armament of E-Boats.

"In view of our treaty obligations and the Disarmament Conference, steps must be taken to prevent the First E-Boat Half-Flotilla ... from appearing openly as a formation of torpedo carriers. I therefore order:

"1. Boats E2 to E5 will be commissioned in the shipyard without armament and will be fitted with easily removable cover sheet metal in the space necessary for torpedo tubes.

"2. The torpedo tubes of all these boats will be stored in the Naval Arsenal for immediate fitting. During the trial runs the torpedo tubes will be taken on board one after the other for a short time to be fitted and for practice shooting, so that only one boat at a time carries torpedo armament. For public consumption, this boat will be in service for the purpose of temporary trials by the Technical Research Bureau."

This order was signed by Raeder, the sour little man with the puckered face who sat next to his fellow navy man, Doenitz, in the second row of the dock.

Hitler came to power in January, 1933. By September of that year there was ready for him an inventory, as it were, of the chicaneries practiced by the German Navy since the day the ink was still wet on Versailles. The document, entitled "Survey List" and marked *Most Secret*, is set up in three columns headed respectively *Measures, Details,* and *Remarks*. Entries include the number of guns, mines, etc., built beyond the number permitted by treaty, the storing of guns which should have been destroyed, the illegal arming of fishing vessels and minesweepers and the details of arrangements with a dozen industrial firms for the production of such forbidden armament items as mechanized detonators and flak shells. Included also as an industrial item is the undertaking of "mass production of engine types essential for war purposes, holding ready the tools, machinery and materials so that the time required for starting work may be shortened."

Notes entered in the *Remarks* column made especially interesting reading at the trial. For example:

"*Measure*: Construction of U-boat parts. *Remarks*: Difficult to detect. If necessary can be denied.

"*Measure*: Arming of Mine Sweepers. *Remarks*: The reply to any remonstrance against this breach: the guns are taken from the Fleet reserve stores, have been temporarily installed only for training purposes. All nations arm their mine-sweeping forces. (Equality of Rights).

"*Measure*: Arming of fishing vessels. *Remarks*: For warning shots. Make little of it."

No one ought to be in a better position, surely, to know what the German Navy was doing between January 10, 1920, when the Treaty of Versailles went into effect, and March 16, 1935, when its naval terms were supplanted by the terms of the Anglo-German Naval Pact, than Vice-Admiral Assmann, a member of the historical section of the German Admiralty.

"But," the historian wrote in a revealing essay on naval operations introduced by the prosecution, "in nearly all spheres of armament where the Navy was concerned, the Treaty of Versailles was violated in the letter and all the more in the spirit—or at least its violation was prepared—a long time before the 16th March, 1935. . . . This probably took place in no other sphere on the one hand so early and on the other hand under such difficult circumstances as in the construction of a new submarine arm. The Treaty of Versailles had only been in force a few months when it was already violated on this point."

Called to the stand, Raeder readily admitted that Assmann was a particularly reliable historian.

No, there never was any need to feel sorry for the supposedly humbled survivors of the Imperial General Staff. They were never humbled. They came home from Versailles with hearts full of deceit and briefcases full of schemes for violating the agreements their government had just signed.

And this illegal rearmament, in the words of navy men themselves, was carried out "with the tacit approval of the Reich Cabinet," at least beginning with 1928. And these were Cabinets of the Weimar Republic, it must be remembered—the Cabinets of the respectable Bruening as well as the tainted Governments of von Papen and Schleicher.

A republic which, whether through ignorance or malice, fails to discipline its military into obedience to its own pledged international word, is no longer a republic. It is a military dictatorship ruled by men in uniform for whom the people have never had the chance to vote. And it was behind this façade of Weimar Republicanism that the military part of the Unholy Alliance—militarism, reaction, nationalism—which was to create Hitler's fascist state, gathered the strength necessary for the tasks ahead.

3.

But guns are not made with schemes alone. Wheels must turn. And in the Ruhr, in Silesia and Saxony, in and around Frankfurt, Stuttgart and the North Sea cities, were Germany's giant industrial wheels ready for turning and Germany's giant industrialists ready to turn them.

I have before me two documents, the first of which was never introduced at Nuremberg at all and the second only partially. The prosecution considered them largely irrelevant because no industrialist sat in the dock. But they are very relevant indeed to the broad picture I am trying to build.

One document is a memorandum prepared by German Army Ordnance *(Heereswaffenamt)*, marked *Secret Command Matter* and dated January 16, 1926—seven years before Hitler came to power and nine years before Germany's first *overt* breaking of Versailles through the remilitarization of the Rhineland. I quote briefly:

"Preparations for industrial mobilization demand trustful cooperation between industry and leading military authorities. For well-known reasons there is no possibility for official cooperation such as our enemy nations have organized. [*Obviously a reference to Versailles; and the reference to* "enemy nations" *six years after the signing of the Peace Treaty is a characteristic note.*]

"After several attempts at cooperation with industry which did not attain the desired aim, we have now succeeded in bringing together, for our purposes, the prominent members of the Reich Association of Industry into a Statistical Association *(Statistische Gesellschaft)*."

The Reich Association of Industry is roughly the equivalent of the National Association of Manufacturers in the U.S.A.

The second document is a secret history of German rearmament by General Georg Thomas, who held high post under Hitler as a war production specialist, in which this Statistical Association is called "an organization of a philanthropic nature, established ostensibly to gather statistical and technical data for interested persons . . . but the real purpose . . . was to procure data required by Army Ordnance on armament production potential." And Thomas added: "In this connection it was essential that participation of military circles or other such authorities should under no circumstances be revealed to the outside world."

To complement the work of the Association, the German Army Office of Supply hired a number of World War I veterans who had since gone back into industry, gave them the title of "Economic Officers," and sent them out to inventory every sizeable factory in the nation for its war production potential. Within a very few years the pertinent military authorities in Berlin had at their disposal:

1. A card index of all important data on each plant that made the plant important for armament, together with notes on production assignments in case of war.

2. A card index for swift location of every machine important for armament, such as revolver-lathes, turning lathes, rifling machines, automatic machines, boring machines, forges, specialty machines.

In his secret history, General Thomas described the extraordinary degree of secrecy with which the work of the Association and of the Economic Officers was carried on, and commented:

"To this strict maintenance of secrecy must be ascribed credit for the success achieved when, during Germany's later open rearmament, the world was surprised at her instantaneous procurement of the most modern equipment produced on a mass-production basis.

"When Reich Chancellor Bruening was reproached, in Paris, for a long series of 'violations' of the Versailles Treaty, the Allied

Powers were not in a position to prove a single case of preparation in the field of armament economy."

Indeed, fooling the Allies became a national pastime in Germany. In 1942 Krupp boasted openly in his house organ, a copy of which is on file at Nuremberg:

"I wanted and had to maintain Krupp, in spite of all opposition, as an armament plant for the later future, even in camouflaged form. . . . Thus to the surprise of many people, Krupp began to manufacture goods which really appeared to be far distant from the former works of an armament plant. Even the Allied snooping commissions were duped. Padlocks, milk cans, cash registers, track repair machines, trash carts and similar small junk appeared really unsuspicious and even locomotives and automobiles made an entirely 'civilian' impression."

Krupp manufactured his first tank in 1928, having first begun with the study of "heavy tractors."

So Big Business with its pots and pans and the General Staff with its innocent briefcases were walking together along the road to war. Hitler was waiting for them around the corner.

4.

The documents collected in Nuremberg, whether used in the courtroom or not, fall into logical place in the known history of the Weimar Republic.

The familiar platform of the Nazi party made good reading for German industrialists and the militarists.

It demanded the abrogation of Versailles and St. Germain (the treaty which had created an independent Austria); it demanded equality of rights with other nations (i.e., expansion of the German armed forces and the right openly to resume munitions-making); it demanded "unification of all Germans in the Greater Germany," it demanded "land and colonies for the sustenance of our people," it opposed "corrupting parliamentary economy" and urged creation of an all-powerful central government.

For the militarists, bigger and better armies, bigger and better weapons; for industry, expanding production, expanding markets; what more could one ask?

There were, it is true, a few points in the platform calculated to disturb the sound, conservative businessman. The total confiscation of all war profits, for instance. This sounded ominous, but did Hitler really mean it? We shall see that he did *not*.

And Point 17 in the platform:

"We demand a land reform suitable to our needs, provision of a law for the free expropriation of land for the purposes of public utility . . ."

This was even worse. This was bolshevism. With this point in his platform, Hitler was automatically cutting himself off from the moneybags of the eastern Junkers, those great landlords whose estates rolled on and on to the four horizons.

The platform was written in 1920. It took Hitler eight years, and undoubtedly much talking to from sundry quarters, to realize what a fool he was. So on April 13, 1928, he proclaimed the following through the Nazi press:

"Regarding the false interpretation of Point 17 of the platform of the NSDAP on the part of our opponents, the following explanation is necessary:

"Since the NSDAP stands on the platform of private ownership, it happens that the phrase 'free expropriation' concerns only the creation of legal opportunity to expropriate, if necessary, land which has been illegally acquired or is not administered from the viewpoint of the national welfare. This is directed primarily against the Jewish land-speculation companies."

The cynics laughed; but what was more important, the Junkers laughed, too, and with much more enjoyment.

But if the party platform made good reading for Big Business, the daily headlines, recounting the exploits of Hitler's Brownshirts, made even better. The Brownshirts didn't like Communists, Social Democrats, trade-union leaders, leftists of all shades, and whenever they saw one they cracked him on the skull.

The Brown Army was the biggest goon squad ever to go to work for union-busting bosses. As early as 1932, during a strike at the huge Krupp foundry at Vorbech, the newspaper *Ruhr Echo* was charging the Nazis with being "strikebreakers and tools of the capitalists."

During the first years, the goon squad did its work *gratis*; later it was paid, and paid well, as documents at Nuremberg showed.

In May, 1928, the Nazis won 12 seats in the Reichstag, gathering 800,000 popular votes. Industrialists, approving in principle Nazi activity, but cautious about yielding support to Hitler until they were convinced he was a man with a future, saw an omen in this election. Hugenberg, a dominating figure in heavy industry and head of the powerful Rightist German Nationalist party, became a Hitler supporter. So did William Keppler, a financier who acted for some years as the Fuehrer's economic adviser.

Within a short time thereafter, testified the defendant Funk, Hitler could count among his friends Emil Kirdorf, Ruhr coal magnate; Fritz Thyssen and other Rheinish-Westphalian industrialists such as Tengelmann, Springorum, Voegler, Knepper, Winkhaus, Buskuehl, Kellermann. Steel and coal, with a dash of chemicals thrown in: Hitler's liaison with I. G. Farben was through von Schnitzler, member of the board, and Dr. Gattineau, private secretary to Duisberg, biggest name in Farben at the time.

In September, 1930, the Nazis increased their number of deputies from 12 to 107, receiving nearly six and one-half million votes. Schacht, the money wizard with a great international reputation in the banking world, and Kurt von Schroeder of the Stein Bank of Cologne, another formidable figure in international banking, swung quietly to Hitler's support.

It's interesting to think back now how, with Schacht and Schroeder in his pocket, Hitler continued blandly in his public speeches to attack international bankers.

In the July, 1932, election, the Nazis won brilliantly, gathering nearly fourteen million votes—37 per cent of the electorate—and 230 deputies.

Hitler was elated, prematurely. The following month he ran against Hindenburg for the presidency, and was trounced. Von Papen took him to see the venerable old man, whose picture looked down from the walls of millions of German homes. Hitler asked for the Chancellorship and was offered the Vice-Chancellery. He refused the offer: "Hindenburg is 85; I can afford to wait." He went home with his hopes and his reputation for invincibility shattered. In November there were new elections, and the Nazis lost 34 seats.

Here was the crisis. Hitler had passed his peak. Would Big Business support him further, or forget him?

The prosecution at Nuremberg showed that Schacht remained loyal: "Permit me to congratulate you," he wrote Hitler, "on the firm stand you took. . . . I have no doubt that the further development of things can only lead to your becoming Chancellor. I am quite confident that the present system is doomed to disintegration."

Back in the Ruhr the industrialists studied the election results and saw more than a setback to the promising Hitler. They saw an increase in Communist strength from 89 to 100 deputies, and a Communist popular vote of nearly six million. To the industrialists, the six million seemed like sixty million, and the sixty million like the end of the world.

One week after this election Wilhelm Keppler reported to Schroeder on discussions among Schacht, Himmler, and von Papen (who had been succeeded by Schleicher as Chancellor) on how best to persuade Hindenburg to make Hitler Chancellor. Result of the discussion: von Papen must intervene on Hitler's behalf. "New elections under the slogan Hindenburg and Hitler would bring the expected result without any doubt." (Keppler in a letter to Schroeder.)

But this wasn't enough. Schacht drafted an appeal direct to Hindenburg: "We recognize in the national movement which penetrates our people, the promising beginning of an era which, through the overcoming of class contrasts, creates the essential basis for a rebirth of German economy. . . . Entrusting the leader of the largest national group with the responsible leadership of a Presidential Cabinet which harbors the best technical and personal talents will eliminate the blemishes and mistakes with which any mass movement is perforce afflicted . . ."

The prosecution proved that this appeal for the appointment of Hitler as head of government was signed by Schacht, Schroeder, Rosterg, and Reinhart, the latter a mining and machinery magnate with important holdings in and around Nuremberg. The prosecution had documents available to show that Albert Voegler, key figure in the German United Steel Works, tried to persuade two other coal and iron men, Reusch and Springorum, to sign, and that these men "shared the views put forward." And there is documentary proof that the appeal was designed for the signature of at least fifty of the foremost men in German industry.

It is difficult to exaggerate the importance of this documentation. The leading money men of Germany wanted Hitler at a time when they still had freedom of choice, when there was no pressure upon them except the pressure of their own conscience and judgment—and greed for money and power. They could not then plead, nor can they plead in the trials which face many of them, that they were merely bending either to majority will or minority pressure. At the time, Hitler was actually losing his hold on the first, and lacked the power to exercise the second.

On January 4, 1933, six men met at Schroeder's house in Cologne and, in a very real sense, brought on World War II. Present, besides the host, were Hitler, Hess, Himmler, von Papen, and Keppler. The meeting—on Schroeder's evidence presented at this trial—was arranged by the banker at von Papen's request; it resulted in an agreement to collaborate in a new government with Hitler as Chancellor, von Papen as Vice-Chancellor and a program calling for "the elimination of Social Democrats, Communists, and Jews from leading positions in Germany and the restoration of order in public life."

The thin-faced, silver-haired von Papen, able diplomat, devout Catholic, with the extraordinary urbanity found only in ambassadors and million-dollar insurance salesmen, sat fourth from last in the second row of the dock. To think of him in association with Nazi gangsters is to think of a swan among buzzards. But the association was of his own choosing. He could not and did not deny that at the trial; he could only assert, as he did, that for him it was a question of Hitler or communism. This is a dilemma which has never daunted the conservative; he relishes the solution so much he is even ready to create the dilemma in order to solve it.

The senile Hindenburg appointed the Hitler-von Papen clique

to office January 30, 1933, and Schroeder termed the new government as "the one he desired, the one he planned, and the one
he considered solely possible."

Three weeks later Goering invited about twenty-five bankers
and industrialists to his house in Berlin. "The purpose of the meeting was not known beforehand," testified Georg von Schnitzler,
member of the Executive Board of I. G. Farben and one of the
guests. "Among those present I remember Dr. Schacht; Krupp von
Bohlen, who at the time was president of the Reich Association of
German Industry; Dr. Albert Voegler, leading man of the United
Steel Works; von Lowenfeld, from an industrial plant in Essen,
and Dr. Stein, head of the Augusta Victoria Works, a mine which
belonged to I. G. Farben. I remember that Dr. Schacht acted as a
kind of host.

"While I was expecting the appearance of Goering, Hitler
entered the room, shook hands with everybody and took a seat
at the head of the table."

Hitler then spoke, and the official text of his speech is available.
When he had finished, there was not one among those who heard
him who did not know exactly what he stood for and what he
proposed for Germany.

He talked dictatorship: "Private enterprise cannot be maintained
in the age of Democracy. It is conceivable only if the people have
a sound idea of authority and personality."

He talked war: "I found [Ideals] in Nationalism, in the denial
of reconciliation between nations. . . . The question of restoration
of the Wehrmacht will not be decided at Geneva but in Germany."

He talked revolution: "Now we stand before the last election.
Regardless of the outcome there will be no retreat. One way or
another, if the election is not decisive, the decision must be brought
about even by other means."

Goering followed his chief, and I quote once more from an
official report of the meeting:

"Goering . . . then led over very cleverly to the necessity for
circles not taking part in the political battle to make, at least, the
financial sacrifices necessary at this time. The sacrifices asked for
surely would be so much easier to bear if it was realized that the

election of March 5 surely will be the last one for the next ten years, probably even for the next hundred years."

I pick up again the evidence given by Schnitzler:

"After Hitler had left the room, Dr. Schacht proposed to the meeting the raising of an election fund of, so far as I remember, three million Reichsmarks."

Schnitzler and his colleagues knew, now, for what purpose they had been called together. Schacht testified that he succeeded in collecting only what he asked for; Funk said the collection may have reached seven million marks. What we do know is that, before the meeting was over, Krupp von Bohlen expressed to Hitler "the gratitude of approximatively twenty-five industrialists present, for having given us such a clear picture of the conception of his ideas.'

The money Hitler got at this meeting was by no means the first from industrial sources, and of course, would not be the last.

He had already been receiving funds from a group known at the time as the "Keppler circle." It included representatives of Germany's most powerful industrial and financial concerns: I. G. Farben, the Bosch company, the Dresdner Bank, Rheinmetal Borsig, Siemens-Halske, North German Lloyd. Both Schroeder and Schacht belonged to the group.

In 1935 or 1936 Keppler fell out of favor with Hitler, and Himmler became "protector" of the circle and with Hitler's consent, got the money. I quote the evidence of Schroeder:

"The circle undertook each year, up to and including 1944, to raise funds for 'special purposes' for Himmler. These funds were paid by the members of the circle or by corporations in which they had leading positions to the Stein Bank to a special account 'S'.

"Each year I wrote to Himmler advising him as to the amount contributed by each person or corporation during that year and Himmler in turn wrote a letter of thanks and appreciation to the contributor."

There exists detailed documentation proving payments of these sums. And there was introduced in evidence the annual report made by Schroeder to Himmler for the year 1943. I quote briefly:

"My very honorable Reichsfuehrer:

"With great joy I learn of your appointment as Reich Minister of the Interior. . . . A strong hand is now very necessary to the operation of this Department and it is universally welcomed, especially by your friends, that it was you who were chosen for this by the Fuehrer.

"I am pleased to inform you that your circle of friends has again placed at your disposal this year a sum slightly in excess of RM 1 million for 'special purposes' . . ."

At the time this letter was written, Himmler and his SS were operating the biggest and most ruthless murder machine in history.

In the meantime, beginning with 1933, German industry as a whole was organized for fund-raising purposes on behalf of the Nazi party. The fund was known as the *Adolf Hitler Spende*; in 1935, industry contributed twelve million Reichsmarks to it under the chairmanship of Krupp. In the early years, individual contributions were voluntary, and it is safe to assume that the first lists of givers represent Hitler's first and best friends among the money men of Germany. Later, the money was levied rather than contributed and the list of contributors loses its significance.

The March, 1933, election turned out successfully for Hitler, who received enough votes and traded for enough more to put through the Reichstag the "Enabling Act" which elevated him from Reich Chancellor to Fuehrer and undisputed dictator of Germany.

Industrial ranks closed in once more to support Hitler in his new role. The following month—on April 25—Krupp wrote a letter to Hitler on behalf of himself and the Reich Association of German Industry, of which he was then chairman. In the letter and in the plan for reorganization of the Association which he enclosed, Krupp announced that his associates had given him "sole authority to hold any necessary conferences with the government of the Reich," and added:

"In reorganizing the Reich Association of German Industry, I shall be guided by the idea of bringing the new organization into agreement with the political aims of the Reich Government. . . .

"The turn of political events is in line with the wishes which I myself and the board of directors have cherished for a long time.

I am convinced that under the threat of impoverishment of our people, the machinery of government must be simplified to the utmost."

In other words, Hitler's idea of simplifying government by destroying the independence of the Reichstag, in which workers and leftists of all stripes might raise a threat to industrial power, was a most welcome change to Krupp and his associates. They would not have to employ goons any longer, not even the SA; now they could have the government working for them.

5.

January 30, 1933, Hitler became Chancellor; February 27-28 the Reichstag burned, the Communists were blamed, and Hitler outlawed the Communist party and threw into concentration camps thousands of its members and hundreds of Social Democrats. The hopes of Hitler's most dynamic opposition in Germany went up in the smoke that hovered that night over Brandenburg Gate.

Who started the fire? Dozens of persons were interrogated on this subject during the course of the trial, some in the secrecy of the interrogation rooms, others on the stand in the courtroom.

Cecilie Mueller, private secretary to the banker Schroeder, said that she was present at a meeting between Hitler and industrialists on January 3, 1933, at which "Goering and Papen plotted to burn the Reichstag in order to make possible the banning of the Communist party, which would be blamed for the fire. . . . Schroeder and Keppler consented to the plan proposed by Papen."

Schroeder denied this, insisted that at no time did he know anything about the burning of the Reichstag until it was actually flaming.

Franz Halder, for a while Chief of Staff of the German Army, testified:

"On the occasion of a luncheon on the Fuehrer's birthday in 1942 the conversation turned to the topic of the Reichstag building and its artistic value. I heard with my own ears when Goering interrupted the conversation and shouted:

" 'I am the only one who really knows the Reichstag story, because I set it on fire.'

"He slapped his thigh with the flat of his hand."

Gisevius, who at the time held office in the Ministry of the Interior, and later became identified with the so-called "Hitler opposition," testified:

"Hitler had stated the wish for a large-scale propaganda campaign. Goebbels took on the job of making the necessary proposals and preparing them, and it was Goebbels who first thought of setting the Reichstag on fire. Goebbels talked about this to the leader of the Berlin SA Brigade, Karl Ernst, and he suggested in detail how it should be carried out.

"Goering gave assurances that the police would be instructed, while still suffering from shock, to take up a false trail. Right from the beginning it was intended that the Communists should be debited with this crime, and it was in that sense that . . . ten SA men who had to carry out the crime, were instructed."

Rudolf Diehls, at the time head of the Gestapo and for a while Goering's relative by marriage, insisted that "Goering knew exactly how the fire was to be started" and that he, Diehls, "had to prepare, prior to the fire, a list of people who were to be arrested immediately after it."

And Goering himself?

He denied any connection with the fire, but admitted the existence of a list of Social Democrats and Communists who were slated for arrest and would have been arrested "regardless of the fire." He "rather suspects Ernst"; in any case, once Van der Lubbe, the dim-witted Dutch Communist, "confessed" to the crime, he dropped the whole affair from his mind.

But whether we know or not who *did* start the fire, it is perfectly clear who *didn't*.

Robert Kempner of the United States Prosecution Staff, who himself had to flee Germany in 1933 because of his outspoken anti-fascism, nailed Goering on this point in a dramatic interrogation:

Q. "How could you tell your press agent, one hour after the Reichstag caught fire and without any investigation, that the Communists did that?"

A. "Did the public relations officer say that I said that?"

Q. "Yes."

A. "It is possible; when I came to the Reichstag, the Fuehrer and his gentlemen were there. I was doubtful at the time, but it was their opinion that the Communists had started the fire."

Q. "Looking back at it now . . . wasn't it too early to say without any investigation that the Communists started the fire?"

A. "Yes, that is possible, but the Fuehrer wanted it that way."

Q. "Why did the Fuehrer want to issue at once a statement that the Communists had started the fire?"

A. "He was convinced of it."

Q. "It is right if I say that he was convinced without having any evidence or any proof of that at the moment?"

A. "That is right, but you must take into account at that time the Communist activity was extremely strong, and that our new Government as such was not very secure."

Yes, of course. And what better way is there for a new government to make itself more "secure" than by destroying the house of parliament, the home of the people in government?

6.

The Enabling Act did to the Reichstag what the fire had done to the building. It ended parliamentary government in Germany; it suspended the constitution and gave Hitler the right to rule by decree.

The story of its passage, as told in the secret documents revealed at Nuremberg, is the story of Nazi brutality and duplicity and the abandonment of democracy by the middle-of-the-road Center party, the great Catholic faction in the Reichstag which held the balance of power.

On March 15, 1933, at a Cabinet meeting presided over by Hitler, Frick as Minister of the Interior pointed out that passage of the Act required a two-thirds majority. He weighed the problem gravely: if the Communist delegates were not disfranchised, it would mean that 432 votes would be necessary for ratification; if they *were* disfranchised, only 378 would be necessary.

He told the Cabinet the moment was not propitious for annulling the communist mandate, but added that "the prohibition of the Communist party is indicated . . . and that, eventually, it might well be necessary to commit to work-camps these persons who remain faithful to communism."

Goering, too, was hopeful about passage of the Act: "Eventually, a majority could be obtained by refusing admittance to a few Social Democrats."

The subject was resumed at the next Cabinet meeting, five days later, and Hitler reported on negotiations with the Center party:

"The representatives of the Center appreciated the necessity of such a law. They had requested that a small Committee be organized which would be informed, regularly, of measures taken by the Reich Government on the basis of the Act. In their opinion, if this request were granted, the Center would doubtless ratify the measure."

And Hitler added: "A ratification of the Act by the Center would mean increased prestige abroad."

The Reichstag met on March 21. Some of its members were missing. A week before, Frick had stated in the Nazi newspaper, *Voelkischer Beobachter*: "When the Reichstag meets, the Communists will be prevented by urgent labor elsewhere from participation in the session. In concentration camps they will be re-educated for productive work. We will know how to render permanently harmless sub-humans who do not want to be re-educated."

This was the political atmosphere under which the Reichstag met. It was the political atmosphere in which the Center party voted for the Act. It was the political atmosphere in which Reinhold Maier, spokesman for a small and supposedly moderate faction in the Reichstag, not only voted for the Act but made a stirring speech in its favor.

The Act was passed and Hitler now had "legal" right to "render permanently harmless sub-humans who do not want to be re-educated."

So came the end of the Weimar Republic.

Chapter IV   Invasion of Germany

In July, 1941, Hitler defined the purposes of invasion of foreign soil: "First, to dominate it; second, to administer it; third, to exploit it."

The Brown Locusts had invaded Germany, and in the elections of March, 1933, their victory was sealed. Hitler's problem henceforth was to administer this conquered territory in accordance with fascist principles, and to exploit it as an instrument of war.

"No two ideologies can live side by side," he had told the industrialists back in February, 1933. "In such struggles the strength of a people eats itself up internally and therefore it cannot act externally."

In other words, internal unity before external aggression.

This chapter is the story of how the Nazis achieved "internal unity;" how Hitler, in his own words, effected "reorganization of the interior, abolishment of the appearances of decay and defeatist ideas, education to heroism."

Education to heroism! It is a noble phrase. I am reminded of the definition used in 1938 by Hitler's Minister of Education, Bernhard Rust, who under the Republic had been fired for incompetence from his job as teacher in a middle grade school. Said Rust:

"The whole purpose of all education is to create a Nazi."

The Third Reich tried to create a Nazi out of Hans Fiegl, a simple man whom I knew in Germany in 1938, and whose subsequent history I pieced together from the accounts given me by mutual friends and from the broader story revealed at the Nuremberg trial.

Hans in 1933 was a rather dull little man in his middle forties who worked as bookkeeper in the welfare department of the Shoemakers Union in Nuremberg. Naturally, he was a Social Democrat, because that was the politics of his union. He himself had no real political convictions, nor thought much about such problems; and, if the truth must be told, he did not altogether share the distaste of his union leaders for the new Hitler Government.

Like most dull little Germans, Hans had a great admiration for strong men, and Hitler certainly was strong.

Indeed, his first official contact with the forces of the new Government was by no means unpleasant. In March, 1933, there had been some trouble at other union headquarters in Nuremberg; SA men had smashed up offices, stolen money, beaten a few unionists. But the Shoemakers Union was not bothered, and Hans put the affair down to a few rowdies, of which even the SA undoubtedly had its share.

Then, on May 2, he walked into his office, and there were SA men there, and their leader announced formally that the Shoemakers Union, and all other trade unions except the Catholic group (which was dissolved later) had been ordered dissolved and that the building and all its contents were now the property of the National Socialist party.

"But," added the spokesman, "you must not think that this is an action against the workers. It is directed only against your Marxist leaders who for years have been swindling and stealing from you through your unions. Another union will take its place; you are to go on working quietly, and nothing will happen to you."

So pretty soon Hans was working for the new "union," the German Labor Front, and he was making the same entries in the same books, only now the book covers were stamped with swastikas.

And he had to confess that this new union was certainly live-

lier than the old, with great parades and blood-red banners and
mass singing and great patriotic orations. And if the union had
lost its right to strike, had indeed become a company union run
by the Government, well, that was not Hans' affair; after all, his
job was to see that Oswald Braunschweig got his forty marks per
month sick benefit, and this job hadn't changed.

So he sat there, making his small entries, and going home at
night he would read about unpleasant things happening to other
people. Indeed, only six weeks after Hitler came to power, he had
read that 16,000 Communists had been imprisoned and that
10,000 prisoners in the jails of Prussia included many Socialists
and intellectuals.

He read a lot about what bad people the Jews were, and he had
himself witnessed the first boycott of the Jews in April, 1933. And
the same year he read in a newspaper an account of a speech by
Goering.

"Whoever in the future raises a hand against a representative of
the Nazi movement or of the State," the genial Hermann had
said, "must know that he will lose his life in a very short while."

And Hans read about concentration camps. Goering pointed
out, in 1934, that the enemies of the party were legion and that
therefore "the concentration camps have been created, where we
have first confined thousands of Communists and Social Democrat
functionaries." When he read that, Hans thought back to that
May 2, 1933, and remembered again that Joseph Simon, the 68-
year-old president of the Shoemakers Union, had been sent to
Dachau, and Simon's son, too. But Hans deliberately did not dwell
on the memory and he tried not to hear the street talk about the
terrible things that were happening in the camps.

Or, when he could not avoid hearing such talk, he told himself
that they must be terrible people, indeed, to deserve such punishment. And he very firmly resolved that he would be very careful
not to bring such punishment upon himself.

So he sat on, making his small entries, and then he would turn
to his newspaper in the evening and he would find that the Nazis
had passed another law. There had been that first one, the Law for
the Protection of the People and State. And as the months and years

passed, others followed: the law outlawing political parties other than the Nazis, the law securing the unity of Party and State, the law centralizing power in the National Government, the law creating Special Courts for political cases, the law merging the Presidency and Chancellorship in the person of Hitler, the law merging the Political Police into the Gestapo, the law putting all police under a single head, Himmler.

But he never thought that these laws had anything to do with him. Indeed, from 1933 until the day of his curious death, he never really understood what was happening to Germany, to the German people, to himself. Totally unattracted by heavy reading, such as *Documents of German Politics* or the *Reich Law Gazette*, he never got to realize, until it was too late, that the foundations of life were being smashed by these laws, that he and every other German had quite literally lost all legal claim to the very right to existence, that for every breath he drew he had to thank not the majesty of German law protecting its citizens but merely the police who didn't happen at the moment to want to kill him.

He never read in the *Reich Law Gazette*, for instance, the Law of June 28, 1935, Amending the Penal Code:

"Any person who commits an act which . . . is deserving of punishment under the fundamental conceptions of the penal code *and sound popular feeling*, shall be punished. If there is no penal law directly covering an act, *it shall be punished under that law which most closely fits*." (My italics—V. H. B.)

And he never read this from *Documents of German Politics*:

"National Socialism . . . considers every attack against the welfare of the people's community . . . as a wrong. Therefore wrong may be committed in the future in Germany *even in cases when no law threatens it with punishment*." (My italics—V. H. B.)

No, Hans failed to see the pattern, or maybe he didn't want to see it. And he was dead six years by the time Goering walked into the witness box in Nuremberg, and with amazing frankness, explained it to the Tribunal:

"The first question was to achieve and establish a different political structure for Germany which would enable her not only to protest against the Treaty of Versailles, but to present an objection of such a nature that it would actually be considered.

"As soon as we had come into power, we were decided to keep that power under all circumstances. We could not leave this to the play of coincidence by way of elections and parliamentary majorities. . . . A further point in the strengthening of power was the elimination of the Reichstag as a Parliament . . . [and] those laws were established which did away with the so-called freedoms.

"The opposition of each individual person was not tolerated unless it was a matter of unimportance. People were arrested and taken into protective custody who had committed no crime, but who one might expect, if they remained in freedom, would do all sorts of things to damage the German State."

So Hans not only could be punished for doing something against which there was no law, but he could be punished even before he did it. The police had become judge and jury; it had, indeed, become the State.

"The decree for the Protection of the People and State," wrote Dr. Walter Hamel, Nazi jurist, in another of those highbrow articles which Hans never read, "has eliminated the negative law barriers of State power. The positive competence of the police to restrict liberty of any kind, especially to order protective custody, flows naturally from the character of the function which it must perform in a National Socialist State."

Dr. Werner Best, another Nazi writer, put it even more simply: "As long as the police carries out the will of the leadership, it is acting legally."

But no one tried to restrict Hans' liberty, because he was never foolish enough to try to assert his right to it. The things he wanted to do, he could do: work and eat and go to the movies and attend the great party rallies at Nuremberg and watch the parades go by. And if the sudden arrest of his Jewish neighbor, Loewe, disturbed him, he angrily told himself that he was not his brother's keeper.

Moreover, whenever he had occasion to feel unhappy about the party, something or other came up that convinced him it wasn't so bad. There was dwindling unemployment, for one thing; there were more radios (even if you had to listen to that interminable

Goebbels); there were the Strength through Joy vacations; there were the grand *autobahns* being built; there was the promise of the People's Car. And above all, permeating the whole atmosphere, riding like a shining flag above the parades, above the new highways, above the smoking chimneys of the busy factories, there was a rekindled pride in being a German, a part of a great and reborn nation.

And if Hans refused to listen to the cries of the tortured in the camps (by 1938, hundreds of thousands of Germans had been arrested for political reasons) he was not alone. The great leaders of Germany, intellectual as well as industrial, saw only the shining flag and would not listen to the cries. Did not Krupp and that world-renowned musician, Wilhelm Furtwaengler, sign a public proclamation calling for Hitler to be made President as well as Chancellor? Did not the proclamation say, "The Fuehrer again has asked us to stand by him faithfully. . . . None of us will be missing when it is up to us to testify to this"?

The Gestapo, of course, was unpleasant; but where, anywhere in the world, is the policeman popular, and especially a political police? On the other hand, surely there was something fine about the SS. The handsomest youth in Germany strode smartly down the street in the shiny black of Himmler's uniform. And the most respectable people in Germany were members, dukes and princes and all sorts of aristocracy.

It is too bad Hans could not have listened to Friedrich Karl von Eberstein testifying, at Nuremberg, in defense of the SS, of which he had been a member since 1929. Defense counsel for the SS as an organization questioned him:

Q. "You are a member of the German nobility?"

A. "Yes. . . . There were a great number of aristocrats and members of German princely houses who were members. After 1933 the Prince of Hohenzollern Sigmaringen became a member, and Prince von Braunschweig, Prince Lippe-Biesterfeld, General Graf von Schulenburg and many others."

Q. "Do you know that the Archbishop Grueber of Freiburg became a member?"

A. "Yes."

Q. "Do you believe that membership of such prominent personages made an impression on members of all classes in Germany, so that one said, 'If such good people belong to the SS and worked for its aims, then it seems certain that these aims must be good and legal'?"

A. "Yes."

The effect of the brief colloquy was a remarkable inversion of its intent. Obviously, defense counsel was seeking to make the murderous SS respectable; all he succeeded in doing was to degrade the aristocracy.

To get back to Hans: SS or no SS, he did not join the party. The traditions, if not the convictions, of Social Democracy, were too strong in him for that.

So the months and the years rolled by, and Hans learned everything that he had to know to keep him safe. He knew, for instance, that the Party Block Leader, in charge of perhaps fifty households, had forwarded to the District Leader a card on each household in the block—how many in the family, what each did, the political opinions of each family member. And Hans knew that this card index was not a static thing, but was continually being added to, because the Block Leader was just a common run-of-the-mill kind of spy who reported everything that happened in his small area, what people said and did and thought and dreamed.

In April, 1938, Hans almost made a very bad mistake. The plebiscite for *Anschluss* was coming up, in Germany as well as Austria, and Hans toyed with the idea of voting No, principally because he had once had very good friends among the Vienna Social Democrats and he thought they would want him to vote No. But as he pondered and talked with his friends and read his newspapers, he changed his mind, for after all the Austrians were German, weren't they, and was not Hitler himself an Austrian? And on voting day he was very glad he had changed his mind, for he found that it wasn't a secret ballot at all.

In the first place, hardly anyone bothered to walk into the voting booth to mark his ballot, but did so openly, and handed the open envelope to the election official who sealed it and dropped it himself into the box. They did this, he realized, to assure the election official that they were voting the right way. Moreover, that evening he had a long chat with his Block Leader, who told him that orders had come down from the party to watch this vote very carefully, to see that everyone turned out for it, and that persons suspected should be given marked ballots. In this instance, the suspects were given ballots marked with a ribbonless typewriter.

And a few days later he was shown a copy of a secret report on an incident which happened near Erfurt in the neighboring province of Thuringia. The report was addressed to the Security Service (SD) of the SS and read as follows:

"This is to notify you that the Jehovah's Witness Robert Siering and his wife appeared in the voting center in Guenstedt on Sunday morning and deposited their vote, after both had been advised of their duty to vote by the police *and had been threatened with the removal of their child in case of non-participation.*"

Apparently things like this had happened all over Germany, so it was with mixed feelings that Hans read the results of the elections. I quote the headlines in the *Thuringer Allgemeine Zeitung* of April 11, 1938:

THE AVOWAL BEFORE THE WORLD:
The United German YES: 99.08%
99.75% in Austria!
The Fuehrer's thanks: "It is the proudest
hour of my life."
Gauleiter Sauckel: "Never before has any
people thus demonstrated their unity."

Then came September and the threat of war, immediately to be dissolved in the bright glory of Munich. And Hans, who didn't want war any more than anyone else, could not help but feel great admiration for the Fuehrer, to whom the great statesmen of the world now came running, instead of Germany having to go to Geneva. And this surge of pride in being part of a strong Germany bore him up even through the November pogrom, which certainly he did not like. By now he had developed a very convenient rationalizing technique by which all the things his country did which he did not like, he automatically blamed on certain people—Himmler and Goebbels and, logically, Gauleiter Streicher, whom practically everyone detested. But Hitler remained above reproach, and as for the genial Hermann—*unser Hermann*—who could not help liking the fat rascal?

Then came March, 1939, and the conquest of the rest of Czechoslovakia, and Hans could look out of his office window and see the tanks rolling by, and the big guns, and the long lines of Wehrmacht green, and he saw the big bombers roar overhead. Block Leaders and other party officials and the SA scurried around and brought everybody into the street, and the townspeople lined up to watch Germany's armed might go by, and after the last platoon had passed, a few SA and SS men in the crowds began to march, too, and Hans was carried along in the rush. And from somewhere, suddenly, an SA band appeared and struck up the *Horst Wessel.*

Hans marched a little while without singing, and men on either side began to look at him, so finally he joined. And pretty soon the cadenced steps and the swinging rhythm and the sound of strong voices in the air, and the sight of the huge red pennants swinging from the housetops, acted like wine in his blood. His step lengthened, and his voice rose, and he thought, "By God, if I can't be a good National Socialist, at least I can be a good and patriotic German!"

It was at this point that two plainclothesmen appeared from nowhere and motioned to him to get out of line. As soon as they got him between them, they snapped handcuffs on him, and before he knew it, someone at Gestapo headquarters was pounding his nose and mouth with a rubber truncheon and shouting at him to confess that he was a member of an underground group in Munich.

Naturally, he could make no such confession, and he was only half-conscious when they stopped beating him and dropped him on the floor of a cell. Somehow, before the guard left, Hans had strength enough to ask, through his blood and tears, for a lawyer, or at least for a hearing before a judge. The guard's answer was to kick him in the groin.

The next day he was at Dachau, still half-drunk with pain, the blood caked upon his face, and every time he saw a man in uniform he stumbled towards him and asked, "Can't I see my lawyer? Can't I get a court hearing?" But the Nazis had been passing laws in

Berlin, remember? So each time the answer was a blow and the fourth time an SS lieutenant grabbed him and said, "I'll teach you to keep your mouth shut, you filthy swine."

They put him in an iron box in the corner of a cell. The box was six feet high and just big enough in width and depth to enable its occupant to bend a little, but not to sit down.

Hans spent the afternoon there, and the night. And in the morning, when an officer came to release him with apologies, for the Gestapo had picked up the wrong Hans, he was dead on his feet in this strait-jacket that was Germany.

Of course the Gestapo could not afford to admit its mistake and it merely sent Hans' ashes back in an urn with the explanation that he had died of pneumonia. The story of the urn got back to Hans' colleagues, naturally, and they put their own interpretation upon it, which was that he certainly must have done something or said something bad. The result was that those among the colleagues who had needed just a little more scaring to get into line, got what they needed.

So in the Nazi regime, even mistakes had their uses. It was all a part of what the defendants at Nuremberg were fond of referring to as the Consolidation of Power in National Socialist Germany.

Chapter V

The Will to War

1.

In 1934-35 the Hearst press published a series of articles by leading Nazis: Goebbels, Goering, Rosenberg. The articles said Hitler wanted peace. Hearst visited Berlin and came back to report that Hitler wanted peace. And what came later to be known as the Newspaper Axis—the New York *Daily News*, the Chicago *Tribune*, the Washington *Herald*—kept on saying that Hitler wanted peace, until Pearl Harbor and Germany's subsequent declaration of war on us discomfited it for perhaps as much as twenty-four hours.

This press was not alone in doing Hitler's work. Out-and-out Fascists, American and German, sedulously propagated the pro-Hitler cult, some for love and many for Berlin pay. The Economic Royalists, hating Roosevelt, could not but feel drawn to a government that had won the support of such eminent financial men as Schacht and Schroeder. The anti-Reds, the anti-Semites, the anti-labor crowd saw in Nazism a dream come true. And in the early years even many liberals, confusing the problem of justice to Germany with justice to Hitler, failed to see that the time for moratoria was over.

Where we were not knaves, what fools we were!

"The plans of Adolf Hitler for aggression," said Jackson in his summation at the trial, "were just as secret as *Mein Kampf*, of which over six million copies were published in Germany."

Mein Kampf (written in 1923) says: "We National Socialists must stick firmly to the aim that we have set for our foreign policy, namely, that the German people must be assured the territorial area which is necessary for it to exist on this earth. . . . The territory on which one day our German peasants will be able to bring forth and nourish their sturdy sons will justify the blood of the sons of the peasants that has to be shed today."

And *Mein Kampf* says: "So also in the future our people will not obtain territory as a favor from any other people, but will have to win it by the power of the triumphant sword."

There it was, six million copies of it distributed in Germany alone. In the U.S.A., two publishers put translations to press and sold hundreds of thousands. The book was praised, reviled, talked and written about endlessly. It attracted everything but credence. "Hitler wants war? Nonsense. That *Mein Kampf* stuff is just diplomatic double-talk. If he really wanted war, do you think he would have said so openly?"

Yes, we were very clever, very sophisticated. We were so sophisticated we refused to believe a statesman when he told the truth; we believed him only when he told lies.

All right. What the Nazis tried and failed to tell us openly, they will now be permitted to tell deviously, in the compelling and fascinating language of their secret archives as revealed at the Nuremberg proceedings.

2.

The moment Hitler came to power, Germany became a giant factory throbbing for war. In German naval files, the prosecution found a *History of War Organizations* in which the statement is made: "Further, Hitler had made a clear political request to build up for him in five years—i.e., by April 1, 1938—Armed Forces which he could place in the balance as an instrument of political power."

A working committee of Delegates for Reich Defense met on May 22, 1933, under the chairmanship of the defendant Keitel, and implemented an earlier Cabinet decision to form a Reich Defense Council, a kind of super War Production Board. These men knew that what they were preparing to do was illegal under the Versailles Treaty. According to the secret minutes of the meeting revealed at the trial, Keitel warned his colleagues:

"The secrecy of all Reich defense work has to be carefully maintained. No document must be lost; otherwise enemy propaganda would make use of it. Matters communicated orally cannot be proven; they can be denied by us in Geneva" (*i.e., at the League of Nations*).

True, and matters communicated orally could also have been denied at Nuremberg. But Schacht, unfortunately for himself, chose to write and not tell Hitler the following on May 3, 1935:

"The following comments are based on the assumption that the accomplishment of the armaments program . . . is *the* task of German policy, and that therefore everything else must be subordinated to this aim.

"The difficulty still exists . . . that to expose the German nation to propaganda for the purpose of winning its support for armament, cannot be undertaken without imperiling our position internationally."

In other words, appeals to the public to buy war or armament bonds, or the direct levying of tax increases to support an armament program, were to be avoided. The Government might get the money, it's true; but the enemy would know what was up. So Schacht, sound businessman and an opponent of inflation, explained to Hitler how he was turning paper into secret gold:

"The Reichsbank has invested the major part of mark deposits owned by foreigners . . . in armament drafts. Our armaments, therefore, are being financed partially with the assets of our political opponents."

But this, of course, was not enough. And the wizard Schacht created the *Mefo* bill, a device for tapping the short-term money market without anyone knowing what the money was to be used for. "This method has as one of its primary advantages," Emil Puhl, a director of the Reichsbank under Schacht, testified at the trial, "the fact that figures indicating the extent of rearmament that would have become public through the use of other methods, could be kept secret through the use of *Mefo* bills." By 1938, there were 12 billion marks worth of these bills outstanding.

In June, 1935, Schacht's wizardry received recognition: he was appointed to the post of Plenipotentiary-General for War Economy to direct all economic preparations for war. And he was ordered to "begin his work already in peacetime." Simultaneously, the Cabinet passed a Law for the Defense of the Reich giving Hitler authority to declare a national war emergency whenever he saw fit. The law was deliberately withheld from publication; indeed, von Blomberg, the War Minister, ordered that copies should be distributed in the Army down to Corps Headquarters only, and added, "I point out the necessity of strictest secrecy once more."

In March, 1936, came the reoccupation of the Rhineland in accordance with military plans laid down a year before. Hitler sought to reassure a questioning world and above all an angry and apprehensive France:

"We have no territorial claims to make in Europe. We know above all that the tensions resulting either from false territorial settlements or from the disproportion of the number of inhabitants to their living space, cannot in Europe be solved by war."

The reassurance went over well, except in France, which hated Germany, and in the U.S.S.R., which hated Nazism. But millions in America and Britain said, "Well, the Rhineland is German, isn't it?" And nobody seems to have sensed the real significance of what had happened, which was not that Germany got back the Rhineland, but that a *fascist* Germany got it back.

"No territorial claims. . . . Tensions in Europe cannot be solved by war." That was March, 1936.

But two months later Goering was telling a meeting of Cabinet ministers, at which Schacht was present, "All measures are to be considered from the standpoint of an assured waging of war."

And in November, 1937, Hitler gathered his war leaders in the

Reich Chancellery and told them (I quote the official report of
Hitler's speech as introduced at Nuremberg):

"The aim of German policy is the security and the preservation
of the nation and its propagation. This is consequently a problem
of space.

"Should the security of our food position be our foremost
thought, then the space required can only be sought in EUROPE.
It would be more to the purpose to seek raw material producing territory in EUROPE directly adjoining the Reich and not overseas.

"The question for Germany is where the greatest possible conquest can be made at lowest cost. The German question can be
solved only by way of force, and this is never without risk.

"The re-arming of the Army, the Navy, and the Air Force, as
well as the formation of the Officers' Corps, is practically concluded. Our material equipment and armaments are modern, and
with further delay the danger of their becoming out-of-date will
increase.

"On the one side the large armed forces, with the necessity
for securing their upkeep, plus the aging of the Nazi movement
and of its leaders, and on the other hand the prospect of a lowering
of the standard of living and a drop in the birth rate, leave us no
other choice but to act. If the Fuehrer is still living, then it will be
his irrevocable decision to solve the German space problem no later
than 1943-45."

Thus spoke the man who was a little later to call Roosevelt a
warmonger. It may be assumed that none among the select group
who heard him—and it included the defendants Goering, Raeder,
and von Neurath—called *him* a warmonger. On the contrary, Goering's contribution to the meeting was characteristic:

"In view of the information given by the Fuehrer, Goering considered it imperative to think of a reduction or abandonment of our
military undertaking in Spain."

The cautious Goering didn't want to drop all his bombs on Spanish democrats; he wanted to save some for the Czechs, just in case.

In the meantime, Hitler's war technicians had drawn up a top
secret directive entitled *Unified Preparation for War of the Armed
Forces,* which envisioned various war possibilities. Continuous pre-

paredness is necessary, said the directive, "to enable the military exploitation of politically favorable opportunities should they occur." It ordered further work on secret mobilization in order to put the Armed Forces in a position to begin a war "suddenly and by surprise."

The economic side of the secret mobilization was Schacht's job. By December, 1937, he could report, among other things, that 300 branches of industry, including 180,000 individual plants, had been inventoried for their war potential; 22 million workers had been indexed and classified for army use or war jobs, and 80 million ration cards had been printed and distributed to county and municipal officials ready for ultimate distribution "within 24 hours."

And Goering's Air Force, on May 2, 1938, prepared a top-secret *Organizational Study for the Year 1950*, which foresaw division of the Air Force into seven group commands with headquarters at Berlin, Brunswick, Munich, Vienna, *Budapest, Warsaw,* and Koenigsberg (My italics—V. H. B.). An attached map showed the Baltics, Poland, Czechoslovakia and Hungary as part of Germany.

Why Goering left out Moscow, I don't know. Certainly he had great ambitions. In midsummer of 1938, a few months after Munich was supposed to have brought peace in our time, he warned a meeting of airplane manufacturers:

"I still am missing entirely the bomber which flies with five tons of explosives as far as New York and back. I should be extremely happy to have such a bomber so that I would at last be able somewhat to stop the mouths of the arrogant people over there."

All through 1938—the year of *Anschluss* and of Munich—war preparations reached a frantic pitch. And knowledge that what was coming was a world war, a life-or-death struggle, was permeating all high levels of Government and the Armed Forces. For example, in September, 1938, Admiral Carls of the German Navy wrote a top secret opinion on a draft study of naval war against England. He said:

"There is full agreement with the main theme of the study. If, according to the Fuehrer's decision, Germany is to acquire a position as a world power, she needs not only sufficient colonial possessions but also to secure naval communications and secure access to the ocean.

"Both requirements can only be fulfilled in opposition to Anglo-French interests. It is unlikely that they can be achieved by peaceful means. The decision to make Germany a world power therefore forces upon us the necessity of making corresponding preparations for war.

"War against England means at the same time war against the Empire, against France, probably against Russia as well and a large number of countries overseas, in fact against half to two-thirds of the whole world."

And a month later Goering, in a meeting at his Air Ministry, laid down the line to industry and to the workers. I quote from a report of his speech prepared at the meeting:

"Goering is faced with unheard of difficulties. The treasury is empty, the industrial capacity is crammed with orders for many years. In spite of these difficulties, he is going to change the situation. If necessary, he will convert the economy with brutal measures in order to achieve this aim. The time has come when private enterprise must show its right to continued existence.

"Goering had received the order to increase armament to an abnormal extent, the Air Force having first priority. Within the shortest possible time, the Air Force is to be increased five fold, also the Navy must get armed more quickly and the Army should get large amounts of offensive weapons at a faster rate, particularly heavy artillery pieces and heavy tanks.

"A retraining of hundreds of thousands of people will have to take place. Much more work will have to be performed by women. Work periods of eight hours a day do not exist any more; wherever necessary, overtime is to be performed; double and triple shifts are a matter of course. Where the workers protest, as in Austria for example, Field Marshal Goering will proceed with forced labor; he will create forced labor camps.

"The Labor Front must not carry false social ideas among the workers. It is a fact that one generation drove the cart into the mud through the mutiny of the workers and by being guilty of not having shot these workers on the spot. Therefore we have to put the thing in order again."

War, war, war! The factories throbbing with war, the workers enslaved for war, the politicians angling for war, the military machine oiled and polished and ready for war down to the last screw. This was Germany in 1938. But inside was a weakness which threatened to spread. Schacht had seen it. Goering saw it when he stormed, "the treasury is empty." He saw it again when, in November, 1938, he told a Cabinet meeting of a "very critical situation of the Reich Exchequer . . . relief initially through the billion-mark fine imposed on Jewry and through profits accruing to the Reich in the 'aryanization' of Jewish enterprises."

But not even the Jew (who was supposed to have all the money in the world) could be made forever to bear the cost of armaments. Armament costs circle viciously: you build a gun, and you must build a bullet. Then you give both to a soldier. Then you must clothe the soldier and feed and house him. And after you have a soldier armed and fed and housed, you have one less worker to produce the arms and food and housing he needs.

There is a way out. Use the armaments you have built; let the guns speak. Then, when you have beaten the enemy, you make him pay your bills.

Was this why Hitler made war when he did—because he was afraid, if he waited too long, he would not be able to make it at all?

I skip now to the text of a speech made by Hitler to his military chieftains on November 23, 1939. There's no need to scan secret German files for what had happened in the meantime. In March, 1938, there was the conquest of Austria; in September, Munich and the occupation of the Sudeten; in March of the following year, conquest of the rest of Czechoslovakia; in August, the Nazi-Soviet Pact and the attack on Poland; in September, the entrance of England and France into the war. By November, Poland had been defeated and the *Sitzkrieg* in the West was on.

Who started all this? Was it the warmonger Roosevelt? The Judeo-Bolshevik-Plutocrats? The Jewish international bankers? Let's listen in to Hitler speaking to his commanders on that November day. It is one of the most revealing speeches of our time:

"When I came to power in 1933, I had to reorganize everything. First reorganization of the interior, abolishment of the appearances of decay and defeatist ideas, education to heroism. While reorganizing the interior, I undertook the second task: to release Germany from its international ties.

" . . . (First) rearmament; in 1935 the introduction of compulsory armed service. After that, militarization of the Rhineland. One year later, Austria came. It brought about a considerable reinforcement of the Reich. The next step was Bohemia, Moravia, and Poland . . . It was clear to me from that first moment that I could not be satisfied with the Sudeten-German territory. The decision to march into Bohemia was made.

"Then followed the erection of the Protectorate and with that the basis for the action against Poland was laid, but I wasn't quite clear at that time whether I should start first against the East and then in the West or vice-versa. Under pressure the decision came to fight with Poland first. One might accuse me of wanting to fight and fight again . . .

"*Basically I did not organize the armed forces in order not to strike. The decision to strike was always in me.*" (My italics— V. H. B.)

The will to war was there from the beginning. It was implicit in the Nazi party program; it was explicit in *Mein Kampf;* it was the driving force, the very *raison d'être,* of the Third Reich. The only question was, would it be war first in the West, or in the East? And the West said, "Go East, young man, go East." But the U.S.S.R., rebuffed by the West in its attempt to form an East-West coalition against Hitler in 1938, would have none of that. That is the real explanation of the Nazi-Soviet Pact.

But in any case there would have been war, pact or no pact. If not in 1939, then in 1940. If not first against Poland, then against France; if not against France, then against the U.S.S.R. But in any case, world war. "*Basically I did not organize the armed forces in order not to strike.*"

3.

Germany's top industrialists shared Hitler's will to war, knew of his plans and worked tirelessly to forge the necessary weapons. Moreover, certain giant concerns—such as Krupp and I.G. Farben, the German Dye Trust—put their worldwide organizations at the Nazis' disposal for espionage and for the transmission of Nazi propaganda.

A series of documents proving these facts were available to the Allied prosecution which were not introduced during the trial because no industrialist was in the dock. They were laid aside for subsequent trials; I was fortunate enough to be given the opportunity to examine many of them.

Big Business worked in intimate relations with the Hitler government chiefly through the various Nazified "Economic Groups," each representing an industry, formed when the Nazis introduced the *Fuehrerprinzip* into the German industrial world. Group leaders and leading industrialists met constantly with Goering as Plenipotentiary for the Four Year Plan, with Schacht and Funk in the Economics Ministry, with Todt and then with Speer in connection with armaments.

The decree creating the Reich Defense Council, issued only a few weeks after Hitler came to power, provided for the presence of industrialists at council meetings whenever it was deemed advisable. Through these meetings and others, German industry was kept informed of the needs of the rearmament program.

In December, 1936, Goering spoke to a gathering of the Reich Association of Industry and dispelled any doubts in the minds of industry as to the direction in which its wheels were turning.

"The stake is our people," Goering said. "We live in a time where the last big conflict looms. We already live in a time of mobilization and war. The only difference is we are not yet shooting."

Goering exhorted the industrialists to new investments because the approaching conflict demanded the greatest possible efforts. And he assured them they need not fear the investments would not be warranted by returns. If Germany is victorious, he explained, German industry will receive its due. What, he asked rhetorically, could be more profitable than armament orders?

I am reminded, reading this Goering speech, of Point 12 of the Nazi Party Platform: "We demand the total confiscation of all war profits." It will not be the last time that I am reminded of it.

In a series of meetings held throughout 1936 and 1937, the Economic Group of the Iron Industry geared itself for imminent war. "It is clear that exports and war needs have first priority," said one member at a meeting in August, 1936. Discussion revealed worry whether war would cut off Swedish ore; stockpiling was planned; a giant program designed ultimately to make Germany self-sufficient in iron and steel was laid out. Goering warned the industry that "we have in Italy a partner who is short of iron." And Roechling, among the biggest of the steel men, uttered another warning: "If you want to achieve autarchy in six years, you must start now."

Poensgen, leader of the Iron Industry Group, wrote a memorandum on August 8, 1937, closing with the words:

"We endorse the military needs. In order to facilitate their fulfillment, we suggest the storage of semi-finished products, pig iron, armor plates, etc., in safe places."

Beginning with the Munich period in 1938, the sense of urgency at the meetings heightened. In September of that year—the month, I repeat, that was to have brought us peace in our time—industrialists were meeting with members of the Army War Economy Staff and of the Economics Ministry and laying plans for the drafting of iron and steel workers by the armed forces, arranging for compensation for eventual damages to certain plants, discussing war prices, war financing and mobilization problems generally.

And two months after Hitler achieved his bloodless victory at Munich, William Zangen, head of the Reich Association of Industry, knew where some of the credit should go. "It is an unfounded reproach," he said in the course of a speech, "to say that German industry has not done everything it could. . . . The great political success we are enjoying now would not have been possible without the cooperation of industry."

This cooperation, as I have pointed out, extended far beyond the borders of the Reich, and in certain instances merged into espionage of the most flagrant sort.

As early as April, 1933, Krupp contributed 20,000 marks to the defendant Rosenberg for propaganda abroad. Rosenberg wrote in thanks:

"I am glad to determine that you, too, welcome the organization of an active counter-action abroad in the interest of the State and of the economy. . . . Very shortly a quantity of material will be sent to you and will subsequently be distributed throughout the world in a comprehensive compilation."

There is documentary proof that by October 12, 1937, industry was engaged in espionage on behalf of the German Combined Services Intelligence Department. On this day a man named Sonnenberg, an employee of Krupp, met with Captain Menzel of the German Navy, representing the Combined Services Intelligence. Sonnenberg wrote a memorandum on the meeting:

"Menzel asked for intelligence on foreign armaments (but not including matters published in newspapers) received by Krupp from their agents abroad and through other channels to be passed on to the Combined Services Intelligence. They have been collaborating for some time in this way in a most satisfactory manner through frequent visits with Messrs. Zeiss of Jena.

"On our part, we undertook to supply information as required. Apart from that, it would be in the patriotic interest if Krupp were kept informed concerning foreign artillery weapons and new methods and constructions. Menzel agreed to that with the reservation that some information had to be kept secret for stringent reasons; he promised to do his best in this direction."

I have already mentioned the Adolf Hitler Fund, to which industry contributed twelve million or more marks a year. Where some of this fund went is disclosed in secret minutes of a meeting held in October, 1939, attended by representatives of contributors and by officials of the Mining Cooperative of the West German Steel Industry.

The Union of Germans Abroad—a Nazi propaganda organization composed of German citizens living abroad—got some of the

money. So did other "cultural" and "ethnical" organizations, such
as the Nordic Society, the German-Italian Students Foundation,
and the German Foreign Institute at Stuttgart.

I.G. Farben, with offices or associate companies in every country
of the world, put its foreign exchange at Hitler's service. There is
available a cable from German Ambassador Ott in Tokyo to the
Foreign Office in Berlin noting that Farben in Japan had placed
one million yen with the Embassy for propaganda purposes. There
is another telegram revealing Farben payments to the German
Embassy in Madrid and warning that if the Spanish Government
discovered the payments, the Farben director in Spain could be
jailed.

On December 29, 1938, certain industrialists met with representatives of the German High Command and of the Economics Ministry and discussed the creation of an agency, to operate under
the Economics Ministry, for the purpose of "disrupting industry
and commerce" in foreign countries. The agency was to be known
as the Research Bureau for War Economy and was to have both
"offensive and defensive" assignments. It was to operate in collaboration with both private and State agencies abroad, and the
channel of contact was chiefly to be the steel industry's Liaison
Office for Press and Literature at Duesseldorf.

The meeting minutes hint that German steel concerns were
actively engaged in intelligence activities for the Nazi Government in France, Britain and the U.S.A., although no details are
given.

Among the industrialists present at the creation of this sabotage
and espionage agency were representatives of Mannesmann, Krupp,
Hoesch A.G., and Bergbaulicher Verein, all steel companies.

Even earlier — in 1937 — a Farben agent reported how his
company was distributing Nazi propaganda and news through its
confidential agents in South America, and recommended that this
propaganda should be directed mainly against the U.S.A.

Presumably, if German industry was thus cooperating with the
Nazis in Europe, Japan and South America, it did so also in North
America. O. John Rogge, chief prosecutor at the sedition trial
in Washington in 1944-45, has reported on various direct links

between our home-grown Fascists and Berlin. At the trial, not much of this evidence was produced, for the prosecution was after other game.

But Captain Sam Harris of the United States Prosecution, in an interrogation only partly introduced into court, drew interesting admissions from Heribert von Strempel, formerly in charge of "cultural relations" at the German Embassy in Washington. Von Strempel admitted:

1. That the Foreign Department of the Nazi party had direct relations with the Bund in the U.S.A.

2. That he was in command of a special press fund, part of which was turned over to the German Library of Information and to Flanders Hall, publishers in America of anti-British and pro-German propaganda.

3. That he dealt with, and gave money to, individual Americans who through their lectures and writings were trying to convince other Americans that only traitors to the U.S.A. would want to go to war against Hitler.

Von Strempel has since been brought to the U.S.A. by the Department of Justice for further questioning.

In this picture of Nazi plotting at home and abroad, industry played its role loyally and well from beginning to end. Indeed, as war came, its role became more dramatic, and more important. And for a while it looked as if its Herculean efforts would indeed, as Goering had promised, be well repaid.

They may still be.

4.

Jackson once said at a meeting of the four-power Prosecution Committee that aggressive war was the core of the prosecution case.

What was the defense against the aggressive war charge?

The defense of the military men—of Keitel and Jodl and Raeder and Doenitz—was "theirs not to reason why, theirs but to do and die." I quote Keitel under questioning by his own counsel:

Q. "It should be clear just what is meant by aggressive war. Can you tell me your views on that subject?"

A. "As a soldier, I must say that the concept does not mean very much to me in that sense. We did know about aggressive action, or defensive action, actions of retreat and how to carry them out, but according to my own personal and soldierly feeling, the concept of 'aggressive war' is a purely political concept and not a military or soldierly one."

Q. "Then you mean to say that . . . in the final analysis, whether a war is a just war or not, that does not fall into the sphere of your professional deliberations?"

A. "That is what I wish to express."

One notes there is no attempt here to deny that Germany waged aggressive war. There is only the assertion that Keitel's sole business, as a soldier, was to fight the war, whether it was aggressive or non-aggressive, just or unjust. It was unfortunate for Keitel that he was not just a common soldier; he was Chief of the High Command of the German Armed Forces. And, as the prosecution pointed out again and again, he was not on trial for fighting an aggressive war, but for having helped to plan it and to bring it on.

Under cross-examination by Jackson, Schacht's admissions were fulsome:

Q. "Well, we found something we agree on, Doctor. You knew of the invasion of Poland?"

A. "Yes."

Q. "As an unqualified act of aggression on Hitler's part?"

A. "Absolutely."

Q. "And of Holland?"

A. "Absolutely."

Q. "And of Denmark?"

A. "Absolutely."

Q. "And of Norway?"

A. "Absolutely."

Q. "And of Russia?"

A. "Absolutely, sir. And of Norway and Belgium, which you left out."

He could afford these admissions, or so he thought. In 1937 he

had gotten into a scrap with Goering and had resigned as Plenipotentiary General for War Economy; in 1939 he had resigned
as Reichsbank president. This absolved him, he argued, from all
responsibility for aggressive war, which he said had begun with
Poland.

Nevertheless, Schacht had remained in Hitler's Cabinet as Minister without Portfolio until 1943; and, in 1940, when Hitler
returned from Compiègne after having witnessed the French sign
their document of defeat, the first to shake his hand at the Berlin
railroad station was Schacht. A German film, shown to the Tribunal, immortalizes the event.

And Schacht could not deny that he had been present at any
number of meetings, prior to 1939, that had to do with preparation for war. He squirmed when the prosecution introduced the
following letter, written to Schacht by Hitler on the occasion of
the former's resignation as Reichsbank president because of technical policy differences:

". . . I take the opportunity to express to you my most sincere
and warmest gratitude for the services which you rendered repeatedly to Germany and to me personally in this capacity during
long and difficult years. Your name, above all, will always be
connected with the first epoch of national rearmament. I am happy
to be able to avail myself of your services for the solution of new
tasks in your position as Reichsminister.

"With German Greetings,

Your

A. Hitler."

The politicians among the defendants, including the politico-
militarist Goering, insisted they never wanted war, aggressive or
otherwise. Indeed, they were slavishly, blindly, devoted to peace.
They had moved heaven and earth to prevent the shedding of a
single drop of blood.

Had not Ribbentrop and Goering — particularly the latter —
maintained contact with London until the very last moment, and
even beyond, to prevent the spreading of the Polish conflict? Had

not Goering been in contact with Lord Halifax by special courier even after German troops had crossed the Polish border?

Yes, of course. However, Goering and Ribbentrop and the other defendants had not been charged with launching aggressive war against England, but against Poland. And there is no doubt that on the eve of the Polish invasion all the defendants, including Goering and Ribbentrop, were indeed slavishly, fanatically devoted to the idea of peace—with England. They were devoted to the idea of peace with everyone except Poland, which they wanted to finish off alone and unhampered.

Back in 1937, in the already mentioned directive *Unified Preparation for War of the Armed Forces,* the course taken by Goering and Ribbentrop had already been laid out: in case Germany's first attack should be towards the east, "the leaders of German policy will endeavor with all possible means to assure the neutrality of England."

As for the rest, the defense against the aggressive war charge was that Germany was seeking merely to correct the injustices of Versailles. All the defendants talked Versailles, Versailles, as if the signers of Versailles were on trial, and not its breakers. Patiently, at first, and later with some acerbity, the Tribunal pointed out to the defendants that Versailles was not germane to the issue. The defendants were not charged with believing that Versailles was an unjust treaty; they were charged with going to war, in violation of international agreements, to rectify it.

But even on its own ground, the defense did not make much sense. The Polish Corridor, it is true, was a creation of Versailles. So was the cession of Alsace and Lorraine by Germany to France and of the Sudeten to the new Czechoslovakia. But what had Bohemia and Moravia to do with Versailles? They were never part of Germany. What had the Soviet Union to do with Versailles? It was never part of Germany.

Indeed, the defense might have done better to insist that none among them, not one, had ever read any one of the six million copies of *Mein Kampf,* and therefore did not know the true aims of this war. Wrote Hitler:

"The claim for re-establishment of the frontiers of 1914 is a political insanity. . . . In reality [these frontiers] did not include all men of German nationality and neither were they more rational from a strategic point of view. They were not the result of a calculated political plan, but rather temporary frontiers; in the course of a struggle by no means ended, they were even partly the result of a gamble.

"The frontiers of the year 1914 have absolutely no value for the future of the German nation. They constituted neither a safeguard for the past nor a power for the future. They will not enable the German people to maintain its inner unity nor to assure its subsistence."

No one would have believed the defendants had they insisted they did not know that Hitler wanted more for Germany than restoration of its pre-Versailles frontiers. But, then, no one believed them anyway.

Chapter VI   Invasion by Telephone

1.

The German High Command, cynically, used for *Anschluss* the code name Case Otto (young Otto of Hapsburg is the Pretender to the Austrian throne). The Nazis had planned it, as the prosecution reminded the Tribunal, as long ago as 1923: *Mein Kampf* begins with the words, "German Austria must return to the Great German Motherland."

I do not want here to enter into a discussion of the merits of *Anschluss per se*. The defendants did, at great length and with greater irrelevance. Nor do I want to defend the Austrian people, who on the record do not deserve any different treatment today than the Germans.

The significance of Case Otto lies in something else. Here is the blueprint of Nazi aggression. Here is the picture of duplicity and terror, of machinations and murder, of unctious diplomacy and brutal gangsterism, which in Nazi Germany and in a sucker world, went by the name of Hitler's foreign policy.

In Case Otto, as in Case Schulung—the remilitarization of the Rhineland—the significance was the acquisition of territory by a *fascist* Germany, which meant that it was another step in the march towards war.

In July, 1934, Austrian Nazis attempted a *Putsch*, assassinating

70

the little Dollfuss, Chancellor of Austria. Berlin instigation was
suspected, but there was no proof. All that the world knew was that
the German Ambassador in Vienna, Dr. Rieth, agreed to "save
bloodshed" — once the *Putsch* was already lost — by offering the
besieged Nazi rebels safe conduct and asylum in Germany if they
would give up fighting.

Nothing fails like failure. Hitler removed Dr. Rieth promptly
and with great publicity, declaring that the Ambassador, in offering aid to the *Putschists,* had acted entirely on his own and
without the knowledge, no less the consent, of the German Government. He then appointed his Vice-Chancellor, the suave von
Papen, as his new Minister to Vienna with the title of Envoy
Extraordinary.

"The assassination of the Austrian Federal Chancellor, which
was strongly condemned and regretted by the German Government," wrote the heartbroken Hitler to von Papen, "has made the
situation in Europe, already fluid, more fluid through no fault of
ours. . . ."

The normal function of a diplomat is to represent his government. But the evidence at Nuremberg showed that von Papen,
being not only an Envoy Extraordinary, but also the reverse, did
infinitely more: he at long last succeeded, where Dr. Rieth had
failed, in overthrowing the government to which he was accredited.
He became at once political saboteur and agent provocateur, a one-
man Fifth Column whose job was made easier by the fact that he
worked in an atmosphere already more than half-fascist under
Dollfuss and his successor, Schuschnigg.

His reports to Hitler are models of the meddling diplomat.

"I suggest," he wrote blandly to Hitler in May, 1935, discussing
the internal Austrian political situation, "that we take a part in
this game." He urged Hitler to offer a new public recognition of
an independent Austria in return for the formation, in Vienna,
of a coalition government containing Nazis and Catholic pan-
German elements. "There should follow," he added slyly, "a
gradual disintegration of the barriers between the two countries."

Two months later he wrote, "National Socialism must and will
conquer the new Austrian ideology." And again, in a report on the

Danube situation: "As a guiding principle, I recommend tactically continued patient psychological manipulations, with slowly intensifying pressure directed at changing the regime." And a year later (May, 1936) he was urging continued support, to the sum of 100,000 marks, for an Austrian Catholic trade union organization known as the Freedom Union, particularly with reference "to continuation of its fight against Jewry."

On July 11, 1936, von Papen drafted one of the series of statements on Austro-German relations by which Hitler sought to convince Austria and the world that his intentions towards Vienna were strictly honorable. This one was in the form of an agreement signed by the two governments. It reiterated earlier Hitler assurances that the Reich Government had no intention of swallowing Austria and added that "internal political matters, including the question of Austrian National Socialism, are regarded by each State as purely the private affair of the other, which it will not seek to influence directly or indirectly."

But five days later, as a secret Nazi report introduced at Nuremberg revealed, Honest Adolf met two of the leaders of the Austrian National Socialist party at his Obersalzberg home and gave them "a clear explanation of the situation and of *(his)* wishes." And the following day, all the Austrian "illegal Gauleiters met in Anif, near Salzburg, where they received a complete report from Ranier on the statement of the Fuehrer and his political instructions for carrying on the fight."

Under such circumstances, one could not expect Austro-German relations to improve. They did not. The Third Reich's intention, clung to with terrible and unshakable tenacity, was to bring Austria back into a Greater Germany. And all the diplomatic machinations, all the public avowals of peaceful intent, were so much eyewash designed to create conditions under which *Anschluss* could take place with world acquiescence and without the shedding of a single German soldier's blood. Why pay for what one could get for nothing?

Nevertheless, Hitler was prepared for all emergencies. The 1937 *Directive for the Unified Preparation for War of the Armed Forces* included provision for special preparations to be made for "armed intervention against Austria (special Case Otto)." And alongside this item, in the original German document, there is a penciled note: "Settled."

The prepared settlement came a little less than a year later. Von Papen induced Schuschnigg to meet Hitler at Obersalzberg, that fairyland of mountain and sky in which Hitler was destined to charm into subservience, with the aid of the beautiful view and the most powerful army in the world, half the countries of Europe.

Hitler had three generals roaming around at this historic Berchtesgaden meeting: Sperrle, Reichenau and the defendant Keitel. Hitler always liked to have generals around when he planned amicable discourse with a guest; their presence, in full-dress and fully bemedalled, undoubtedly helped to induce in the visitor a most reasonable frame of mind.

The defendant Jodl, although not present at the meeting, summed up what happened with admirable precision in his diary: "Feb. 11: In the evening and on 12 February General K. [Keitel] with General v. Reichenau and Sperrle at the Obersalzberg. Schuschnigg together with G. Schmidt *(Austrian Foreign Minister)* are again put under heaviest political and military pressure. At 2300 hours, Schuschnigg signs protocol."

Schuschnigg went back with the protocol to Austria's President Miklas, its acceptance practically assured. But Hitler took no chances. Through Keitel, he ordered that military pressure should be kept up until February 15 at least by shamming military action all along the frontier. And so Austrian Intelligence agents, for the next few days, were picking up all kinds of planted stories: that the Wehrmacht was cancelling furloughs, that rolling stock was being assembled in Munich, that frontier police had called up reinforcements.

Miklas yielded, of course, and the Nazis were on the rise again in Austria. A few weeks later Schuschnigg, realizing at last that his country was no longer being run from Vienna but from Berlin, determined on a showdown. He would call for a plebiscite on the continued existence of a sovereign and independent Austria.

He announced the plebiscite plan on March 10. Hardly twenty-four hours later, there was no more Austria.

On the morning of the 11th two things happened: Hitler ordered his Army alerted to march (preparations for Case Otto "settled," remember?); and Goering got on the telephone.

I suppose this is the first time in history that a country was conquered by telephone. Goering, undoubtedly filled with a sense of history, had his conversations transcribed for the future, which at the moment did not seem likely to include a Nuremberg trial. That is why he had to hear so many of his words all over again in the courtroom. He did not seem to mind. A less vain man would have collapsed under the weight of this self-indictment; Goering merely smirked, occasionally looking sideways, grinning, at his co-defendants, as if to say, "I did all right, that time, didn't I?"

Goering spoke intermittently from two o'clock in the afternoon until ten at night. He was in Berlin; at the other end of the line was Vienna. He did not speak to any member of the Austrian Government except Seyss-Inquart, the ostensible "non-party" Minister of the Interior in Shuschnigg's cabinet, who had actually paid Nazi party dues as early as 1934. For the rest, his conversations were with various Austrian Nazi leaders who were working at top speed to destroy their country.

Goering's demands increased as the day wore on. He wanted cancellation of the plebiscite. When he got that, he demanded Schuschnigg's resignation. When he got that, he demanded that Seyss-Inquart be made the new Chancellor of a new all-Nazi Cabinet, including his (Goering's) brother-in-law as Minister of Justice. President Miklas balked at appointing Seyss-Inquart, and Goering grew very angry.

"You go immediately," he ordered Seyss-Inquart, "and tell the Federal President that if the conditions which are known to you are not accepted immediately, the troops who are already stationed at and advancing to the frontier will march in tonight along the whole line and Austria will cease to exist.

"Please do inform us immediately about Miklas' position. Tell him there is no time now for any joke. . . . Call out the National Socialists all over the country. They should by now be in the streets. Remember, an answer must be given by 7:30. If Miklas could not understand it in four hours, we shall make him understand it now in four minutes."

The Austrian Cabinet, with the exception of Seyss-Inquart, abdicated in a body, but Miklas still stood firm. Goering telephoned to Lieutenant General Muff, military attaché at the German Embassy in Vienna:

Goering: "The invasion is going to happen now. He *(Seyss-Inquart)* should take over the Government and should carry through quietly. The best will be if Miklas resigns."

Muff: "But he won't. He declared that he will under no circumstances yield to force."

Goering: "What does this mean? So he just wants to be kicked out?"

Muff: "Yes, he does not want to move."

Goering: "Well, with fourteen children one cannot move as one likes. Tell Seyss that he is to take over."

A few minutes later he was talking with Keppler, leader of the Austrian Nazis, who reported that orders had gone out to the Austrian Army not to oppose the invading Germans.

Goering: "I do not give a darn. Listen carefully. The following telegram should be sent here by Seyss-Inquart: The provisional Austrian Government . . . sends to the German Government the urgent request to help it to prevent bloodshed. For this purpose, it asks the German Government to send German troops as soon as possible."

Keppler: "Well, the SA and the SS are marching through the streets, but everything is quiet."

Goering: "He should send the telegram as soon as possible."

Keppler: "I will send the telegram to Seyss in the office of the Federal Chancellery."

Goering: "Show him the text and tell him that we are asking him—well, he does not even have to send the telegram. All he needs to do, is to say: 'Agreed.' "

Keppler: "Yes."

So that's how the German Army came to march into Austria in response to a telegram which was never sent, to quell disorders which never occurred. And one of the first things the Nazis did, after they got into Vienna, was to unveil a memorial plaque to the killers of Dollfuss—that Dollfuss whose assassination four years before had been "strongly condemned and regretted" by the German Government.

But Goering was not through with his telephone yet. Two days later he was on the line speaking to the defendant Ribbentrop, then Hitler's Ambassador in London. As he spoke, he was quite well aware that the British might be listening in:

"Tell the following to Halifax and Chamberlain: It is not correct that Germany has given any ultimatum. This is a lie by Schuschnigg, because the ultimatum was presented to him by Seyss-Inquart. . . . And as far as I know, just a military attaché came along, asked by Seyss-Inquart for technical reasons—to let Seyss know whether, if German troops were asked for, Germany would grant this request.

"Furthermore I want to state that Seyss-Inquart asked us expressly by telephone as well as by telegram, to send troops because he did not know about the situation in Wiener-Neustadt, Vienna and so on, because arms had been distributed there."

(Goering's defense on this point was characteristic. From the witness stand, under questioning by his attorney, he said: "During a conversation which I had with Foreign Minister Ribbentrop . . . I stressed that the ultimatum had been put not by ourselves, but by Seyss-Inquart. That was absolutely true. Legally, in fact, I put it, but that telephone conversation was heard on the English side and I had to conduct a diplomatic conversation.").

Ribbentrop answered that he had "the best impression of Halifax and Chamberlain" and foresaw no trouble from that quarter. Goering enthusiastically agreed and, undoubtedly still thinking of a possible British eaversdropper, continued:

"We have a clear conscience and that is the decisive factor. Before world history we have a free conscience. . . . Come over, it is beautiful here. The weather is wonderful. Blue sky. I am sitting here on my balcony—all covered with blankets—in the fresh air, drinking my coffee. Later on I have to drive in, I have to make the speech and the birds are twittering and here and there,

I can hear over the radio the enthusiasm which must be wonderful over there."

Yes, it was rather wonderful in Austria at the moment. Hitler, his feet again on his beloved native soil, was laying flowers on his mother's grave. The "liberated" Austrians, swastikas suddenly emerging on their lapels, surged through the market places shrieking *Heil Hitler* and singing the *Horst Wessel Lied,* and throwing flowers at their liberators, the marching Wehrmacht. And in Vienna cellars, men with black uniforms and rubber truncheons were beating out the brains of anti-Fascists, and on the streets and in cafés Jews were forced to clean spittoons and latrines with their lips while the jolly Viennese, lovers of music and of laughter, watched and chuckled.

And in the vast cool recesses of the War Ministry in Berlin, the generals checked off Case Otto as finished, noting with satisfaction how, on the new map of the Greater Reich, Czechoslovakia looked like a prone figure with its head between the jaws of the Nazi wolf.

Out of *Anschluss* was to come eventually the death of thirty million people. But before world history, Goering, sitting under the blue sky and listening to the twittering of the birds, had a clear conscience.

2.

Germany's new and strategically much improved eastern frontier was only six weeks old when Hitler and the defendant Keitel sat down to discuss Czechoslovakia.

In the language of the Nazi politicians, and before the world, the case of Czechoslovakia was the case of extending the protective and beneficent arm of the Third Reich over the Sudeten Germans, who were so persistently and shamefully persecuted by the savage Czechs.

But in the language of the German military, Czechoslovakia was merely Case Green, another piece in the mosaic of aggression. "The bloodless solution of the Czech conflict in the autumn of

1938 and the spring of 1939 and the annexation of Slovakia," the
defendant Jodl was to say in a speech delivered some years later,
"rounded off the territory of Greater Germany in such a way that
it now became possible to consider the Polish problem on the basis
of more or less favorable strategic premises."

Keitel and Hitler, meeting on April 21, 1938, didn't have to
waste time talking about the "persecuted" Sudetens. They were
both undoubtedly aware that the Sudeten Germans were the most
fairly treated minority in Central Europe. The problem at hand
was something else: under what circumstances should the invasion
of Czechoslovakia begin? The top secret minutes of the meeting,
revealed at the trial, show how carefully the problem was weighed.

Should the attack begin suddenly, without cause or possible
justification? No. Hitler and Keitel agreed that a consequent
hostile world opinion might lead to a critical situation.

Should it begin as the result of a long series of diplomatic
clashes leading naturally to crisis? No. Hitler and Keitel agreed
that such a course would forewarn Czechoslovakia and give her
time to take security measures.

There was a third way, and this was the plan which was approved
in principle:

"Lightning-swift action as the result of an incident (e.g.,
assassination of German Ambassador in connection with an anti-
German demonstration)."

Very simple, very effective, and apparently, so far as that old
soldier Keitel was concerned, perfectly in spirit with the code of
German military honor.

And an eminently practical plan, too. For Hitler and Keitel
knew they could have an anti-German demonstration in Czechoslovakia any time they wanted it. All they had to do was to tell
Konrad Henlein and his Sudeten German party, and they would
provoke one.

The Sudeten German party—the party of the assertedly persecuted Sudeten German minority — had been on the payroll of
Hitler's Foreign Office since 1935. Fifteen thousand marks monthly
is what the party received: twelve thousand in Prague, disbursed

through the German Embassy in Prague; and three thousand more in Berlin, paid out to the party office there.

So thoroughly were the Sudetens under the thumb of Berlin, in fact, that they even behaved themselves when so ordered. Immediately after *Anschluss*, according to an entry in Jodl's diary, Hitler felt that the Czech question ought to remain quiescent because "Austria has to be digested first." So the order went out from the German Legation in Prague:

"The line of German Foreign Policy is exclusively decisive for the policy and tactics of the Sudeten German party. .... The party leadership abandons its former intransigent line and adopts a line of gradual promotion of Sudeten German interests."

But this temporary quiet on the Czech front didn't blind certain European capitals to Hitler's ultimate intent. As early as March 4, 1938, a week before the Austrian adventure, the buzzards in Budapest were suggesting German-Hungarian military talks on "possible war aims against Czechoslovakia." (The talks were politely refused by the Germans because of the danger of third parties hearing of them.) And some time during the same Spring, and again in July, Mussolini asked Hitler when he intended to move against the Czechs so that the Italian Army could take precautionary measures along the French frontier.

So if Budapest and Rome smelled aggression against Czechoslovakia, it was not surprising that some of the ugly odor should penetrate into Prague. In May, the wary Czechs, under continued vituperative attack by the Nazi press and feeling themselves under momentary danger of war, suddenly mobilized.

This made the righteous Hitler and that indefatigable Pepys, the defendant Jodl, very indignant. The latter wrote in his diary:

"The intention of the Fuehrer not to touch the Czech problem as yet is changed because of the Czech strategic troop concentration on May 21, which occurs without any German threat and without the slightest cause *(sic!)*. Because of Germany's self-restraint, the result is a loss of prestige for the Fuehrer, which he is not willing to take once more. Therefore, on May 30, the new order is issued for Case Green."

The new order was signed by Hitler himself and began bluntly:

"It is my unalterable decision to smash Czechoslovakia by military action in the near future. It is the job of the political leaders to await or to bring about the politically and military suitable moment.

"The proper choice and determined and full utilization of a favorable moment is the surest guarantee of success. Accordingly the preparations are to be made at once."

Yes, Hitler was irritated, as irritated as a man can be who, having planned to commit murder on Sunday, is charged by his prospective victim with having tried to do it on Saturday.

From the May 30 directive to the September crisis and Munich, developments were foreordained by the Nazis, shaped and compelled by them. And when I think back now on the columns and columns of tripe which appeared in the American and British and French press of the period, the columns on border incidents, on Hitler "peace" speeches, on the "murders" of "peaceful Sudetens" by the mad Czechs, on the solemn British Runciman mission to "investigate" Prague, on the editorials of the London *Times* pleading righteously for the rights of a minority to autonomy, I want to weep with shame and despair. For the border fights were provoked by Henlein's Sudeten Free Corps; the Nazis not only admit this, they boast of it. And as for all that high-sounding talk of autonomy, that wasn't a Nazi idea at all; the Nazis—to be exact, the defendant Ribbentrop—borrowed the notion from the British.

So there was Munich, and the Big Four departed afterwards to their respective capitals and were greeted everywhere with wild acclaim. For was not here the perfect solution? Was not Germany getting its Sudeten Germans, the Sudetens getting their Germany, and the world its beloved peace? A great gift, peace! And three weeks after this magnificent boon was granted by Chamberlain and the magnanimous Hitler, the latter was issuing Top Secret Order No. 236/38, dated October 21:

"The future tasks for the Armed Forces and the preparations for the conduct of war resulting from these tasks will be laid down by me in a later Directive.

"Until this directive comes into force the Armed Forces must be prepared at all times for the following eventualities:

"1. The securing of the frontiers of Germany. . . .

"2. The liquidation of the remainder of Czechoslovakia.

"3. The occupation of the Memelland."

From then on, as had happened with the Sudeten, events shaped themselves into a foreordained pattern. I have already quoted Hitler's speech made two years later, in which he reviews this period: "It was clear to me from that first moment that I could not be satisfied with the Sudeten-German territory. The decision to march into Bohemia was made." After Munich, the rump of Czechoslovakia had five months to live.

The technique was essentially the same. There were the same charges leveled against the Czechs of mistreatment of Germans, of generally anti-German policy, of the Czech Army—how weak now without its Sudeten fortifications, without even proper railway communications!—constituting a standing menace to the Third Reich.

And in the Slovaks, Hitler found his new Sudetens; and in Slovak State Secretary Karmasin, his new Henlein. Like the Sudeten leader, Karmasin was on Hitler's payroll; and like Henlein's, his job was to weaken Prague, this time by inflaming the traditional Slovak independence movement.

By March, in 1939, Hitler was ready to move. But this time he was not going to move alone. He had already promised a small piece of Czechoslovakia—the Teschen area—to the Poles; and the Budapest buzzards had been promised the easternmost province of Ruthenia. On March 13 he received a touching acknowledgment of his generosity from Horthy of Hungary:

"My sincere thanks. I cannot tell you how happy I am because this Head Water Region is of vital importance to the life of Hungary. . . . The dispositions have already been made. On Thursday, the 16th of this month, a frontier incident will take place which will be followed by the big blow on Saturday.

"Your devoted friend,

Horthy."

On the same day Hitler got this letter, he called in Tiso, chief of the province of Slovakia, and warned him that if the Slovak

Parliament did not sever relations with the Prague Government, and declare itself independent, he would leave Slovakia to the mercies of Hungary.

Within three days, Slovakia broke with Prague; and in the place of Tiso, in Hitler's office in the Reich Chancellery, sat the aged Hacha, President of Czechoslovakia, and his Foreign Minister, Chvalkavsky.

The events of this conference, like those of the Berchtesgaden meeting with Schuschnigg, have been no secret for years. The old President walked into Hitler's study bearing his country in his outstretched, pleading hands, an Indian bearing gifts. One cannot blame him too much; one can blame him only for having gone to Berlin at all. Once he was there, pressure was more than a human being could stand.

At six in the morning the German Army would march into Czechoslovakia, Hitler told him. He was almost ashamed to say that there was a German division for almost every Czech battalion. Goering, smiling affably, said he would be sorry if he had to bomb beautiful Prague. Hitler said the Czechs could offer resistance and be destroyed in two days or they could yield peacefully and put Czech-German relations on a new and mutually profitable basis. "We intend," said Hitler, "no denationalization."

The Fuehrer expressed himself as particularly horrified by the size of the Czech Army compared to the country which it served. "Why did not Czechoslovakia immediately reduce her army to reasonable strength? Such an army represented an enormous burden. Czechoslovakia's foreign policy had no mission to fulfill, so there was no point in retaining such an army."

On this point the aged Hacha offered his only argument. He asked whether the whole purpose of the entrance of German troops into his country was to disarm the Czech Army. Could this not, he asked plaintively, be done some other way?

Foolish, vain talk! "My decision is irrevocable," said Hitler. "Everyone knows what a decision of mine means. The only possibility of disarming the Czech Army is by the German Army."

The talk lasted all night. The old man, who had neither physical nor spiritual strength, went into an anteroom for a moment and conferred briefly with his Foreign Minister. When he returned, he signed a document that was handed to him. The document read:

"The President of the Czechoslovak State declared that, in order to reach a final pacification, he confidently placed the fate of the Czech people and of their country into the hands of the Fuehrer and the German Reich."

Lidice, Lidice!

I am reminded at this stage that, on the occasion of the march into Austria one year before, Goering had given his word of honor to the Czech Ambassador in Berlin that nothing would happen to Czechoslovakia.

I want to present Goering's own explanation of this point, given from the witness box at Nuremberg, as revelatory of what a Nazi means by his word of honor.

"The Czechoslovakian Ambassador, Dr. Massny, came to me, very excited, shaking," testified Goering, "and I told him in the presence of others: 'Your Excellency, listen carefully now, I give you my personal word of honor that this is a question of the annexation of Austria only and that not a single German soldier will come anywhere near the Czechoslovakian border.' . . . At no time did I tell him, I give my word of honor, that for all time we will never have anything to do with Czechoslovakia."

The Tribunal was presented with that kind of defense for more than six months.

3.

The monstrous Goering sat under the blue sky sipping coffee, at peace with his conscience. Yet it is a mistake to think of him and his Nazi colleagues as the only protagonists in this drama of infamy.

I have said that Hitler moved towards war inexorably, calculatingly, deliberately. This is true. But it is also true that he wanted this war to come under his own conditions, when *he* was ready and the enemy unprepared, when he could strike the sudden blow with the aid of that most powerful of modern secret weapons—surprise.

And today we know, from the Nazis' own secret archives revealed at the trial, that these conditions were not 100 per cent present for Hitler until 1939, and that any time before that date he could have been stopped in his tracks—at worst with a short war, at best without a single shot having been fired.

Until he had Austria and all of Czechoslovakia, Hitler remained in mortal fear of a general war. Only his profound conviction that the West was paralyzed by lassitude and the fear of communism encouraged him, against the judgment of many of his generals, to risk his first aggressions.

It is a matter of history that Hitler forced through the remilitarization of the Rhineland despite his generals' fears that France would march. "Militarization of the Rhineland," Hitler said in 1939, "was again a process believed to be impossible at the time . . . the number of people who put trust in me was very small." But apparently it was enough.

Austria?

I want to quote from two documents. The first is a letter, introduced by defense counsel, written by von Papen to Hitler on June 1, 1937, reporting the writer's conversation with Sir Nevile Henderson, who had just been appointed British Ambassador to Berlin.

"Sir Nevile . . . was in complete agreement with the Fuehrer," wrote von Papen, "that bolshevism was the foremost and greatest danger to the existence of Europe and that this point of view should take precedence over all others.

"When I explained the German-Austrian problem to the Ambassador, he said that he was convinced that England fully comprehends the historic necessity of a solution of this question in the Reich German sense."

Von Papen then reminded Sir Nevile that the British Ambassador in Vienna did not share this view and was "doing everything to support the thesis of Austrian independence." Von Papen quotes Sir Nevile's answer as follows:

" 'But my opinion is quite different and I am convinced that my opinion will prevail in London, too. . . . But please, do not betray to my Viennese colleague that I hold this view.' "

I don't for a moment think that this letter made Hitler feel friendly towards England. It simply helped lead him to the belief —in which time proved him right—that whatever the eventual cause of war between England and the Third Reich, it would *not* be Austria.

Yet he remained worried. There was France, and there was Italy — Catholic, like Austria, governed by a similar type of fascism, and with a possible common fear of a mutual neighbor growing more powerful by the day.

A few hours before the German Army crossed the Austrian border, Hitler spoke by telephone to his Ambassador in Rome, Prince Philipp von Hessen. There is an hysterical note to the conversation which reveals clearly Hitler's real feelings at the time, in contrast to the boasting and self-confident attitude he assumed before his public:

Hessen: "I have just come back from the Palazzo Venezia. The Duce accepted the whole thing in a very friendly manner. He sends you his regards. He said that Austria would be immaterial to him."

Hitler: "Then please tell Mussolini that I will never forget him for this, never, never, never, whatever happens. . . . As soon as the Austrian question is settled, I shall be ready to go with him through thick and thin, nothing else matters."

Hessen: "Yes, my Fuehrer."

Hitler: "Listen, I shall make any agreement—*I am no longer in fear of the terrible position which would have existed militarily in case we had gotten into a conflict.*" (My italics—V. H. B.)

But there was no conflict because Sir Nevile's opinions did indeed prevail in London, and without London Paris would not move.

Czechoslovakia?

As early as 1937, in his oft-quoted November speech to the Nazi military chieftains, Hitler's position was made quite clear:

"The Fuehrer believes personally that in all probability England, and perhaps also France, have already silently written off Czechoslovakia, and that they have gotten used to the idea that this question would one day be cleaned up by Germany."

This is the frame of mind in which Hitler entered the Austrian adventure, the prelude to Czechoslovakia, and this is the frame of mind in which, on May 30, 1938, he made his "unalterable decision to smash Czechoslovakia by military action in the near future." However, three weeks after the unequivocal May directive, Hitler added a cautious qualification:

"There is no danger of a preventive war by foreign states against Germany. Germany has not committed herself to any military alliance which might automatically force Germany into warlike conflict.

"The immediate aim is a solution of the Czech problem by my own free decision. This stands in the foreground of my political intentions.

"However, I will decide to take action against Czechoslovakia only if I am firmly convinced, as in the case of the occupation of the demilitarized zone and of the entry into Austria, that France will not march and therefore England will not intervene."

He might better, perhaps, have put it the other way: that England would not march and therefore France would not intervene. In any case, he could safely reckon that one would not march without the other.

As the military plans for the Czechoslovakian campaign were developed by the Nazi chieftains, stress was laid again and again upon a surprise beginning and a quick ending to avoid a general European crisis. Hitler knew that when once a warlike step is taken, things move rapidly and today's Chamberlain can become tomorrow's Churchill.

This was his great worry, and he shaped his military plans accordingly, but always with the conviction that he was merely insuring himself against the unlikely and unexpected.

He had no need to worry. London saw no reason to go to the rescue of that small country whose name, as Chamberlain had publicly pointed out, the average Englishman could not even spell. London did not send an army to help the Czechs; instead, it sent a Runciman Mission to help the Sudetens.

And Hitler? A little more than a year later, on the eve of his attack on Poland, he was able to say proudly to his generals:

"The creation of Greater Germany was a great achievement politically, but militarily it was questionable, since it was achieved through a bluff of the political leaders."

No bitterer epitaph could have been written on the policy and spirit of Munich.

Part II
AGGRESSION

Chapter VII   Case White

1.

From the moment Hitler seized power, an evil triumvirate of Nazis, militarists and Big Business was pushing its country deliberately and inexorably towards war. But what war? Against England? France? Russia? Poland?

For the first six years, Hitler himself was not certain against whom this war would begin. The year of decision was 1939.

The documentary evidence of the preceding two years, presented by the prosecution, showed how and why this decision was reached.

In his November, 1937, speech, Hitler expounded to his generals his plan to acquire *in Europe* — preferably from territories adjoining the Reich—the necessary "living space" for the German people. And he made perfectly clear that this territory could only be acquired by war.

"We live in a period of economic empires," Hitler said then. "In Japan and Italy economic motives are the basis of their will to expand, and economic needs will also drive Germany to it."

Against the fulfillment of this program, Hitler said, stood "two hateful enemies, England and France, to whom a strong German colossus in the center of Europe would be intolerable." He knew then that the showdown one day would have to come from the

West, just as he knew that one day there would have to be a show-down with the Colossus of the East, the Soviet Union.

The already quoted Admiral Carls' memorandum of 1938, fore-seeing and accepting the concept of war against England, France, and Russia, in order for Germany to regain its place as a world power, was the logical development of the "showdown" thesis. Hitler's application of the principle was simple enough: Show-down, yes, but with one side at a time. *No two-front war.*

So from 1937 through the first months of 1939, Hitler's policy was one of defense against the West and aggression against the East—Austria and Czechoslovakia. And in the war plans of the period Case Red—code name for war against the West—was developed as a defensive campaign to come into force only if the West should attempt to interfere with the Vienna and Prague adventures.

But with the final, bloodless acquisition of the rump of Czecho-slovakia in March, 1939, Case Red momentarily lost its defensive character and Hitler considered developing it as an aggressive plan for the showdown in the West.

"I wanted to establish an acceptable relationship with Poland in order to fight first against the West," Hitler explained to his generals on August 22, 1939. "But this plan, which was agree-able to me, could not be executed because essential factors changed. It became clear to me that Poland would attack from the rear in case of conflict with the West."

In other words, he feared a two-front war should he attack in the West; more certain of it, indeed, than if he first attacked to the East. For if Munich and the preceding five years had told him anything, it was that in all the world there would be no more quiescent and amiable observers than England and France if he would only keep moving eastward and attack the U.S.S.R.

So out of the unwholesome atmosphere of Munich, a pact whose effects were as dangerous to Soviet security as it was fatal to Czecho-slovakia's, there grew the Nazi-Soviet non-aggression pact of August, 1939, and the place and time of the first battles of World War II were duly entered by Hitler's generals in a little folder labeled Case White—Poland.

2.

The Germans are the most long-suffering people on earth. Once away from their native soil, they are oppressed by everyone. Dollfuss and Schuschnigg beat them and imprisoned them in Austria. The Czechs cut their throats and burned down their houses. The Poles cut off their ears and their tongues.

These atrocities always happened at the most opportune time for Hitler. It is astonishing how, when one examines closely secret German archives as well as German newspaper clippings, the atrocities always seemed to multiply on the eve of a planned German invasion. It was so in Austria, in Czechoslovakia, in Poland.

But treatment of the German minority was only one of the ostensible causes of German-Polish friction. There was also the Polish Corridor and Danzig. Particularly Danzig. If one put together the transcripts of the conversations on Danzig that Hitler and Ribbentrop had with Polish diplomats from the year 1937 onward, one could walk across the Atlantic on a bridge of paper.

Indeed, the problem of Danzig did walk across the Atlantic. It became a burning international issue. It became, to all intents, the only issue. And on the first Sunday after Hitler's attack on Poland, the Hearst press in America published a two-page map of Europe, with Danzig pictured as the tiny insignificant dot on the vast continent over the possession of which the world was being plunged into war.

But in May, 1939, more than three months before the outbreak of war, Hitler secretly told his generals:

"Danzig is not the subject of the dispute at all. It is a question of expanding our living space. If fate brings us into conflict with the West, the possession of extensive areas in the East will be advantageous."

There are none so blind as those who will not see. Was not Hitler making peaceful speeches? Had he not publicly told his Reichstag, on September 26, 1938, that "We have assured all our immediate neighbors of the integrity of their territory. . . . We have no interest whatever in a breach of the peace"? Was there not a Polish-German non-aggression pact dating back to 1934? And did not Hitler say publicly, as late as January 30, 1939, that "During the troubled months of the past year, the friendship between Germany and Poland has been one of the most reassuring factors in the political life of Europe"?

Then, in March, Hitler finished with what was left of Czechoslovakia, and two months later he called in his generals, and told them, in secret session, of his decision to attack Poland. Present at this conference of May 23, 1939, were the defendants Goering, Raeder, and Keitel, as well as others of the Nazi High Command. The minutes were kept by Lieutenant Colonel Schmundt, the adjutant on duty, and I want to quote from them at some length, for they constitute what was perhaps the key document in the prosecution's case on aggressive war:

"It is questionable whether military success in the West could be achieved by a quick decision; questionable, too, is the attitude of Poland.

"The Polish Government will not resist pressure from Russia. Poland sees danger in a German victory in the West, and will attempt to rob us of the victory.

"There is therefore no question of sparing Poland, and we are left with the decision: *To attack Poland at the first suitable opportunity.* We cannot expect a repetition of the Czech affair. There will be war. Our task is to isolate Poland.

"Fundamentally, therefore: Conflict with Poland — beginning with an attack on Poland—will only be successful if the Western Powers keep out of it. If this is impossible, then it will be better to attack in the West and to settle Poland at the same time.

"It is not impossible that Russia will show herself to be disinterested in the destruction of Poland. Should Russia take steps to oppose us, our relations with Japan may become closer.

"If there were an alliance of France, England, and Russia against Germany, Italy, and Japan, I would be constrained to attack England and France with a few annihilating blows. The Fuehrer doubts the possibility of a peaceful settlement with England. We must prepare ourselves for the conflict. England sees in our development the foundation of a hegemony which would weaken her. She is therefore our enemy and the conflict with her will be a life and death struggle.

"The Dutch and Belgium air bases must be occupied by armed force. Declarations of neutrality must be ignored. . . .

"An effort must be made to deal the enemy a significant or the final decisive blow right at the start. Considerations of right and wrong, or treaties, do not enter into the matter."

This is the grand scheme, the fruit of the fascist mind. One notes above all the unshakable will to attack, whatever the contingency: With Russia neutral, or, failing that, with Japan co-belligerent; with the West neutral, or failing that, with Italy co-belligerent. The vivid nightmares of the megalomaniac take on shape and form, the shape and form of hard steel and marching men. Krupp's pots and pans have not been in vain. Nothing has been in vain—not the ideological gibberish of the defendant Rosenberg, the obscene mouthings of Streicher, the counting-house legerdemain of Schacht and Funk. All contributed, willingly and knowingly, to the physical and spiritual molding of a country to the point where its leader could get up and say: "Tomorrow we attack, Poland alone if we can, but half the world if we must."

A month before this conference, Hitler had asked General von Brauchitsch to draw up an operational plan for Case White. The plan was drawn with careful emphasis on the surprise element and was made operational "anytime from September 1 onwards." A little later—June 14—the operational time was advanced to August 20: "All preparations must be concluded by this date."

On August 13, Mussolini's Foreign Minister and son-in-law, Ciano, came up to visit Hitler and Ribbentrop at Obersalzberg. The visitor was informed of Hitler's determination to settle the Polish problem once and for all. Ciano said he didn't like the idea; the time was not ripe. Italy, he insisted, was not ready for war; Spain needed a rest and more battleships; the whole political situation would improve for the Axis as time went on. But Hitler would have none of that argument.

"The Fuehrer had come to two definite conclusions," say the official notes on the conversation, "(1) In the event of any further provocation, he would immediately attack Poland and (2) If

Poland did not clearly and plainly state her political intentions, she must be forced to do so." And Hitler added that, because of weather conditions, Poland's answer must come before the end of August.

What Hitler didn't tell Ciano was that the "provocation" needed for attack had already been arranged. The affidavit of Alfred Neujocks, member of the SS, which was presented to the Tribunal in the course of the trial, furnished another glimpse of the fascist mind at work—the mind which a year earlier had planned the assassination of the German Ambassador in Prague to furnish reason for the invasion of Czechoslovakia.

"On or about August 10, 1939," testified Neujocks, "the chief of the Sipo and SD, Heydrich, personally ordered me to simulate an attack on the radio station outside of Gleiwitz near the Polish border and to make it appear that the attacking force consisted of Poles.

"Heydrich said, 'Practical proof is needed for these attacks of the Poles for the foreign press as well as for German propaganda purposes.'

"I went to Gleiwitz and waited there fourteen days. I went to see Heinrich Mueller, head of the Gestapo, who was then near by at Oppeln. In my presence, Mueller discussed with a man named Mehlhorn plans for another border incident, in which it should be made to appear that Polish soldiers were attacking German troops. Germans in the approximate strength of a company were to be used.

"Mueller stated that he had twelve or thirteen condemned criminals who were to be dressed in Polish uniforms and left dead on the ground of the scene of the incident, to show that they had been killed by attacking. For this purpose they were to be given fatal injections by a doctor employed by Heydrich. They were also to be given gunshot wounds.

"After the incident, members of the press and other persons were to be taken to the spot.

"Mueller told me that he had an order from Heydrich to make one of those criminals available to me for the action at Gleiwitz.

The code name by which he referred to these criminals was 'Canned Goods.' "

On the eve of war, both incidents went through as planned. The schemes were accomplished with the aid of that honorable soldier, Keitel. For Keitel, as Chief of the High Command, relayed from Hitler to his Intelligence men the order to furnish Heydrich with the Polish uniforms. The Chief of Intelligence, Admiral Canaris, talked to Keitel about the schemes and Canaris' notes of the conversation were introduced at the trial: "He [Keitel] does not think much of actions of this kind. . . . However, there is nothing else to be done if they have been ordered by the Fuehrer."

That is a typical Keitel defense. It is typical of the defense in general. Hitler ordered it, Himmler ordered it, Bormann ordered it. The only guiltless men in Germany were the twenty-one in the dock, all of whom were innocent messenger boys. In uniform-loving Germany, where postmen look like Field Marshals, why shouldn't Field Marshals act like postmen?

On August 22, Hitler made two speeches to his generals. The first, a lengthy one from which I have already quoted, comprised an appraisal of the world situation as favorable to immediate German aggression. He closed it with the announcement of the Nazi-Soviet pact and added:

"Now Poland is in the position in which I wanted her. We need not be afraid of a blockade. The East will supply us with grain, cattle, coal, lead and zinc. . . . A beginning has been made for the destruction of England's hegemony.

"*I am only afraid that at the last minute some Schweinehund will make a proposal for mediation.*" (My italics—V. H. B.)

In the second speech, Hitler grew even tougher. The document on this speech introduced at the trial is in the form of terse notes probably taken by Schmundt, who took down the minutes of the May meeting.

"Destruction of Poland in the foreground," say these notes of Hitler's speech. "The aim is elimination of living forces, not the arrival at a certain line.

"I shall give a propagandistic cause for starting the war — never mind whether it be plausible or not. The victor shall not be asked later on whether we told the truth or not. In starting and making a war, not the Right is what matters, but Victory.

"Have no pity, take a brutal attitude. Eighty million people shall get what is right. The strongest has the Right."

This was nine days before the attack. On the surface, much happened in those nine days. In and out of the Reich Chancellery and Ribbentrop's Foreign Office scurried frantic diplomats, bearing proposals, counter-proposals and new proposals. The British, the French, the Poles chased each other's long coat-tails in this diplomatic merry-go-round. The wires burned from Berlin to Rome to London to Paris to Washington. Goering and Ribbentrop maintained last-moment communication with Lord Halifax or others in London, seeking not peace, but the guarantee of a one-front war.

Came England's promise that it would help Poland if attacked. Came a few days' delay by Hitler to give his minions a further chance to isolate Poland politically. Came long and solemn communications by the wire services and star correspondents: the war was on, it was off, it was postponed, it *will* come, it *won't* come. Came the dignified Sir Nevile to the German Foreign Office and the reading, with such haste that not one word in ten could be understood, of a pages-long ultimatum by a snarling Ribbentrop.

It was all sound and fury, signifying nothing. For Case White was already in process of evolving. The gray-green columns of the German Third Army Group were at their posts at or near the Polish border. Heydrich had his Polish uniforms, and the men who were to wear them, all ready, and a physician stood by with his syringe. And Neujocks was already at Gleiwitz, waiting for the code words, "Canned Goods."

Came the appointed hour—4:45 A.M., September 1, 1939—and the Wehrmacht and Heydrich and Neujocks moved into action. And the Wehrmacht continued to move until Poland was smashed in twenty-two days. Hitler was proved right again. Although he failed to keep France and England neutral, he was right in having prophesied that there would be no two-front war. The French and British did not or could not move out of the Maginot Line; Munich and Maginot arose out of the same spiritual sickness of the period.

I do not want to forget, in the midst of these grave events, a

very unhappy gentleman who during the trial sat towards the
end of the first row in the dock, between Streicher and Schacht.
This was the defendant Funk, successor to Schacht as Economics
Minister.

Funk wept openly in court when the prosecution reminded him
of atrocities committed by the National Socialist party. But on
August 24, 1939, on the eve of war, Funk was in quite a different
mood, and he wrote as follows to Hitler:

"My Fuehrer:

I thank you sincerely and heartily for your most friendly and
kind wishes on the occasion of my birthday. . . . The information
given to me by Field Marshal Goering that you, my Fuehrer, yes-
terday evening approved in principle the measures prepared by
me for financing the war . . . made me deeply happy. I hereby
report to you with all respect, that I have succeeded in making
the Reichsbank internally so strong and externally so unassailable,
that even the most serious shocks in the international money and
credit market cannot affect us in the least.

Heil My Fuehrer

Walter Funk."

Despite this letter, Funk denied on the stand that he knew that
war was coming. And he insisted, anyway, he was just a small man
who never had any power.

They were, indeed, all small men in the dock, but not precisely
in the way Funk meant.

Chapter VIII   Weser, Yellow, Marietta, and "25"

1.

The trial held interest at high level for a fortnight. Everything was still new and fascinating: Goering's mugging, Sauckel's leer, the Caligari mask of Rudolf Hess; Lawrence's sliding spectacles and the gorgeous mustachios of the French Justice, M. de Vabres; the daily wrestle of the black-gowned counsel with unfamiliar court procedure and the still stranger earphone system; the taut voices of inexperienced interpreters working under strain; the bustle of newsmen and photographers; the neighborly chatter of the defendants during the recess periods.

It was exciting to recognize the smaller dramas within the greater one: to watch Kempner, an American prosecutor, gazing at the defendant Frick, his former persecutor in Germany; to see Albert, an American interpreter, sitting two feet away from the defendant Fritzsche, who had dismissed him from the Vienna radio in 1934; to watch a young Czech-born Jew, now in the uniform of a United States Army lieutenant, bring a glass of water to the witness Ohlendorf, who had just finished telling how he had killed 90,000 Jews in a single year.

But most of all, it was exciting to hear the secret, unfamiliar voice of Fascist Germany intoning its own guilt in its own words.

The excitement could not and did not last. The novelty wore

away; one grows weary of watching faces and gestures, even if they be of world-famous criminals. Lawrence's spectacles never did fall off. There were too many documents and not enough flesh-and-blood witnesses, too many long speeches and not enough sharp argument.

Humankind's capacity for boredom is often the least rewarding of its virtues. It took more than six years, and very nearly her existence, for England to learn that the Nazis were liars and meant her nothing but evil. The British prosecution, giving names, dates, places, texts, proved the details in six days, and lots of people yawned (as England and the world had yawned for six years).

Yet it is a story that must be told again and again and again—in this book, and other books, in magazines and lectures and school courses and history texts. There must be left no loophole for the fascist apologists for Hitlerism, who have by no means been crushed in the U.S.A. any more than in Germany, and who will grow in arrogance and in numbers as time heals the pains and lulls the passion left by this war.

These apologists are saying now—and I have heard it said by members of the American prosecution staff in Nuremberg—that we should never have indicted Germany for violating treaties and attacking neutrals. Their argument is that countries have always violated treaties, and always will; that, had not Germany attacked Norway and Belgium and Holland first, England and France would not have hesitated to do so if it became a matter of life and death. And this school of hard-boiled political realists—is it "realism" always to be ready to give the Fascists a better-than-even break?—point triumphantly to the evidence that England was about to invade Norway at the very moment the Nazi invasion took place.

I agree that international morality has not yet reached the point where it supersedes the law of self-preservation. But what right had the Nazis to decide that it was a matter of "self-preservation" for them to attack and destroy Poland, a nation of thirty million people? And what right had the Nazis to decide that it was a matter of life and death for them to invade Holland and Belgium in order to reach the British in France? Who and what had brought the British to French soil in the first place? And as for Norway, prove that the British had planned to invade Norway *before* the war had started, prove that George VI secretly coveted Haakon's throne—only then would the apologists be on sound ground.

The most that can be said for Germany is that, once launched on aggressive war and having met serious resistance, she is geographically incapable of honoring her treaties or of refraining from further aggressions. She is like the bank robber who, having shot the night watchman, must kill six policemen before he can break into the clear. Is he excused the six murders because, without any doubt whatsoever, they were a matter of his life or the policemen's?

The Nazis, when they decided to make war, were perfectly well aware of Germany's geographical peculiarities and the resultant strategic inducement to overrun neutrals. They knew these problems not only from the memory of 1914 and the Kaiser's rape of Belgium. Their knowledge was much more intimate and immediate; they studied these problems, prepared for them, *planned* once again to tear up treaties and throw them to the winds of war.

The documents produced at Nuremberg prove this up to the hilt.

2.

In May, 1939, Hitler told his generals:

"If England intends to intervene in the Polish war, we must occupy Holland with lightning speed . . . the Dutch and Belgian air bases must be occupied by armed force. Declarations of neutrality must be ignored."

One notes the cautious qualification: *if* England intervenes. Actually, Hitler did not believe that England would intervene. And most emphatically he did *not* believe there was any imminent danger of England violating the neutrality of either Belgium or Holland. He said that plainly to Ciano on August 12, 1939, and again to his generals on August 22.

On his own part, he had no intention of stirring up trouble in the West until he had finished with Poland. So, five days before the Polish onslaught, he publicly reassured Belgium and Holland that their neutrality would be respected. And, undisturbed by the paper war declaration which England and France had made against him, he proceeded to the business of finishing off Poland.

But this was only a preliminary business. The "life and death struggle" with England, already nominally at war with Germany, remained. And even as the Wehrmacht was razing Poland, the War Ministry in Berlin was perfecting plans for the execution of Hitler's decision of the previous May: "Declarations of neutrality must be ignored."

Warsaw fell on September 23. Hitler waited exactly sixteen days—only long enough, presumably, to make certain that redeployment of his forces from Warsaw to the West was well under way. Then, on October 9, he issued *Directive No. 6 for the Conduct of the War:*

"Preparations should be made for offensive action on the northern flank of the Western Front crossing the area of Luxembourg, Belgium, and Holland. The object of this attack is to defeat as strong a section of the French Fighting Army as possible, and that of her Ally and partner in the fighting, and at the same time to acquire as great an area of Holland, Belgium, and Northern France as possible, to use as a base offering good prospects for waging aerial and sea warfare against England and to provide ample coverage for the vital district of the Ruhr.

"The time of the attack is dependent on the operational readiness of the armored and motorized units and on the state of the weather."

Thus the policy of defense in the West changed definitely to attack; in the code of the Wehrmacht, Case Red became Case Yellow. And within a month of the directive, the "operational readiness" which was one of the two prerequisites for its execution, was achieved.

But the other prerequisite, the weather, was something else.

Thanks to Nuremberg, the world now knows, at least in part, the explanation of that peculiar suspension of activity in the winter of 1939-40, the something that was war and yet not war, which came to be known as the *Sitzkrieg*. Whosever plan it was, it was not Hitler's. For the trial revealed that fifteen times between

November, 1939, and May, 1940, Hitler ordered the attack, and that each time weather postponed it.

Whether, during this period, the Anglo-French leaders were as assiduous as Hitler in consulting the meteorologists or whether they were merely content to consult each other, the trial did not show. At any rate, nobody moved until May 10 when the Wehrmacht green, burgeoning suddenly in the spring weather, sent its swift, choking tentacles across Luxembourg, Holland, and Belgium.

This is not to say that Hitler wasted the winter months entirely. Part of the time, at least, he spent inventing reasons for invading neutral countries that would be more palatable to world opinion than mere "operational readiness" and good weather. And simultaneously with his army, his propagandists moved to make his inventions public.

"On the basis of the evidence," said an ultimatum delivered to Belgium dated May 9, but not delivered until the following day, "and particularly on the basis of the attached reports from the Ministry of the Interior of the 20th March and the German High Command of the 4th May, the German Government establishes . . ."

There followed a long list of allegations that the Anglo-French forces were about to overrun Belgium and that Belgium herself had been guilty of innumerable unneutral acts. The ultimatum did not add, naturally, that, weather permitting, the invasion would have taken place six months ahead of the reports which were supposed to justify it.

I want to quote briefly from the official Belgium account of the meeting which took place on the morning of May 10 between the German Ambassador at Brussels and the Belgium Foreign Minister, M. Spaak, now President of the General Assembly of the United Nations:

"At 8:30 A.M. the German Ambassador came to the Ministry of Foreign Affairs. When he entered the Minister's room, he began to take a paper from his pocket.

"M. Spaak stopped him: 'I beg your pardon, Mr. Ambassador.

I will speak first.' And in an indignant voice, he read the Belgian Government's protest:

" 'Mr. Ambassador, the German Army has just attacked our country. This is the second time in twenty-five years that Germany has committed a criminal aggression against a neutral and loyal Belgium.

" 'No ultimatum, no note, no protest of any kind has ever been placed before the Belgian Government. It is through the attack itself that Belgium has learned that Germany has violated the undertakings given by her on October 13, 1937, and renewed spontaneously at the beginning of the war.

" 'The act of aggression committed by Germany, for which there is no justification whatever, will deeply shock the conscience of the world. The German Reich will be held responsible by history.' "

3.

The Norwegians shot Quisling. Did his bosses rate milder treatment?

The defendant Rosenberg, as head of the Nazi Party Foreign Office, kept close contact with Quisling during the winter of 1938-39. He thought highly of this Norwegian "patriot" who had founded, in his country, a pro-German, fascist party with a laudably strong anti-Semitic platform.

By January, 1939, Quisling had joined the growing list of immortal payroll patriots who received Reich gold to help them betray their countries. In that month the defendants Rosenberg and Ribbentrop, working in collaboration, awarded him 200,000 gold marks for the furtherance of his good work.

It was Rosenberg's plan, at that time, that Quisling should engineer a coup in Norway, with the help of Fascists (German and Norwegian) trained for the job on German soil. Then, as Seyss-Inquart had been told to do in Vienna, Quisling was to get on the telephone and ask Berlin for troops to help "maintain order."

Undoubtedly Rosenberg was drawn to Norway because, behind his brunette complexion and brown hair, he had an absolutely blond mind with an incorrigible Nordic bent. The German Navy was also drawn to Norway, but for reasons less genetic than geographical.

Evidence brought out at the trial showed that in this connection there occurred, during September and October of 1939, a fascinating sequence of developments in Germany:

1. On September 2, the Reich Government sent an *aide memoire* to Oslo in which it pledged "under no circumstances to prejudice the inviolability and integrity of Norway and to respect the territory of the Norwegian State."

2. Four days later the defendant Raeder, then commanding the German Navy, discussed the whole Scandinavian problem with Hitler and learned that the Fuehrer's ultimate intention was to establish a "north Germanic community with limited sovereignty in close dependence on Germany."

3. On October 3, Raeder—undoubtedly recalling his talk with Hitler and also having more immediate plans for Norway—asked his War Staff for an opinion on which Norwegian harbors might be suitable as U-boat bases.

4. Three days later the Reich Government gave Norway another open reassurance that there existed "no conflicts of interest or even points of controversy with the Northern States."

5. And on October 9, again three days later, the defendant Doenitz, then commanding the German U-boat fleet, proposed taking the Norwegian port of Trondheim as the best possible submarine base.

All of which proved, among other things, that the worst possible thing that could happen to a European State was to have friendly words bestowed upon it by Hitler. With the Third Reich, an open reassurance was practically a guarantee of a secret menace.

In December, Rosenberg brought Quisling in to see Ribbentrop and Hitler, and the converging political and military aims of the party and of the navy met and merged. Thenceforth events moved swiftly. In January, 1940, the defendant Keitel, as Chief of the Supreme Command of the Armed Forces (OKW), started planning for the Norway invasion under the code name Weser Exercise. The following month von Falkenhorst was offered command of the operation and accepted "gladly."

And on March 13, that tireless diarist, the defendant Jodl, jotted down an extremely interesting item: "The Fuehrer does not yet give the order for Weser. He is still looking for an excuse."

With the possible exception of Versailles, I don't suppose that any point in the Nuremberg evidence brought out so much and such acidulous comment as this little entry. The prosecution rightly threw it at Raeder, Doenitz, Jodl, Keitel, Rosenberg, and Ribbentrop, all of whom had direct or indirect hand in the Norway attack.

But the defendants stood firm: it was not an *excuse* that Hitler was looking for, but a *justification*. For, said the defendants, Hitler didn't really want to invade Norway, he only wanted to make sure that England did not do so first. And what he was waiting for was documentary proof that England really meant invasion.

Yet the diary of Admiral Assmann, who was the Pepys of the German Navy as Jodl was for the army, says the following about a meeting between Hitler and Raeder on March 23:

"British landing in Norway not considered serious. Raeder suggests invasion by German forces at the next new moon, to which Hitler agrees."

Sir David Maxwell-Fyfe, the able Scots member of the British prosecution, cross-examined Raeder on this item:

Q. "Do you remember that?"

A. "I haven't seen the document, but it is quite improbable."

Q. "But the second part, the second sentence, is right, isn't it: 'Raeder suggests invasion by German forces at the next new moon,' the 7th April?"

A. "But yes, of course. I was in favor of carrying out the landings in Norway at the easiest possible time, when ice conditions had improved, as we had previously decided and as had been ordered by Hitler."

Q. "Well, again I must argue with you, but the point comes to this, that you are saying that Admiral Assmann, who is right in his second sentence, is not only wrong, but entirely wrong, when he says that 'British landing in Norway not considered serious.' "

Anyway, on April 2 Hitler finally fixed the date for Weser, which included Denmark as well as Norway, for April 9. And before the dawn of that day, under a new moon, the German Armada sailed across the North Sea, its warships flying British flags and its troopships disguised as British merchantmen, and with standing orders that any Norwegian challenge should be answered in English by some such phrase as "Calling at Bergen for a short visit, no hostile intent."

Somewhere behind Norway's dark coasts awaited the Quislings, eager to welcome the invaders. But the Quislings weren't the Norwegian people; and what had been planned as a bloodless invasion cost the armada its flagship, and what had been planned as a bloodless occupation turned out to be a bed of thorns for the Germans for the duration of the war.

It is perfectly true that at the last moment the British and French were planning operations in Norway. Apprehensive, after the Soviet-Finnish war, of any further extension of influence into Scandinavia by either Germany or the U.S.S.R., and determined to stop the steady flow of Swedish iron ore south along Norwegian waters from Narvik, the British planned to occupy the latter port with three or four battalions of infantry and some anti-aircraft batteries.

"If opportunity offers," reads the British operations order, which the defense introduced on behalf of Raeder, "the Commander intends to advance into Sweden and occupy the Gallivare oil fields and important centers in that area. On no account will armed forces advance across the frontier without express orders from Force Headquarters."

But this order is dated April 6, four days after Hitler had definitely set the date for his own invasion, and months after the Germans had definitely decided upon invasion (although without setting a date).

And years before—in 1934—Goering, Hitler, and Raeder had agreed, at a meeting, that "no war could be carried on if the navy was not able to safeguard the ore imports from Scandinavia." Did the Nazis think that, regarding the importance of Swedish ore, the British were less intelligent than themselves? And did they expect that the Allies would forever refuse to fight on any ground except that of the Nazis' choosing?

Hitler thought neither, of course. He knew, the moment he determined to destroy England, that sooner or later either Norway or Sweden or both would eventually be dragged into the war, just as he intended that Belgium and Luxembourg should be. He wanted both Swedish ore and Norwegian bases; the British wanted him to have neither.

Of course, the Nazis could always say, as some of the defendants did imply, that nobody would have bothered the neutrals if only England and France had given up. I am reminded of that German woman who, looking around the smoking rubble of Aachen as the the Americans moved in, cried bitterly, "If you would only have let Hitler have his way, all this would not have happened."

After all, Hitler's war aims in the West were really very modest. "The German war aim," he had told the members of his Armed Forces High Command back in October, 1939, "is the final military dispatch of the West, i.e., destruction of the power and ability of the Western Powers ever again to be able to oppose the State consolidation and further development of the German people in Europe."

4.

On October 28, 1940, Mussolini began to feed his Italian soldiers, with shocking profligacy, to Greek cannon guarding the Albanian border. Two weeks later Hitler wrote the Duce a chiding note:

"Allow me at the beginning of this letter to assure you that my heart and thoughts have been, in the last fourteen days, more than ever with you. . . .

"I wanted to ask you, first of all, to postpone the battle to a more favorable time of year, in any case until after the American presidential election.

"In any case, however, I wanted to ask you, Duce, not to undertake this battle without a previous lightning-like occupation of Crete, and for this purpose I wanted also to offer you practical suggestions for the commitment of a German parachute division and a further airborne division."

Still, the Duce was not only an ally, but a friend *("Please tell Mussolini I shall never forget him for this, never, never, never")*. And a conquest of Greece would certainly offer certain definite advantages to the Axis. So about the time Hitler wrote so plaintively to Mussolini, he also ordered his generals to prepare plans for occupying the Greek mainland north of the Aegean Sea in order to "make possible the use of the Luftwaffe in the Eastern Mediterranean, in particular against those English air bases which threaten Romanian oil."

Undoubtedly Hitler hoped the Duce would be able, in the end, to accomplish this alone. But by December, the winter war in the Albanian-Greek mountain passes made it seem more likely that the Italians would see the Adriatic again before they ever saw Athens. And so Hitler ordered hastening of preparations for Greece under the code name Marietta, and, winter war being what it was, set the jump-off time for the following March.

Meanwhile Nazi politicians got to work on Yugoslavia, whose army lay on the flank of Hitler's planned route to Greece via Bulgaria. And on March 26, the *Voelkischer Beobachter* boasted in big headlines to its German readers:

"Yugoslavia Also in the Tri-Partite Pact.

"Minister Churchill Again Has Lost a Battle."

But the people of Yugoslavia had other ideas. Within a few days revolution swept Belgrade and the fascist pact-signing government was out, replaced by one which might go with England or the U.S.S.R., or might stay neutral, but which would never under any circumstances go with the Nazis.

Berlin's reaction was instantaneous. The following day Hitler called his generals together and the faithful Colonel Schmundt kept his usual careful notes of what was said at the secret session:

"The Fuehrer is determined, without waiting for possible loyalty declarations of the new government, to make all preparations in order to destroy Yugoslavia militarily and as a national unit. No diplomatic inquiries will be made nor ultimatums presented.

"Politically, it is especially important that the blow against Yugoslavia be carried out with unmerciful harshness. The war should be very popular in Italy, Hungary, and Bulgaria, as territorial acquisitions are to be promised to these states.

"The main task of the air force . . . is to destroy the Yugoslav air force ground installations and to destroy the capital, Belgrade, in waves."

No declarations, no ultimatums, no mercy. Ghengis Khan must have been an Aryan, too.

The Yugoslav development, labeled Operation 25 by the Germans, did not fundamentally alter plans for Marietta. The only change was that the Wehrmacht, instead of deploying towards Greece through friendly Bulgaria, marched chiefly through unfriendly Yugoslavia, smiting as it went.

But the Yugoslav development did alter matters in another direction. I cite an additional line from the Schmundt notes quoted above:

"The beginning of the Barbarossa operation will have to be postponed up to four weeks." (Italics as in original.)

Barbarossa was the Wehrmacht code name for attack on the Soviet Union.

Chapter IX   Barbarossa

1.

In June, 1940, at Compiègne, Hitler danced his jig on the corpse of Western Europe. So many of us, by now, have seen the film—the mincing step, the hand on hip, the face wreathed in smiles under the fabulous forelock. What the camera could not catch was the bright lust for England in his eyes.

The Armistice that brought the French campaign to its close was signed June 21. Nine days later the defendant Jodl prepared a memorandum entitled the *Continuation of the War Against England:*

"A landing in England can only be contemplated after Germany has gained control of the air. [Its] sole purpose should be to provide the *coup de grâce,* if necessary, to a country whose war economy is already paralyzed and whose Air Force is no longer capable of action.

"This situation will not occur before the end of August or the beginning of September."

Poland had fallen in 22 days, France in 42. England would take a little longer, perhaps as much as 60 days. Does this sound, shall we say, a trifle over-confident? One must remember the time. Germany, having fed so long on victory, was fat with confidence. After the conquest of half a continent, what was a little island?

So in August, Goering's Luftwaffe—the Goering who said his name would be Meyer if ever an Allied bomb landed on Germany —went up and the bombs came down on London and southern England. But, unfortunately for Goering, so did his Luftwaffe. The RAF was in the skies, the RAF which Churchill later was to immortalize in his brilliant phrase, and the end of August came, and the beginning of September, and the air over the Channel still belonged to England.

There came again a shift in Hitler's plans.

"The fear that control of the Channel sky could no longer be attained in the autumn of 1940," the defendant Raeder noted in a memorandum written in 1944, "led the Fuehrer to consider whether—even prior to victory in the West—an Eastern campaign would be feasible with the object of first eliminating our last serious opponent on the Continent."

Not, of course, that this was the first time the Nazis had thought about an attack on Russia. Such an attack was foreshadowed in *Mein Kampf*, and in every speech the Nazis ever made against the "Bolshevist menace." It was implicit in the very rise of Nazism, in the theory of Lebensraum and in the simple fact that the Ukraine was the breadbasket of Europe. It was foreshadowed in the signing of the Nazi-Soviet pact itself.

"In view of previous statements made by the Fuehrer," wrote Raeder in the same memorandum, "and of the contrasts in ideology, I personally have always doubted that the Fuehrer believed from the beginning that the Russo-German pact would endure. I think that the pact arose solely out of the need of the moment and that the Fuehrer *in no wise* intended it to be a *permanent* solution of the Russian problem." (Italics in original.)

Hitler himself had said as much in his speech to his generals in November, 1939.

There is no doubt that many of Hitler's military advisers (including Raeder) did not, for one reason or another, relish Barbarossa very much. For one thing, they dreaded a two-front war. But Hitler persisted, and on the basis of his not unreasonable calculations, he was right.

For Barbarossa was planned as a *blitz* which would smash the

U.S.S.R. in a few months. Hitler did not believe the Allies would or could launch any large scale attack of their own within that period. And it turned out that the Allies gave him not merely a few months but a year and a half—until November, 1942, when our forces landed in North Africa. And if Hitler mistakenly thought he could beat the Russians in a *blitz* campaign, he must not be judged too harshly; a lot of people made the same mistaken judgment, including the Chief of Staff of the United States Army.

At any rate, in August, 1940, while the bombs—and the Stukas —were dropping on England, a part of the Wehrmacht that had conquered France was quietly transferred eastward to a new staging area: the General Government in Poland and the Czech Protectorate. And just as quietly, almost casually, the chief of German Army Ordnance was told by Goering that deliveries of war materials to Russia under the Nazi-Soviet trade pact should be made punctually only until the spring of 1941: "Later on we will have no further interest in satisfying Russian demands."

In connection with the transfer of troops to the East, the defendant Jodl laid down the propaganda line to be followed by his Counter-Intelligence services:

"These regroupings must not create the impression in Russia that we are preparing an offensive in the East. On the other hand . . . she should draw the conclusion that we can at any time protect our interests, especially in the Balkans."

So, in August and September, while the German people were still singing *Wir Fahren Gegen England,* the warmakers in Berlin began to look in another direction. Operation Sea Lion — code name for the invasion of England—was shelved, if only (as the OKW then thought) temporarily. And in the mind's eye of the generals and the map-makers, the white cliffs of Dover gradually gave way to the Pripet marshes and the great fortresses of Leningrad, Kharkov, Kiev.

On December 18 the final decision was made, and over Hitler's signature was issued *Directive No. 21:*

"The German Armed Forces must be prepared *to crush Soviet Russia in a quick campaign* before the end of the war against

England (Case Barbarossa).... Preparations are to be completed
by 15 May 1941." (Italics as in original.)

Thenceforth plans developed with extraordinarily successful
secrecy, considering that the deployment of more than 100 divisions—perhaps one and a half million men—was involved. Hitler
did not even take Mussolini into his confidence. The tremendous
deployment of the Wehrmacht towards the East was made to appear
as merely a feint for the cross-channel drive into England; the
OKW planned it as "the greatest deception in the history of warfare." The sudden Balkan maneuver in the spring further complicated the picture and aided deception. Even so, world capitals
were rife with rumor, and in Moscow the British Ambassador
astonishingly and accurately forecast the exact date of the attack:
June 22. What is so astonishing is that he made his forecast on
April 24, whereas Hitler did not actually settle the date of A-Day
until April 30.

Then, at 3:30 A.M. on June 22, the Wehrmacht threw itself
upon the U.S.S.R. in wave after wave. And it came to pass as
Hitler had prophesied to his generals on the previous February 2:
"When Barbarossa commences, the world will hold its breath."

2.

Hitler said his war on Russia was defensive. Many of the defendants repeated this from the witness stand.

What is a defensive war? Is it one that forestalls attack today,
tomorrow, in five years, ten years?

Whatever might have been the ultimate outcome of the great
conflicting forces then dominating Europe, the evidence is conclusive that, in the summer of 1941, Russia was *not* preparing to
attack Germany.

The defendant Raeder, looking back on Barbarossa in his memorandum of 1944, wrote that "Stalin cannot have intended to take
the initiative in attacking this strong Germany in 1941."

Two weeks before June 22, the Nazi Ambassador reported to
the defendant Ribbentrop, then Foreign Minister, that the Soviet

Government was doing everything "to avoid a conflict with Germany."

General Thomas, chief of the German Army Armaments Office, notes significantly of the period:

"The Russians carried out their deliveries *(under the Nazi-Soviet Trade Pact)* as planned, right up to the start of the attack. Even during the last few days, transports of India rubber from the Far East were completed."

And when, just a few hours before attack, German Navy reconnaissance nosed through the Baltic Sea, it found lacking not only all signs of attack, but also any sign that attack was expected: "Battleships still continue target practice!"

What is a defensive war?

Is it one the objective of which is to crush the enemy forever? To destroy it not only militarily but also as a nation? To steal its lands and enslave its peoples? To harness its resources to the victor's own war-making machine? To murder its fighters after capture, to burn its towns and seek to destroy, through killings and other measures, its biological vitality?

These were the goals of Barbarossa.

Hitler had set the tone in *Mein Kampf:*

"The goal of our future foreign policy must not be 'orientation to the East or West' but Eastern policy in the sense of procuring the necessary land for our German people."

In the three months preceding June 22, the military preparations were paralleled by politico-economic planning designed to effectuate this policy.

On March 13, in connection with Case Barbarossa, Himmler was entrusted with "special tasks" arising out of the "struggle which has to be carried out between two opposing political systems." The "special tasks" were not defined in the appointment order. And at this point I do not want to say more than that they were typical SS tasks, carried out in typical SS manner.

Within a few weeks, the defendant Rosenberg was appointed Reich Commissioner for the Eastern Occupied Territories, in charge of political development, while the defendant Goering was named chief of the Economics Staff East, charged with the over-all direction of economic operations in the conquered territories.

Six weeks before the "defensive" war began, Rosenberg wrote some general instructions for the Military Governors who were to take over the conquered Russian areas:

"The only possible political goal of war can be to free the German Reich from Great Russian pressure for centuries to come. Therefore the German Reich must beware of starting a campaign on the basis of an historical injustice, i.e., the reconstruction of a Great Russian Empire, no matter of what kind.

"Therefore this huge area must be divided according to its historical and racial conditions into Reich Commissariats. The Reich Commissariat Eastland *(the Baltic states)* including White Ruthenia, will have the task to prepare, through development of the area into a Germanized protectorate, a progressively closer cohesion with Germany.

"The Ukraine shall become an independent State in alliance with Germany; Caucasia, with the contiguous Northern Territories, a Federal State with a German plenipotentiary. Russia proper must put her own house in order for the future."

By "Russia proper," of course, is meant Great Russia, with Moscow as its capital. And when Rosenberg said that this area shall be permitted to put its own house in order, he was, to put the matter moderately, indeed, speaking euphemistically. For meanwhile Goering's Economic Staff East, created specifically to bring about "the immediate and highest possible exploitation of the occupied territories in favor of Germany," was developing its own ideas about what was to be done with the Moscow region.

On May 23, the Agricultural Group of Goering's staff laid down the general lines of economic policy which was to be applied to the conquered eastern lands. The report points out that European Russia is divided into two great complementary regions: the industrialized "forest belt" of Great Russia, which runs roughly from the Moscow-Leningrad region in the West to the Urals in the East, and the agricultural "black soil belt" of Southern Russia (the Caucasus and the Ukraine).

Heretofore, Goering's experts emphasized, the great urban centers of the industrial region depended for their food upon Southern Russia, paying for it in manufactured goods. In other words, without the Ukraine, the Moscow worker must starve.

This was a very pleasant thought to Goering's experts, who proceeded to capitalize upon it:

"All industry in the *(food)* deficit area, particularly the manufacturing industries in the Moscow and Petersburg regions, as well as the Ural industrial region, will be abandoned.

"Destruction of Russian manufacturing industries in the forest zones is also indispensable to Germany's more remote peacetime future. In future, Southern Russia must turn its face towards Europe. Its food surpluses, however, will only be paid for if it purchases its industrial consumer goods from Germany or Europe. Russian competition from the forest zone must therefore be eliminated.

"It follows that the German administration *(in the forest zone)* may well attempt to mitigate the consequences of the famine which will undoubtedly take place . . . Many tens of millions of people in this area will become redundant and will either die or have to emigrate to Siberia.

"Any attempt to save the population from death by starvation by importing surpluses from the Black Soil zone would be at the expense of supplies to Europe. It would reduce Germany's staying power in the war and would undermine Germany's and Europe's power to resist the blockade. This must be clearly and absolutely understood." (Italics in the original.)

It *was* clearly understood, even by the fuzzy philosopher Rosenberg, who preferred politics to economics and polemics to either. "We see absolutely no reason," he told members of his political staff two days before invasion, "for any obligation on our part to feed the Russians with the products of the food surplus zone. . . . It is certain that the future will hold very hard years in store for the Russians."

Besides destroying Great Russia's industry and deliberately imposing famine upon its people, the Nazis planned to confiscate from the U.S.S.R. all meat, cut or on the hoof; all pigs, fish, oil, seed, flax, sugar, alcohol, hides, leather, and "industrial consumer goods such as coal, kerosene, etc." From these stocks the German Army was to be supplied first; what was left over was to be shipped to the Reich.

3.

A defensive war?

"Therefore we shall emphasize again that we were forced to occupy, administer, and secure a certain area. Nobody shall be able to recognize that it initiates a final settlement. This need not prevent us from taking all necessary measures—shooting, resettling, etc.—and we shall take them."

Thus Hitler at a meeting at his headquarters when the war on Russia was twenty-four days old, and the smashing Wehrmacht was ahead of even the most optimistic schedule.

"But we do not want to make any people prematurely into enemies," Hitler added. "Therefore we shall act as though we wanted to exercise a mandate only. *At the same time we must know clearly that we shall never leave those countries.*" (My italics—V. H. B.)

Present at this meeting were the defendants Goering, Rosenberg, and Keitel. The defendant Bormann was also present and obligingly left for posterity—and the Nuremberg trial—the notes from which I am quoting.

A defensive war? Listen to Hitler again:

"On principle we have now to face the task of cutting up the giant cake according to our needs in order to be able,

"First, to dominate it;

"Second, to administer it;

"Third, to exploit it.

"Never again shall it be possible to create a military power west of the Urals, even if we have to wage war for a hundred years. *We must never permit anybody but the Germans to carry arms.*" (Italics in original.)

A defensive war?

"The Reich Marshal *(Goering)* thinks it right to incorporate into East Prussia several parts of the Baltic country. The Fuehrer emphasizes that the entire Baltic country will have to be incorporated into Germany. At the same time the Crimea, including a considerable hinterland . . . the Volga colony . . . the district around Baku . . . will have to become Reich territory.

"The Finns wanted East Karelia, but the Kola Peninsula will be taken by Germany because of the large nickel mines. The annexation of Finland as a Federated State should be prepared with caution. The area around Leningrad is wanted by the Finns; the Fuehrer will raze Leningrad to the ground and then hand it over to the Finns."

A defensive war?

"The Russians have now ordered partisan warfare behind our front. This partisan war again has some advantage for us; it enables us to eradicate everyone who opposes us. . . .

"The Reich Marshal was going to transfer all his training fields to the new territories, and if necessary even Junker 52s could drop bombs in case of riots. Naturally this giant area would have to be pacified as quickly as possible. *The best solution was to shoot anybody who looked sideways.*" (My italics—V. H. B.)

On the last day of the trial one of the defendants, in his final statement, declared that Germany's guilt had been "expiated" through Russian, Polish, and Czech post-war treatment of Germans. The speaker was Hans Frank who, as Governor General of Poland, had once said that if he wanted to put up a poster for every Pole shot by the Germans—presumably for "looking sideways"—there would not be enough wood in all the Polish forests to supply the necessary paper.

4.

One could argue that the Nazi-Soviet pact, which Red-baiters still insist "started the war," actually assured Germany's defeat. For without the pact, it is more than likely that the Nazis would have attacked the Soviet Union earlier, a development which the West would have watched with tranquillity. Could the Red Army alone have defeated the Wehrmacht? And could the West, granting the ultimate clash, have defeated a Germany strengthened by Ukrainian bread, Caucasian oil, Donets coal and steel?

But *with* the pact, the U.S.S.R. got half of Poland, the Baltic states, Bessarabia. And few military men will disagree that Soviet possession of these buffer areas saved Moscow, Stalingrad and possibly the whole East Front for the Allies.

This is the pragmatic argument and it satisfies many people, including, naturally, the Communists. It does not satisfy the people who would have preferred a fascist victory over the U.S.S.R. to a coalition victory over Hitler. And it also does not satisfy the liberal and the idealist, to whom it is a shocking thing that Stalin should, under any circumstances, have teamed up with Hitler.

The liberal draws the parallel between the United States' shipment of scrap iron to Japan prior to Pearl Harbor, and the Soviet shipment of rubber into Germany up to the eve of war. If the first was "appeasement," why not the second?

Perhaps it was. It depends upon one's definitions. The Nazi-Soviet pact was by no means a one-sided affair; the Soviet Union got out of it not only the immensely important strategic buffer areas, but also steel for the naval guns that defended Leningrad. At any rate, it is evident that the Germans did not consider the pact as "appeasement" on the part of Russia; the German Naval War Diary refers, at one point, to Stalin as a "cold-blooded blackmailer."

The key to Nazi-Soviet relations between the fall of 1939 and the summer of 1941 lies, of course, in the pact itself. If the pact was justified, then one must expect all that followed: an attempt by Russia to establish at least a minimum friendly relation with Germany, meanwhile rearming and possibly waiting *(a)* for American entry into the war and *(b)* a show of attacking strength, and the will to use it, by the Anglo-American coalition.

As regards justification for the pact, I want to quote again from Hitler's speech to his commanders on August 22, 1939, in which he announced that the accord would shortly be signed. This time I cite from notes of the Fuehrer's talk taken by Admiral Hermann Boehm, present as representative of the German Navy:

"Among the Western Powers there was hope for the cooperation of Russia, which aside from material support was also of psychological significance. The decision to shed blood is difficult. One is apt to ask: Why just I? So the hope of England was directed towards Russia.

"But only a blind optimist could believe that Stalin would be so crazy as not to see through England's intentions, namely, to wage only a kind of stationary war in the West and to let Russia carry the bloody burden of the war in the East.

"*For these reasons the Western Powers did not wish to enter into any definite commitments and every time the concrete question about it came up, the negotiations came to a deadlock, as no positive answer was given.*" (My italics—V. H. B.)

The strength of this interpretation, of course, is that it can hardly be attacked as coming from a communist source, or even that of a fellow traveler.

Chapter X   Hirohitler

1.

What is he doing here, this American boy who lies so still beneath strange soil? What brought him all the way from Middletown to this little crooked street in this little crooked town of Oberpfaffenhofen, in southern Germany, here to stop a bullet with his stomach?

Nash-Kelvinator, if you remember, implied he died for modern refrigerators. Someone else, I forget who, said he died for apple pie and ice cream. The Aluminum Corporation of America, whose cartel agreements delayed our plane production program, said he died for Free Enterprise. But the Nazis said he died for the warmonger "Rosenfeld" and the British Empire, and isn't it curious how many of our isolationists said the same thing?

Some people had another answer: this boy died, they said, by gunfire in Germany so that eventually his whole family would not have to die by bombings on Middletown. But most Americans would not accept this answer. Our oceans are too wide, our consciousness of strength too great, for us to scare easily.

So we preferred to believe Senator Borah, who a week before the attack on Poland said that there would be no war. And as time went on, with untiring obstinacy, so many of us objected to fortifying Guam, to "plowing under every fourth American boy," to fighting "to save India for the British and Europe for the Bolshevists." Too many of us preferred Father Coughlin's anti-Semitism to FDR's anti-Nazism; too many were impressed by the isolationist line of the Newspaper Axis and the pro-German line (which, in the end, amounted to the same thing) of the Berlin-paid Nazi propagandists who were working among us.

Well, things are plainer now, thanks to the secret German plans revealed at Nuremberg. We now know what the result would have been had we stood on the sidelines while the Fascists won the war. *We know now that the Nazis were planning to take over Iceland, the Azores and a huge chunk of Central Africa, as well as sufficient of Europe's coast line to assure naval as well as aerial domination of the Atlantic.* We know that the Nazis planned to run Europe north of Italy, that the Italians were to dominate the Mediterranean and that part of Africa that didn't fall to the Germans, and that Japan was to run the Far East.

I leave it to the defendant Ribbentrop to picture for us America's brilliant place in the projected Axis world order. In 1941, urging the Japanese to join in the attack on Russia, he wrote:

"After the collapse of Russia, the position of the Three Power pact members will be so gigantic that the question of England's collapse or the total destruction of the English islands will only be a matter of time. *An America totally isolated from the rest of the world would then be faced with our taking possession of the remaining positions of the British Empire which are important to the Axis.*" (My italics—V. H. B.)

Not an isolationist America any more, but an isolated America. We would have lain like a choice nut between the jaws of an intercontinental cracker. And Goering, who had wanted those bombers that could fly to New York and back, would have had his problem vastly simplified: Iceland is a thousand miles nearer New York than the nearest German soil. And who can doubt, by the time Goering was ready to send his planes off, that their pay-load would have been atom bombs?

2.

In the evolution of the Nazis' plans for world conquest, neither the U.S.A. nor Japan was ever very far from the minds of the warmakers, the former as a potential enemy, the latter as a potential ally.

As early as November, 1937, Hitler was noting happily the "weakening of the British position in the Far East by Japan."

In August, 1939, Italy's Ciano urged Hitler to delay war for a while: "The position of Japan would be strengthened, while the position of Roosevelt in America would be undermined by tranquillity . . . whereas his election was certain if war broke out."

But Hitler would not listen to this argument; he was convinced that the Western Democracies would shrink from plunging into a general war. (Curious how, a year later, Hitler was to use precisely the same argument against Mussolini's march into Greece: "I wanted to ask you to postpone the battle . . . until after the American presidential election.")

Then, in November, 1939, when Hitler announced to his generals the decision to swing westward from crushed Poland to attack England and France, he reminded his listeners:

"America is still not dangerous to us because of its neutrality laws. The strengthening of our opponents by America is still not important."

Our neutrality laws, of course, had originally been designed to assure non-intervention in Spain, and had worked in favor of Franco. But there is an old adage—or is it new?—that anything that helps Fascists anywhere, helps them everywhere. The Nazis were very grateful for our neutrality laws.

Yes, the Nazis quite early must have developed a deep affection for many Americans. They adored our non-intervention in Spain while their planes were bombing Guernica. They loved those who loved Munich. They cheered the Americans who wouldn't fortify Guam, who opposed the draft law, who opposed Lend-lease.

The whole drift of the American isolationist press emboldened Hitler to note in a memorandum dated August, 1939:

"The attempt of certain circles of the U.S.A. to lead the Americas in a direction hostile to Germany is definitely unsuccessful at this moment, but could still in the future lead to the desired result. Here, too, time is to be viewed as working against Germany."

In other words, strike while isolationism is still hot in America. One is tempted to point out that the policies pursued by the Newspaper Axis had at least as much to do with starting the war as the Nazi-Soviet pact which these newspapers so bitterly attacked.

And in the same memorandum in which the Nazis were thus discounting any immediate American danger to their plans, they were counting on ultimate help from Japan:

"It will be her *(Japan's)* interest to make use of every weakening, in Eastern Asia, of the European States with the minimum expenditure of her own power."

In plain English, what this meant was that Germany expected Japan to strike at Singapore and the Dutch East Indies and other European possessions in East Asia the moment the Wehrmacht offensive against the West began. Thus the defensive strength of the Allies would be dissipated over the globe, while the Wehrmacht could concentrate its strength on France and England.

It is so clear today, so simple to understand. It was not Hitler alone who threatened America, and not Hirohito alone, but both together, a gigantic Hirohitlerian Fascism. The goals of the two war-minded nations were, at least for the moment, complementary; anything that Germany did against England and France and Holland helped Japan; anything Japan did against Singapore or French Indo-China or the Dutch East Indies *or the Philippines,* helped Germany.

All this must, however, have seemed very complicated at the time, at least to the isolationists, and so they adopted the sturdy slogan: *Let's stay out of one war at a time.* And they urged appeasement of Hirohito when *that* suited the Nazis right down to the ground. And, after Pearl Harbor, they urged that the Yanks stay out of the European war and concentrate on the Far East.

This was so much up Hitler's alley that one might almost think the isolationists had heard—and were obeying—a secret OKW directive issued March 4, 1941 (ten months before Pearl Harbor):

"The aim of our collaboration," said the directive in reference to German-Japanese relations, "will be to induce Japan to intervene actively in the Far East as soon as possible. Strong English forces will thereby be tied down *and the focus of U.S. interests will be shifted to the Pacific.*" (My italics—V. H. B.)

From the moment Tokyo entered the Rome-Berlin pact, the Nazis angled for Japanese help in their own aggressive plans. What they asked varied with their own front lines. They began by wanting Hirohito to attack Singapore and the British, proceeded to encourage attack on America, ended by demanding attack on the U.S.S.R.

"Japan must take steps to seize Singapore as soon as possible," the defendant Raeder urged in the spring of 1941, "since the opportunity will never again be as favorable (whole English fleet contained, unpreparedness of U.S.A. for war against Japan, inferiority of the United States fleet vis-à-vis the Japanese). If Japan has Singapore, all other East Asiatic questions regarding the U.S.A. and England are thereby solved (Guam, Philippines, Borneo, Dutch East Indies)."

About the same time that this Raeder memorandum was written, the defendant Ribbentrop had a heart-to-heart talk with Oshima, the Japanese Ambassador to Berlin. He told the Ambassador that America was no good as a military power, and that, in any case, the best assurance for continued American neutrality was a powerful Japan in possession of Singapore.

But the Japanese were wary not only of the Americans but of the Russians. Ribbentrop promptly reassured Oshima: Germany would strike immediately should Russia attack Japan. It was an easy promise for Ribbentrop to make; he knew, even as he made it, that the date for Barbarossa had already been fixed.

At the end of March, 1941, Hirohito sent his Foreign Minister, the pro-war Matsuoka, to Berlin. Ribbentrop gave him another sales talk on Singapore; told him, too, that "U.S. submarines are so bad that Japan need not bother with them at all." And Hitler bluntly promised him support wherever the Japanese chose to attack, whether it be Singapore or Hawaii or the Soviet Far East Command.

"Germany has made her preparations so that no American could land in Europe," Hitler said glibly. "I would not hesitate a moment to reply to any widening of the war, be it by Russia, be it by America. Providence favors those who will not let dangers come to them, but who will bravely face them."

In the midst of the brilliant early German successes against the Russians, Nazi interest switched from Singapore to Siberia. "I ask you to employ all available means in further insisting upon Japan's entry into the war against Russia," Ribbentrop ordered the German Ambassador in Tokyo. "The natural objective . . . that we and Japan join hands on the trans-Siberia railroad before winter starts."

But Japan had other plans, equally as helpful to Hitler and more suitable to her own tactical situation. Matsuoka had returned to Tokyo with exactly what he wanted: assurance that Germany would declare war on America should Japan attack the Philippines or Hawaii. As late as November 29, a week before Pearl Harbor, he was reassured on this by Ribbentrop:

"As Hitler said today, there are fundamental differences in the very right to exist between Germany and Japan on the one hand, and the United States on the other. . . ."

Read now from the brief entry for December 8, 1941, in the diary of the Italian Foreign Minister, Ciano:

"A night telephone call from Ribbentrop; he is overjoyed about the Japanese attack on America. He is so happy about it that I am happy with him, although I am not too sure about the final advantages of what has happened.

"One thing is now certain: America will enter the conflict, and the conflict will be so prolonged that she will be able to realize all her potential force. This morning I told this to the King, who had been pleased about the event; he ended by admitting that in the 'long run' I may be right.

"Mussolini was happy, too."

They were all happy. Hitler, at a reception given in honor of Germany's new "honorary" Aryan brothers-in-arms, jovially threw his arms around the Japanese Ambassador's shoulders and said, "You gave the right declaration of war!"

But at this moment, a thousand miles to the east, the Wehrmacht was faltering in its drive for Moscow, and a reinvigorated Red Army began to push it back. And three thousand miles to the west an angry America, in line with the knowing Ciano's prophecy, at last repudiated the isolationists and united for war.

The forces of Hirohitler, in contrast to the traditional British style, were always destined to win every battle but the last.

3.

We gave in to Japanese demands for expansion, and Pearl Harbor never happened. We gave in to Hitler's demands, and never sent convoys to Britain. We gave in to the isolationists' demands, stayed home, minded our own business.

The Fascists have won the war. What do they do with Europe?

I quote from a memorandum prepared on June 3, 1940, by the German Naval War Staff entitled *Questions of Territorial Expansion and Bases:*

"The solution appears to be to crush France, to occupy Belgium, part of North and East France, to allow the Netherlands, Denmark, and Norway to exist on the basis indicated above *(i.e., dependent on Germany).*

"The possession of Iceland would mean material strategic expansion for Germany.

"Contiguous possessions in Central Africa are considered extremely desirable. They comprise the French possessions south of the Senegal, the former German colonies of Central Africa and the Belgian Congo.

"The acquisition of one or more bases on the group of islands off Africa would be of the greatest importance, and besides this the possession of Madagascar and the French group of islands in the Indian Ocean.

"Time will show how far the outcome of the war with England will make an extension of these demands possible." (My italics— V. H. B.)

Four months later a Major von Falkenstein wrote from Hitler's headquarters:

"The Fuehrer is at present occupied with the question of the occupation of the Atlantic Islands *(Canaries, Azores, Iceland)* with a view to the prosecution of the war against America at a later date."

What the Nazis planned to do with the Soviet Union, Nuremberg has told us. And we have a pretty shrewd idea of what the Japanese were planning to do with victory in the Far East.

And what does the Chicago *Tribune* and the Hearst Press say on this day of final fascist victory? I can see the giant black headlines: "LAST RED STRONGHOLD WIPED OUT."

Peaceful America, untouched by war, its young men still whole, its tax (and VD) rate down, its humming factories showering cars and refrigerators upon the populace, reaffirms the Monroe Doctrine in—what is the phrase?—no uncertain terms.

And from Berlin and from Tokyo come reassuring replies: The New World of Europe and the New World of Asia will respect absolutely the political integrity of the Old World of America.

That's when the trade missions begin to arrive.

I can see the German mission now, stiffly and in step, climbing to the entrance of the old and ugly State Department Building in Washington. Goering, present as Plenipotentiary for the new German Four Year Plan, is the only one who wears a uniform. With him are Funk (or maybe it's Schacht) and Oswald Pohl (who as business manager of the Nazi concentration camp system fancies himself as an economist) and a few lesser specialists. Bormann is there, too, as the Fuehrer's Deputy and head of the Nazi party Chancellery: party interests must be protected.

I can see them, for the next several weeks, going in and out of the old building, always correct, always stiff, always in step, and each time coming out with another piece of America in their briefcases.

I can see the Bund paper in New York carrying a banner line: American National Socialist Party Formed. Why not? Why should Germany do business with a country that permits persecution of a peaceful political party?

I can see a Brown House going up across the street from the German Embassy to house the party leadership.

I can see the Riker's Island penitentiary in New York harbor turned into a concentration camp for political prisoners. Why not? Weren't two German nationals just beaten up by some Communists in Union Square? Why should Germany do business with a country that permits persecution of the peaceful citizens of a friendly State?

By and by Himmler flies over from Berlin to give the FBI some friendly advice. How can we say no? Don't we prefer trade missions to Goering's bombers?

Or do we meet the issue bravely, sign a pact of mutual assistance with Canada, Mexico, Costa Rica and Uruguay, and declare war on Europe and Asia?

Part III
TODESRAUM

Chapter XI   Genocide

1.

The story of Nazi atrocities is supposedly an old one. Long before the war ended, indeed before it began, we were hearing the story—through the press, through the radio and occasionally through the testimony of eyewitnesses who managed miraculously to escape the giant abbatoir which was Europe to reach America in safety.

Many of us believed what we read and heard, some of us half-believed, some of us—blinded by a faith, political or otherwise—refused to believe.

The scores of thousands of GI's who liberated Buchenwald, Dachau, Nordhausen, Mauthausen, did not need the evidence produced at Nuremberg to dispel doubts. They saw the evidence on the spot—saw it and smelled it and helped to bury it in common graves so big they looked like subway cuts.

But Nuremberg did more than furnish incontrovertible documentary proof for today's skeptic and tomorrow's historian. *It showed that the Nazi atrocity technique was as modern a weapon of war as the V-bomb, and infinitely more sanguinary.* The difference was that it was less designed to win this war than the next, *the war which Germany,* having established hegemony over

Europe, *planned ultimately to wage for domination of the globe.*

So modern, indeed, was Nazi "barbarism," that in no language did there exist a word to describe it until shortly before the Nuremberg trial began. In 1944, Raphael Lemkin, expert in international law and historian of the legal aspects of Nazi territorial expansion, invented and formulated the concept of the word *genocide*, defining it as the purposeful destruction of "nations, races, or groups."

The authors of the Nuremberg Indictment incorporated the new word into their document as part of Count IV (Crimes Against Humanity). The word was used repeatedly during the trial, especially by the British prosecutors. It has become as significant a contribution to our vocabulary as *quisling, coventrize* or *blitz,* and with a far firmer etymological foundation.

So I think it misleading to refer to Nazi "barbarism," which implies a reversion to something out of the past. Genocide is a *new* concept, part and parcel of that newest and most dangerous of the socio-political diseases of our time: fascism. It is a concept involving specific socio-political goals, specific techniques and specific and terrible consequences for all mankind.

2.

The theoretical basis for the practice of genocide existed in the corroding Nazi doctrine of race and in Haushofer's geopolitical gibberish which called for German expansion on the continent of Europe. Its practical application was assured on October 7, 1939, when Hitler appointed Himmler as Reich Commissioner for the Consolidation of German Nationality with orders to

(1) bring back from conquered areas all "racial" Germans and German citizens and settle them in the new communities of the Greater German Reich;

(2) eliminate the "harmful influence of such alien parts of the population which represent a danger to the Reich and German folk community."

In point 2, of course, lies the genesis of genocide as applied to non-Germans. And in the light of the evidence produced at Nuremberg, this second point really meant:

(1) destruction of the *nationhood* of conquered areas and curtailment of the propagation of conquered "non-Germanic" peoples;

(2) destruction throughout Europe of all "non-adaptable" peoples, including Jews, gypsies and intellectuals who might provide leadership for the renaissance of national spirit;

(3) enslavement of the European masses, chained by ignorance and semi-starvation (both deliberately imposed), in support of the fascist struggle for world domination.

These are not inferences; they are facts written plainly upon the Nuremberg record in the Fascists' own words. Himmler, as chief architect of this New Blood Order in Europe, made three speeches in the course of 1943 before his SS colleagues in which he revealed Germany's blue print for the world of the future. I quote from relevant portions:

"We will create the necessary conditions ifor the whole German people and the whole of Europe, controlled, ordered and led by us, to be able to stand the test in her battles of destiny against Asia. We do not know when that will be. Then, when the mass of humanity of one to one-and-a-half billion line up against us, the Germanic people, numbering I hope a total of 600 to 700 millions, and with an outpost area stretching in a hundred years beyond the Urals, must stand the test in its vital struggle against Asia."

Again:

"What happens to a Russian, to a Czech, does not interest me in the slightest. What the nations can offer in the way of good blood of our type, we will take, if necessary, by kidnapping their children and raising them here with us. Whether nations live in prosperity or starve to death interests me only insofar as we need them as slaves for our Kultur. . . . We Germans, who are the only people in the world who have a decent attitude towards animals, will also assume a decent attitude towards these human animals. But it is a crime against our own blood to worry about them and give them ideals, thus causing our sons and grandsons to have a more difficult time with them."

And again:

"How can we take the most from the Russians, dead or alive? We shall do it by killing them or taking them prisoner and putting them to work. Only by this means can the Continent be made a Germanic Continent capable of daring to embark on the conflict with Asia which spews out hordes of humanity. Perhaps we shall also have to hold in check other colored peoples and thus preserve the world of our children and grandchildren."

And yet again:

"Our purpose is to create an order which will spread the idea of Nordic blood so far that it will attract all Nordic blood in the world, take away the blood from adversaries, absorb it so that never again will Nordic blood . . . fight against us. We must get it and the others cannot have it."

In Europe, of course, the greatest single stream of "non-Nordic" blood runs through the veins of the Slav. His role in the *Pax Germanica* was made quite clear in an incredible memorandum prepared in 1942 by the defendant Bormann, who by that time had taken over Hess' job as Hitler's deputy and active head of the party. Bormann wrote in substance:

"The Slavs are to work for us. Insofar as we don't need them, they may die. Therefore compulsory vaccination and German health services are superfluous. The fertility of the Slavs is undesirable. They may use contraceptives or practice abortion, the more the better.

"Education is dangerous for them. It is enough if they can count up to 100. At best an education which produces for us useful stooges is admissible. Every educated person is a future enemy. Religion we leave to them as a means of diversion. As for food, they won't get any more than is necessary.

"We are the masters, we come first."

No, to speak merely of Nazi "barbarism," of Nazi bloodlust, or even of Nazi atrocities, is to miss the significance of the Nazi crematory and mass grave. It is as superficial as to speak glibly of Nazi "imperialism," in the accepted sense of the word, or—and how many times has this been done in recent years?—to liken Hitler to Napoleon. The Nazis themselves knew better. I quote from the SS newspaper *Das Schwarze Korps*, dated August 20, 1942:

"Imperialism as an aim of State, best represented up to the year 1940 by Napoleon, saw in the acquisition of space only the widening of the power of the State, the enlarging of the number of its subjects, workers, taxpayers, soldiers. Whether this increase of population belonged racially to the people making up the State did not matter! Anyone who spoke broken French was a Frenchman, anyone who spoke broken German was a German.

"One cannot make Germans out of foreign individuals; conversely, one cannot make foreigners out of Germans. The Reichsfuehrer SS [Himmler] has written the following:

" 'It is our task, not to Germanize the East in the old sense, i.e. to teach the people living there the German language and German laws, but to see to it that only people with Germanic blood should live in the East.'

"Thus in the East we are now securing our future, and this security will not be achieved until the land won by sacred sacrifice of blood—insofar as the land is to be settled by us at all—is *German* land, German because of the people who inhabit and cultivate it, German because of the industrious work of the German plow."

3.

What did genocide mean in terms of flesh and blood? The Nazis' own files, introduced at Nuremberg, give us a vivid answer.

Himmler, speaking to the officers of a *Waffen SS* regiment in 1943, described what it meant in Poland:

"Very frequently the members of the Waffen SS think about the deportations of people here [*in Lorraine*]. Exactly the same thing happened in Poland in weather forty degrees below zero, where we had to haul away thousands, tens of thousands, hundreds of thousands; where we had to have the toughness—you should hear this but also forget it immediately—to shoot thousands of leading Poles, where we had to have this toughness, because otherwise they would have taken revenge on us later."

Three years before, the defendant Frank, Governor General of Poland, had already noted this fact in his diary:

"We are taking advantage of the focussing of world interest on the Western Front by wholesale liquidation of thousands of Poles, first the leading representatives of the Polish intelligentsia."

What did it mean in Czechoslovakia?

The Nazis were for long uncertain what to do with this stubborn little people. Back in 1938, Hitler had said, "We don't want any Czechs!" But now he had them, and their valuable industry, and their rich land, and their rich culture, and his industrialist advisers were telling him to do one thing, and his party advisers another, and his militarists still another.

But then one day he received a plan which had been approved by the man he had appointed as Protector of Bohemia-Moravia, that respectable and venerable career diplomat, the defendant von Neurath:

"Absorption of about half of the Czechs by the Germans," the memorandum advises, "this half to be determined by their value from a racial or other standpoint. The other half must be deprived of its power, eliminated and shipped out of the country by all sorts of methods. This applies particularly to the racially mongoloid part and to the major part of the intellectual class.

"The intellectuals can scarcely be converted ideologically and would represent a burden by constantly making claims for leadership over other Czech classes and thus interfering with rapid assimilation."

This is the plan Hitler finally approved.

And what did genocide mean in the U.S.S.R.?

You will recall, as part of Goering's plan for the exploitation of Russia, the scheme for deliberate starvation of millions of Russians in the so-called Moscow region. But the Nazis were also on the track of Soviet leaders, political and intellectual, whether they came from the Moscow region or not.

On July 17, 1941, a top-secret directive was issued to special units which were to be placed by the Chief of the Security Police and the SD (then Heydrich, later the defendant Kaltenbrunner) in all prisoner of war camps. I quote from the directive:

"The task of the special details is the political examination of all camp inmates. It is above all important to ascertain all important functionaries of the U.S.S.R. and the Communist Party, especially professional revolutionaries, functionaries of the Comintern, functionaries in the Central, Territorial and District Committees, all People's Commissars and their deputies, all former Political Commissars in the Red Army, leading personalities of the Central and Intermediate Courts, leading personalities in economic life, Soviet Russian intellectuals, all Jews and all persons who can be identified as agitators or fanatical Communists."

And once the identity of these has been ascertained, what then? The directive is quite specific:

"Executions are not to take place in the camp nor in its immediate vicinity. If the camps are located within the Government General or in the immediate vicinity of the border, the prisoners are to be moved, if possible, to former Soviet Russian territory for special treatment."

It is a curious thing about this genocide business. It was committed nowhere and everywhere, by no one and by everyone. The defendants at Nuremberg did not and could not deny the dead. But, by their own reckoning, there could not have been any dead, because there were no killers.

The SS did it, said the SD. The Gestapo did it, said the SS. The Waffen SS was guiltless because it was part of the army. But the army insisted it had nothing to do with the Waffen SS.

The Nazis had no single Genocide Squad. Genocide was not a specific function; it was a general policy. It underlay or overrode all other policies—for a while. It was dominant in extermination camps, subordinate in other camps. It was dominant in the activities of the *Einsatzgruppen*, subordinate in the slave labor program. It was dominant, during the first years, in the handling of Soviet war prisoners, subordinate in the handling of hostages and reprisals. But dominant or subordinate, it was always there.

The *Einsatzgruppen*—Special Task Forces—were the nearest thing to an out-and-out Genocide Squad the Nazis had. There were four such groups, each serving a sector of the Eastern Front.

"I was chief of Special Task Force D," testified Otto Ohlendorf at Nuremberg. "Himmler stated that an important part of our task consisted of the extermination of Jews—women, men and children—and Communist functionaries.

"According to an agreement with the OKW [Armed Forces High Command] and the OKH [Army High Command], units of the Special Task Forces were assigned to certain Army Corps and Divisions. The Army designated the areas in which these units were to operate. The units themselves were commanded by personnel of the Gestapo, the SD or the Criminal Police. Additional men were detailed from the regular police and the Waffen SS.

"When the German Army invaded Russia, I was leader of Special Task Force D in the Southern sector, and in the course of the year the unit liquidated approximately 90,000 men, women and children. The majority liquidated were Jews, but there were among them some Communist functionaries, too."

Who was responsible for the *Einsatzgruppen*? The Tribunal wanted to find out. Lord Chief Justice Lawrence, of the Tribunal, questioned counsel for the SD.

Chief Justice Lawrence: "Dr. Gawlik, the Tribunal understands that the SS, the Gestapo and the SD all disclaim responsibility for the *Einsatzgruppen*. Could you tell the Tribunal who is responsible?"

Dr. Gawlik: "The *Einsatzgruppen* were subordinated to — the responsibility may be seen from my statement on Page 61. I should like to refer you to the testimony of Dr. Best, Schellenberg, Ohlendorf and Document—

Chief Justice Lawrence: "Dr. Gawlik, the Tribunal would like to know who you say was responsible for the *Einsatzgruppen*. They don't want to be referred to a cloud of documents and a cloud of witnesses. They want to know what your contention is."

Dr. Gawlik: "They were, in my opinion, organizations of a special kind which were directly under Himmler, and for the rest, the testimony of the witnesses diverges as to how far they were subordinate to the Army. As far as this question is concerned, I cannot define my attitude."

What this exchange did not bring out was that *however much or little the German Army controlled the activities of the* Einsatz-gruppen, *it was fully aware of these activities and directly or indirectly shared in them.* I quote from an official report of *Einsatzgruppe A*:

"*Einsatzgruppe A* has just reached the region of the concentration of forces, as ordered on June 26, 1941. [Note the date: only four days after the opening of hostilities against the U.S.S.R.]. The Northern Army Group consisted of the 16th to 18th Armies and the 4th Panzer Division. Our problem consisted of establishing liaison with the Commanders-in-Chief of these groups. *It might be noted that relations with the Armies are of the best and closest. Frequently liaison is so close that operations can be planned almost individually . . .*" (My italics—V. H. B.)

But Dr. Gawlik could not, or would not, define his "attitude." In this he was no different from any of the defendants. Responsibility, that unpleasant little insect with the sharp bite, spent a most unhappy and tiring eleven months in the courtroom; no one would let him alight to rest his weary, bloodred wings.

4.

"*We are the masters,*" Bormann had written in 1942.

Who are the *we?* The so-called blond Nordics of which Nazi anthropologists prated so much? No, not quite. In February, 1943, the SS Committee on Labor, which included representative scientists, frowned on the use of the term *Nordic.* "In regard to the words *Nordic* and *Germanic,*" said the Committee report, "the first expression must be used less and less. With the expression *Nordic,* too high a position has been granted Norway, Sweden and Denmark at the expense of the West Germans."

So the *we* refers to all *Germanic* peoples? Again, not quite. Himmler, in one of his 1943 speeches, made plain that not all *Germanic* blood is of equal value, either; there is a "leading blood" which flows exclusively through the veins of the members of the SS and of the Leadership Corps of the National Socialist party.

"We stand or fall with this leading blood of Germany,"

Himmler said, "and if this blood is not reproduced we will not be able to rule the world."

It is difficult to estimate the combined membership of the SS and the party leadership, because the figures overlap. A half-million persons would be a generous estimate.

It is these half-million then, who are the *we*, the masters, the rulers of the world, for whom the three billions in the rest of the world are to become slaves—yellow and white and black, Americans and British and Chinese and Nigerians and, in due course of time, those honorary Aryans and comrades-in-arms, the Japanese.

Now I am not an anthropologist and I confess complete inability to recognize common run-of-the-mill German blood when I see it, no less *leading* German blood. What I do know is that Goering was blond and round-headed and still, after having lost seventy pounds in the Nuremberg jail, quite a big man; that Goebbels was dark and long-headed and quite small, and that Streicher looked like one of his own caricatures of a Jew. And I bet I could take any number of the hated Slavs—Russian or Czech or what have you, all of them blond—and put them in SS uniforms, and I guarantee they would look more impressively "German" than, say, the sallow Rosenberg, or for that matter, the fantastically undistinguished-looking Himmler himself.

Is there really such a thing as German blood, leading or otherwise? I suspect that neither Himmler nor Hitler, for all their talk, ever knew or ever really cared very much. After all, in a pinch, they could create their own anthropological laws and establish the existence of "leading" German blood merely by encasing its owner in a black suit. I think the whole business, as the Nazi leadership tackled it, was not a question of race but of rationalization. What better way is there of rationalizing the taking of other people's lands, and the acquisition through enslavement of cheap labor, than to insist that you are taking both at the expense of "inferior races"?

Indeed, the evidence at Nuremberg produced repeated examples of the Nazis enthusiastically violating their own racial theories. Himmler not only refused to ban "fraternization" between members of the Wehrmacht and Dutch and Norwegian women, but actually encouraged procreation by offering financial support to women who would consent to bear children by German fathers.

Even more sensational was the so-called *Heu Aktion*, by which, in the last year of the war, thousands of Czech, Polish, Russian and Yugoslav children from five years and up were torn from their parents, brought into the Reich and given to German parents for rearing as *German children*. Apparently the only criteria were that the children should be healthy and be able to pass as German, which means that blonds were preferred.

Anyone who is familiar with Eastern Europe knows what wide sections of "purely" Slav peoples are blonds—*and how many blond Jews can be found in every country of the Old World!*

Chapter XII   KZ

1.

The concentration camp (KZ for *Konzentrationslager*) was Big Industry, turning out chiefly corpses and war goods. The products were not complementary; the more corpses, obviously, the fewer workers to produce the war goods.

Here was a striking contradiction which baffled the Americans in the closing weeks of the war. I saw the liberation of Nord-hausen, Buchenwald, and a number of smaller camps; to Dachau I came late, though not too late to count the last unburied corpses and to choke on the stench of death. Everywhere we noted the same paradox: in a land desperate for lack of labor, labor was being slaughtered like cattle in a time of famine.

There was another facet to the paradox: The Third Reich spent huge sums building factories in contemplation of the use of camp labor, and then proceeded to decimate the camps.

We understood nothing, at the time. The camps had the quality of grisly nightmare, of something dreamed up out of stale marihuana and a sick stomach. It was neither the time nor the place to search for method in this madness; there was room only for horror and a vast and futile rage—futile because we knew even then, however dimly, that what we were here witnessing was beyond all atonement.

Nuremberg could not resolve the paradox, but did reveal its origin in the Nazis' mutually conflicting concept of genocide, aimed at victory in the next war, and a production program aimed at victory in this. The Nazis wanted both mass murder and mass production, and what resulted was a dualism in policy which was reflected not only in the concentration camps, but in the slave labor program, in the treatment of prisoners (especially Soviet) of war and even in the program for the extermination of Jewry.

The trouble was that the war lasted too long, much longer than the Nazis had anticipated. As the months of conflict rolled into years, their early zest for murder was diminished, although never extinguished, by the growing need to replace both the labor and the stockpiles they were expending so lavishly on the field of battle.

Himmler, addressing a group of SS generals in 1943, summed up the dilemma admirably:

"The Russian Army was herded together in great pockets, ground down, taken prisoner. At that time we did not value the mass of humanity as we value it today, as raw material, as labor. What, after all, thinking in terms of generations, is not to be regretted, but is now deplorable by reason of the loss of labor, is that the prisoners died, in tens and hundreds of thousands, of exhaustion and hunger."

2.

Goering, as head of the Prussian police, started the concentration camp system in 1933 to take care of political prisoners—including, as Goering testified at the trial, not only persons who had committed overt acts against the State or party, but persons who *might* do so if left free.

A glimpse into the disciplinary regulations for Dachau, dated October 1, 1933, is illuminating:

"Tolerance means weakness. In the light of this conception, punishment will be mercilessly handed out whenever the interests of the Fatherland warrant it. Authority for ordering punishments lies in the hands of the Camp Commander.

"The following are punishable with eight days close confinement and twenty-five thrashings to be administered before and after the serving of the sentence: anyone making deprecatory or ironical remarks to a member of the SS, deliberately omits the prescribed marks of respect, or in any other way demonstrates unwillingness to submit to measures of discipline and order.

"The following will be hanged: anyone who talks politics, who holds inciting meetings, forms cliques, loiters around with others, or who, for the purpose of supplying the propaganda of the opposition with atrocity stories, collects true or false information about the concentration camp and its institutions."

Murder and torture of inmates began early in the camps. There were examples in Dachau in 1933, and a naive German civil servant, the Attorney General of Bavaria, preferred charges against the guilty camp guards. He succeeded only in losing his job.

There were similar instances at Hohenstein camp the following year, instances which impelled even the Reich Minister of Justice to write at the time, in a personal letter, that "the nature of the mistreatments, particularly the use of the drip apparatus, is evidence of coarseness and brutality completely alien to German sensibility and feeling."

But the Minister's own sensibilities were not sufficiently aroused for him to resign at once; nor did he resign when twenty-two Hohenstein guards, convicted of murder and torture by ordinary criminal courts, were promptly pardoned by Hitler; nor did he resign when the party, as a mark of disapproval of the whole proceeding, forced the public prosecutor in the case to resign from the SA.

At war's outbreak, six major camps existed in Germany. Their population, at that time, was some 50,000, although hundreds of thousands had passed in and out in the preceding six years. By 1944 the number of camps, including the so-called "daughter camps" which were grouped around the larger ones, rose to more than 300; they housed 1,200,000 living inmates, plus the rotting cadavers, or bones and ash, of perhaps ten times as many dead.

In the months following the beginning of the war, the function of the camps, at least theoretically, underwent fundamental change. "The custody of prisoners for reasons of security, education or prevention is no longer the main consideration," it was officially explained. "Mobilization of all prisoners who are fit to work for war purposes now and for reconstruction in the forthcoming peace, comes to the foreground more and more."

What this official report, introduced as part of the prosecution's slave labor case, does not describe is how slowly the new concepts came to the foreground. So long as the Wehrmacht was slicing through Poland, and through France, and then through the Red Army, so long as each succeeding dawn promised final victory, there was no dualism in high Nazi policy. The first gas chambers were put to use in the summer of 1941; there is no documentary evidence that anyone objected at the time. There is no documentary evidence that anyone objected to the shocking waste of labor—as Himmler put it—in the death by starvation of hundreds of thousands of Soviet war prisoners.

Why should there be objection? Everyone knew that the only good Jew or good Russian was a dead one. Besides, corpses do not eat, and that was a hard, tangible and extraordinarily favorable argument in support of corpses.

Unfortunately, the Nazis couldn't create corpses quickly enough. The concentration camps kept filling up. This was perfectly natural because imported slave labor and the teeming prisoner-of-war camps formed natural reservoirs for the KZ. The Polish farm worker caught talking to a German woman, the Soviet war prisoner guilty of the slightest infraction of camp rules, found themselves behind the electrified wires of Buchenwald or Treblinka or Gross Rosen.

But crowded camps meant increasing illness, and increasing illness meant danger of epidemics, not to speak of useless mouths to feed. So on November 12, 1941, commanders of the principal concentration camps received the following communication from Himmler's office:

"As the Camp Commandants of Dachau, Sachsenhausen, Buchenwald, Mauthausen and Auschwitz have been informed, the said camps will be visited in the near future by a Board of Physicians who will pick out prisoners for detachment.

"As the physicians available are very busy the examination at the camps must be shortened as much as possible.

"After completion of the examination, a report is to be submitted to the Inspector of Concentration Camps stating the number of prisoners allocated to special treatment '14 f 13'. The exact date of arrival of the Board of Physicians will be made known in ample time."

In Nazi language, "special treatment" meant death. We will come across the phrase again.

The dream of early Nazi victory faded in the grim winter of 1941-42. It faded with the entrance of the U.S.A. into the war, with a resurgent RAF hammering at German cities, and with an astonishing Red Army that not only saved Moscow but actually began pushing the Wehrmacht back along the tank-littered, corpse-covered frozen roads to Smolensk.

With the prospect of a long war there emerged the dualism of German policy, the problem of somehow merging the work of the architects of race with the architects of armament. The whole problem was put into sharp focus in a secret report, dated December, 1942, found in the files of the defendant Rosenberg's Reich Ministry for Occupied Eastern Territories:

"Since the Eastern war has turned out unexpectedly long, it is the opinion of civilian and military commanders that German Eastern policy must be changed. Food rations allowed for the Russian population are so low that they fail to secure mere existence. The Russians are faced with death by starvation.

"The position at one time taken by Germans that there were too many people in the East, and that their extermination would be a blessing, must now be changed, since the Wehrmacht lives by the work performed in the Eastern cities . . . Roads are clogged by perhaps a million people wandering around in search of nourishment. Since these wanderings deprive the German war industry of valuable man hours, it is necessary to feed the urban population essential to German war industry."

In the sping of 1942, a characteristic half-step was taken in respect to the *KZ*. Administration was taken out of the hands of the Gestapo, which up to that time had exercised primary authority, and put into the hands of a new organization, the SS-Main-Office Economics and Administration (WVHA). It was a half-step because the WVHA was still SS, and the primary business of the SS was murder; all else was sideline.

Then, in September the same year, the agile-minded Goebbels laid down the formula which, in general, was adhered to until the end of the war:

"With regard to the destruction of asocial life, the following groups should be exterminated: Jews and gypsies unconditionally, Poles who have been sentenced to 3-4 years of penal servitude, and Czechs and Germans who have been sentenced to death, life imprisonment or life 'security custody.'

"The idea of exterminating them by labor is the best." (My italics—V. H. B.)

By agreement among Hitler, Himmler and the Minister of Justice, the Goebbels formula was amended only to include Russians and Ukrainians among the groups to be exterminated "unconditionally." They, like the Jews and gypsies, were to die working.

Close examination reveals that this formula did not obviate the need for the gas chamber and the gallows. In the first place, it was obviously foolish to sentence to "extermination by labor" prisoners who, at the outset, were incapable of working. Among such were the aged, the sick, the very young, and many women — especially pregnant and nursing mothers.

In the second place, it wasn't always economic to let a prisoner die on the job. Generally, long before he died, he had ceased producing enough to warrant even his starvation ration.

It was for such as these that the extermination camps—Auschwitz, Treblinka B, Mauthausen, Hartheim—were provided.

3.

"I, Rudolf Franz Ferdinand Hoess, being first duly sworn, depose and say as follows:

"I am 46 years old and have been a member of the NSDAP since 1922, a member of the SS since 1934.

"I have been constantly associated with the administration of Concentration Camps since 1934, serving at Dachau until 1938; then as Adjutant at Sachsenhausen from 1938 to May 1, 1940, when I was appointed Commandant of Auschwitz.

"I commanded Auschwitz until 1 December, 1943, and estimate that at least 2,500,000 victims were executed there by gassing and burning, and at least another 500,000 succumbed to starvation and disease, making a total of 3,000,000. This represents about 70-80 percent of all persons sent to Auschwitz, the remainder having been selected and used for slave labor in the camp industries.

"Included among the executed and burned were approximately 20,000 Russian prisoners of war, previously screened out of PW cages by the Gestapo, who were delivered at Auschwitz in Wehrmacht transports operated by regular Wehrmacht officers and men. The remainder of victims included about 100,000 German Jews, and great numbers of citizens, mostly Jewish, from Holland, France, Belgium, Poland, Hungary, Czechoslovakia, Greece and other countries. We executed about 400,000 Hungarian Jews alone in the summer of 1944.

"I was ordered to establish extermination facilities at Auschwitz in June, 1941. At that time there were already in the General Government three other extermination camps: Belzek, Treblinka and Wolzek.

"I visited Treblinka to find out how they carried out their exterminations. The Camp Commandant at Treblinka told me that he had liquidated 80,000 in six months. He was principally concerned with liquidating all the Jews from the Warsaw Ghetto.

"He used monoxide gas and I did not think his methods were very efficient. So when I set up the extermination building at Auschwitz, I used Cyclon B, which was a crystallized prussic acid which we dropped into the death chamber from a small opening. It took from 3 to 15 minutes to kill the people in the death chamber, depending upon climatic conditions. We knew when the people were dead because their screaming stopped.

"After the bodies were removed, our Special Commandos took off the rings and extracted the gold from the teeth of the corpses.

"Another improvement we made over Treblinka was that we

built our gas chambers to accommodate 2000 people at one time, whereas at Treblinka their ten gas chambers only accommodated 200 each. The way we selected our victims was as follows: we had two SS doctors on duty to examine incoming transports. The prisoners would be marched past the physicians who would make spot decisions as they walked by. Those who were fit for work were sent into the Camp. Others were sent immediately to the extermination plants.

"Children of tender years were invariably exterminated, since by reason of their youth they were unable to work.

"Still another improvement made over Treblinka was that at Treblinka the victims almost always knew that they were to be exterminated and at Auschwitz we endeavored to fool the victims into thinking that they were to go through a delousing process. Of course, frequently they realized our true intentions and we sometimes had riots.

"Very frequently women would hide their children under their clothes, but naturally [*natürlich*] when we found them we would send the children in to be exterminated.

"We were required to carry out these exterminations in secrecy, but the foul and nauseating stench from the continuous burning of bodies permeated the entire area and all of the people living in the neighboring communities knew that exterminations were going on at Auschwitz."

4.

On how many hands, besides those of Hoess and his co-workers and of the dead Himmler and Hitler, was the blood of Auschwitz?

Head of the WVHA was Oswald Pohl. The WVHA, I have stated, ran the camp system. But Pohl would say that was not a strictly accurate statement. He insisted on the witness stand that he was merely a businessman. He had charge of billeting, feeding, and medical care in the camps; he ran the SS camp factories.

But blood? Never were cleaner and more beautifully manicured hands held up in horror and protest.

All right, not Pohl. The defendant Kaltenbrunner? He was chief

of the Reich Security Main Office (RSHA) which did everything
else with the camps that the WVHA did not do: signed the commitment warrants, signed the death warrants, signed the punishment orders.

The prosecution produced evidence to show that Kaltenbrunner's
name was signed to many such warrants and orders.

That didn't feeze the gaunt Kaltenbrunner. *He* never signed such
warrants; he was active only in the Intelligence Branch of the organization of which he was top man. If his name were signed to
death warrants, *he* didn't put it there; it was his deputy Mueller,
chief of the Gestapo, who signed the warrants for him and never
told him.

Amusing? The joke doesn't stop there. Attorney for the Gestapo
took umbrage:

"In reality the concentration camps were at no time administered by the Gestapo. It was rather the Reich Leadership of the
SS which was responsible. . ."

Has that unpleasant little insect, responsibility, really alighted
at last? Ah, no! Listen now to counsel for the SS:

"A reign of terror may well have been exercised through arrests
and commitment of individuals to concentration camps, but that
was not a matter of any branch of the SS, but rather of the Ministry of the Interior and the Gestapo. . ."

No, Kaltenbrunner was clean of camp blood, the SS was clean,
the Gestapo was clean. So, they insisted in turn, were Goering,
who started the camps; and Ribbentrop, who in 1943 had told
Horthy that the Hungarian Jews "must either be exterminated
or taken to concentration camps"; and Jodl and Keitel, whose
Wehrmacht had transported 200,000 Soviet war prisoners to
Auschwitz; and Frank, who admitted to the Tribunal that he had
once visited Auschwitz but was convinced it was a labor camp
because he "saw people digging a ditch. . ."

Still, if these people insisted on their innocence, at least they
did not try to deny what had taken place. Different was the testimony of Georg Morgen of the SS Legal Department. Under
questioning by SS defense counsel, he said:

"A concentration camp is not a site for the extermination of human beings. I must say that my first visit to a camp, the first one was at Buchenwald, was a great surprise to me. The camp is on wooded heights with an excellent view. The installations were clean and thoroughly painted. There were grass and flowers. The prisoners were healthy, normally fed and brown."

Chief Justice Lawrence: "When are you speaking of?"

Morgen: "I am speaking of July, 1943. The installations were in good order, especially the hospital. The Commandant was ordered to provide the prisoners with an existence worthy of human beings. They had regular meal service. They had a large book store, even with foreign books. They had variety shows, motion pictures, sporting events. They even had a bordello. All the other camps were similar to Buchenwald."

Chief Justice Lawrence: "What did you say they even had?"

Morgen: "A brothel."

That was true, too. The brothel at Buchenwald was presumably like Oranienberg's, which charged two marks, of which a half-mark went to the woman (a camp inmate, of course) and the other one-and-one-half marks went to the businessman Pohl, head of the WVHA. Need I add that the majority of the brothels' patrons were SS guards and the dread Kapos, camp inmates who sucked up to the SS guards and thereby became bosses over their fellow prisoners?

As I listened to Morgen's description of Buchenwald, its lovely view and fresh painted houses and its grass and flowers and library and brothel and good food and movies, I thought back to my own visit there. Strangely, I didn't think of the pile of bodies I saw in the crematories; I didn't think of the dead and half-dead I saw lying shoulder to shoulder on wooden planks in the unpainted barn that was the so-called "quarantine" hospital. I thought only of a youngish man who had come out of the camp to meet the entering Yanks. One GI had apparently given him a piece of cracker out of a K-ration, for when I saw him he was sitting on a rock just outside the main camp gate, and half the cracker was still in his hand and there were crumbs clinging to his lips and unshaven chin. And although he had been dead more than a day, he was still sitting, because there had been no wind and he was too frail to fall of his own weight.

There was no mark of violence on him, either, so I must presume he died of a broken heart at having to leave that paradise which was Buchenwald.

Chapter XIII   Ghoul's Gold

1.

In the winter of 1945-46, a section chief in United States Military Government at Munich told me:

"What Germany needs is a non-political administration. All other things being equal, I'll appoint the simple German businessman every time."

Well, I presume members of the firm of I. A. Topf & Sons, Erfurt, Germany, are simple businessmen. I have seen the metal plate bearing the firm name on products all over Germany. It manufactures heating equipment—boilers, furnaces, fancy living room stoves and, I think, kitchen stoves. But it also, for a while, manufactured other things, and I quote from a letter dated February 12, 1943, introduced at Nuremberg by the Soviet prosecution:

"To the Central Construction Administration of the SS and Police, Auschwitz.

"Subject: Crematoria for the second and third prisoner camps.

"We again confirm receipt of your order for five three-part cremation furnaces, including two electric elevators for the transportation of corpses. A practical installation for heating with coal and an apparatus for the removal of ashes have also been ordered.

(Signed) I. A. Topf & Sons."

Or perhaps my Military Government friend would prefer the firm of H. Korn AG, the management of which, on the basis of long experience in the field, seemed able to anticipate the needs of its clients even better than the clients themselves. I quote from a letter written by H. Korn AG to the SS in Belgrade:

"In addition to our conference regarding the delivery of equipment of simple construction for the burning of bodies, we are submitting plans for our perfected cremation ovens which operate on coal and which have proved to be extremely satisfactory.

"In connection with the intended construction, we offer two such ovens, *but would request you to reply whether two ovens will be enough.*

"We guarantee the effectiveness of the cremation ovens as well as their durability, the use of the best material and our faultless workmanship. Heil Hitler!"

The Belgrade job was much sought after, incidentally; there is on the Nuremberg record a competitive bid from the firm of Didier Werke AG of Berlin, and I quote a few lines only to indicate the economy and efficiency which the practiced hand can achieve in any field:

"Every furnace provides for a cremation space of only 24 inches in width and 18 inches in height, the use of coffins not being planned. We suggest the use of light transport trucks running on wheels for carrying the corpses from the store room to the furnaces and we include a sketch of the dimensions of the trucks."

Other firms were involved in what might be termed the disposal end of the Nazi corpse industry. A Danzig firm named Arrd manufactured an electrically-heated tank for the manufacture of soap out of human fat: "The recipe called for 12 pounds of human fat, ten quarts of water, and eight ounces to a pound of caustic soda . . . all boiled for two or three hours and then cooled." Crushed bone was sold to fertilizer firms for the manufacture of phosphate. A Berlin manufacturer turned out those mobile murder machines called gas vans. Millions of garments, carefully sorted in extermination camp warehouses, were turned back for reprocessing to the German textile industry. A chemical

firm named Degesch supplied camps with prussic acid ampoules
for fatal injections.

Hair was not wasted, either. I quote from a directive sent to all
camp commandants on August 6, 1942:

"Chief of the SS-Main-Office Economics and Administration,
SS Major-General Pohl, orders that all human hair cut in concentration camps be utilized. Human hair is spun into industrial
felt and yarn. Out of combed and cut hair of women, hair-yarn
stockings for U-Boat crews are made, as well as hair-felt stockings
for Reich railway workers."

But business competition for the raw material of the corpse
industry—the labor potential of the million inmates of the KZ
system—was even livelier. Hundreds of thousands of inmates were
farmed out to labor camps attached to industrial plants, some
Government-owned but most privately owned, and in these plants,
the State's *work-to-death* order was carried out under the beneficent banner of Private Enterprise.

I do not have a complete list of German firms which employed
camp labor: it would read, undoubtedly, like a Directory of Directors. The Nuremberg witness Hoess, ex-Commandant of Auschwitz and later attached to Pohl's SS-Main-Office of Economics and
Administration, prepared a partial list for the use of the American
prosecution in the post-Nuremberg trials of industrialists.

The list included the giant electrical firm of Siemens-Schuckert,
which employed 1500 women inmates at Auschwitz for piece work
inside the camp, and set up other enterprises at or near the camps
at Neuengamme and Flossenburg. It included the Mauser Works,
which employed women from Natzweiler; the German Weapons
Works, which used Buchenwald prisoners; Daimler-Benz, auto-
mobile and engine manufacturers, which got part of its labor supply from Sachsenhausen; the Henschel Locomotive Works, the
Laura Smelting Mines, the giant Borsig steel plant and various
State projects such as the Reich Railways and H. G. (*Hermann
Goering*) Works, in Berlin, all of which drew heavily on labor
from various camps.

And the list included I. G. Farben, which built and operated
with camp labor a buna rubber plant less than a mile from Ausch-

witz, and in all employed at least 20,000 workers from Auschwitz alone. Moreover, Farben plant managers worked closely with the camp commandant *and knew what was going on.*

"I often visited the Farben plants," testified Hoess, "and very often the managers visited me in my office, which was located at the camp entrance. Dr. Duerrfeld was temporary director of the buna plant in Auschwitz. He also visited the camp personally. He knew about the gassing of people and was worried about how to explain these dreadful things to his colleagues and subordinates."

It would seem that Dr. Duerrfeld was worried unnecessarily. Every business executive who ever came near Auschwitz, whether on behalf of Farben or any other firm, must have known by his nose what was going on. Remember Hoess's earlier testimony:

". . . the foul and nauseating stench from the continuous burning of bodies permeated the entire area and all the people living in the neighboring communities knew that exterminations were going on at Auschwitz."

I want to mention one additional firm which occupied a rather unique place in the corpse industry. Tesch and Stabenow, an affiliate of the International Insecticide Co. of Hamburg, manufactured a powerful crystallized prussic acid fumigant known as Cyclon B. Perhaps you recall the name; it is the stuff Hoess was dropping into his gas chambers at Auschwitz. I quote Hoess again:

"Cyclon B in cans, used for the gassing of human beings at Auschwitz, was procured continuously and exclusively from Tesch and Stabenow. I assume with certainty that this firm knew the use of the Cyclon B which it was delivering. This they would have to conclude from the great quantities continuously being ordered . . . at least 10,000 cans, that is about 22,000 pounds, in three years.

"This figure is arrived at by computing the number of gassed people at 2,500,000 and figuring an average consumption of six cans—about 13.2 pounds—for each 1500 people."

2.

Krupp von Bohlen, the armaments king who was saved from the Nuremberg dock by senility and a paralytic stroke, earned more than his share of ghoul's gold. Why not? He had helped to plan it that way, with his secret tank building during Weimar, his invaluable aid to Hitler in 1933, his leadership in Nazifying industry.

The great Krupp works at Essen asked for concentration camp labor in 1942; for unexplained reasons, no shipments were forthcoming until 1944. But long before—since shortly after the attack on the U.S.S.R. in 1941—the firm was getting slave labor shipped to it directly from the conquered areas in the East.

"In the middle of 1941, the first workers arrived from Poland, Galicia and the Polish Ukraine," testified Adam Schmidt, a Reich railway employee at Essen, in an affidavit. "They came to Essen in freight cars jammed full. The Krupp overseers laid special value on the speed with which the slave workers got out of the train. They were beaten and kicked . . . I could see with my own eyes that sick people who could scarcely walk were taken to work."

I quote from the sworn statement of Dr. Wilhelm Jaeger, who in 1942 became senior camp doctor in the workers' camps which dotted the landscape around the Essen plant:

"Conditions in all camps were extremely bad. They were greatly overcrowded . . . the diet was altogether insufficient. Only inferior meat, such as horse meat or tuberculin-infested meat rejected by veterinaries, was distributed.

"Clothing was likewise completely inadequate. They worked and slept in the same clothing in which they had arrived from the East. Virtually all . . . had to use their blankets as coats in cold and rainy weather; many workers had to go to work barefoot, even in winter.

"Tuberculosis was particularly widespread. The TB rate was four times the normal rate. The causes were bad housing, the poor quality and insufficient quantity of food, overwork."

Records found in the Krupp files show that beating and torturing of war prisoners and foreign workers were deliberately prescribed by Krupp officials. Steel switches for beatings were distributed in accordance with instructions from Herr Kupke, head of the Krupp slave labor camps. But Krupp genius went far beyond steel switches. I quote the testimony of three German employees who attached photographs to their affidavit:

"Photograph 'A' shows an iron cupboard which was specially manufactured by Krupp to torture Russian civilian workers. Men and women were locked in one compartment of the cupboard, in which a man could scarcely stand, for long periods. The compartments were approximately five feet high, breadth and depth 16 to 20 inches. People were often kicked and pressed in pairs into one compartment. At the top of the cupboard, there were air holes through which cold water was poured on the unfortunate victims during the ice-cold winter."

The above affidavits against Krupp were included in the legal case against him prepared at Nuremberg, but never presented because at the last moment he was dropped from the list of defendants.

3.

Yes, by all means let's do business with German businessmen. Almost any American Military Government official will tell you that they are capable, honest and conservative, just the type to whom we ought to entrust the Fourth Reich.

What, for instance, had the German Ministry of Economics, or the great Reichsbank, both highly technical and non-political institutions serving the admittedly far from indigenously German god Mammon, to do with murder and concentration camps and torture?

As to the Ministry of Economics:

"I, Oswald Pohl, after being duly sworn, state the following:

"Since February 1, 1934, I was Chief of the SS-Main-Office

Economics and Administration. In the year of 1941 or 1942, I received an order from Himmler, who was my chief, to get in touch with the Reich Economics Minister, Walter Funk, to obtain a higher allotment of textiles for SS uniforms. I visited Funk in his office. I informed Funk of my instructions that I was to ask him for more textiles for Waffen-SS uniforms, inasmuch as we could deliver so many old textiles from the actions against Jews. It was openly discussed that we earned perhaps privileged treatment on account of the delivery of old clothes from dead Jews. It was a friendly conversation between Funk and myself and he said to me that he would settle the matter favorably with the gentlemen concerned."

As to the Reichsbank:

"Emil Puhl, being duly sworn, deposes and says:

"I was appointed a member of the board of directors of the Reichsbank in 1935 and Vice-President of the Reichsbank in 1939, and served in these positions continuously until the surrender of Germany.

"In the summer of 1942, Walter Funk, the President of the Reichsbank, told me that he had arranged with Himmler to have the Reichsbank receive on safe deposit gold and jewels for the SS. Funk directed that I should work out the arrangements with Pohl who, as head of the SS-Main-Office Economics and Administration, was in charge of the economic aspects of the concentration camp program.

"I asked Funk what the source was of the articles to be turned over by the SS. Funk replied that it was confiscated property from the Eastern Territories but that I should ask no further questions and that we were to keep the matter absolutely secret.

"Deliveries [by the SS] were made from time to time, beginning in August, 1942, over the following years. The material deposited by the SS included jewelry, watches, eye-glass frames, dental gold and other gold items in great abundance taken from Jews, concentration camp victims and other persons by the SS. This was brought to our knowledge by SS personnel who attempted to convert this material into cash and who obtained, in this connection, the assistance of the Reichsbank personnel with Funk's approval and knowledge."

The names Oswald Pohl and Emil Puhl are, perhaps, slightly confusing; but their evidence wasn't, not to anyone except, possibly, Funk himself. For Funk had been simultaneously Reich Economics Minister and President of the Reichsbank, and at Nuremberg he was put into the position of having to defend himself against a simultaneous two-flank attack.

Funk did not do very well on either flank.

As former Minister of Economics, he denied vigorously on the witness stand that Pohl had ever talked to him about textiles. He explained that he never concerned himself with specific matters of this kind, and in the next breath added that when he did so concern himself, it was always in the presence of his State Secretary. Then he insisted that things like old clothes from concentration camps were exclusively a matter for the Reich Commissar for Used Materials, "an office outside" the Economics Ministry; and a minute later he added that, "the office worked quite logically with the textile experts of my ministry." And in the end he explained that his memory was not quite what it used to be, and maybe Pohl *had* talked to him about textiles, in which case "I most certainly would have turned over this matter to my State Secretary so that he would handle it and do the necessary thing."

Poor Funk! He was so intent on contradicting himself that he forgot to contradict the evidence.

As former Reichsbank president, Funk ran into even graver difficulties. Under brilliant cross-examination by Tom Dodd, United States Chief Trial Counsel, he admitted the deal with Himmler to accept SS deposits, admitted that he knew that some of the deposit material might have come from concentration camps, admitted that he thought it best not to inquire too closely into the nature of the deposits. But he insisted that he thought the deposits consisted only of gold coin, foreign exchange and certain types of banknotes which all Germans, and not only camp prisoners, had to give up under law.

Justice Biddle interjected a few questions:

Q. "Was it Himmler's business to see that gold and notes were brought into the bank under German law?"

A. "Yes, if these things, for example, had been taken from the inmates of concentration camps."

Q. "That is exactly what I meant. So that you knew, or suspected, since Himmler was dealing with you, that the gold and notes had come from concentration camps which were under Himmler?"

A. "Yes."

Q. "He said these gold and notes were part of other property; there was other property, too?"

A. "No, he said they were confiscated valuables. He told me: 'We have confiscated a large amount of valuables, especially in the East, and we would like to deposit them in the Reichsbank.'"

Q. "This was not one of your regular deposits, was it? It was unusual?"

A. "It was a special case."

Q. "You didn't ask him any questions about it at all? You weren't curious about it? It didn't interest you?"

A. "No. Once or twice I talked to Puhl, and once to Wilhelm quite briefly."

Q. "Thank you; that is all."

And while the incurious Funk sat in his President's office, deeply immersed in ignorance, his Chief Treasurer, on September 15, 1942, was sending to the Municipal Pawnbroker in Berlin, with the request "for the best possible utilization," a "second shipment" of valuables as follows: 660 rings, including wedding rings; 1900 watches; 2500 pairs of earrings; 1058 bracelets, necklaces and other pieces of jewelry; 469 candelabras, knives, forks and pocketbooks, *and 160 diverse dentures*, partly of gold.

There were many such shipments; but even so, the Reichsbank was getting the stuff faster than the Municipal Pawnbroker could dispose of it. And when the Allies finally overran Germany, they recovered—from salt mines in which the Nazis had hidden the material—enough to fill three huge vaults of the Frankfurt branch of the Reichsbank.

A film of this recovered material was shown at the trial. The

Tribunal saw watches and wedding rings and jewelry. They saw eyeglass frames and silver shoebuckles and alarm clocks. And they saw ghoul's gold: false teeth, fillings, bridgework, inlays, yanked from the mouths of the dead.

4.

It must not be thought that German business circles were exclusively money-grubbers, devoid of all nobler sentiment. Nothing could be further from the truth. There were, for instance, no greater patriots to be found anywhere in Germany than among certain industrialists who worked unceasingly for their fascist government at very real—if perhaps only temporary—financial loss to themselves.

Hitler had been in power only a few months, as an example, when the deputy manager of the German Iron Producing Industry was urging upon member firms the necessity for disseminating abroad, as widely as possible, an "uncut version" of a speech by the Fuehrer before the Reichstag. "The Reich Ministry of Propaganda," the deputy manager reminded members, "has made available translations of the speech into English, French, and Spanish, which could be attached as leaflets to members' correspondence with their foreign agents, or could be sent in bulk to branches abroad."

That was in May, 1933. A month later members of the Association of German Iron and Steel Industries, which of course included many giant industrial complexes with affiliations all over the world, were putting into the foreign mails another Goebbels literary effort, this one a pamphlet designed "to counteract foreign boycotting of German products resulting from the elimination of Jews from the political and economic life" of Germany.

Heavy industry by no means monopolized collaboration with Goebbels. In 1940, thirty chemical firms—including the very large Metzler Tire Co., presumably listed as a chemical firm because at the time it was manufacturing buna—requested propaganda material for distribution abroad in various languages.

From propaganda to espionage is but a short step, and German industrialists were not loath to take it. In an amazing letter addressed to the Reich Group Industry, the all-over organization of German industrialists, the High Command of the German Navy complained that certain businessmen-spies abroad were not acting with sufficient discretion.

The letter was dated September 23, 1939—shortly after the outbreak of war—and I quote from a summary:

"The Naval High Command informs Reich Group Industry that German technicians working for German firms outside Germany have been able to procure detailed information on the technical organization of the Armed Forces in foreign countries. Unfortunately, however, these technicians were careless enough to report their observations by letter. The Naval High Command therefore requests all firms concerned to instruct their technicians working abroad to act with extreme caution."

A year later, espionage developed into something even more sinister. A cable from the German Ambassador in Buenos Aires to the Foreign Office in Berlin noted planned formation of a huge German industrial syndicate for the secret delivery of arms to Argentina. The cable did not reveal who was to get the weapons, but did name as members of the syndicate the following firms and industrial organizations: Krupp, Koeln Rottweil, Borsig, Siemens, the Association of Airplane Manufacturers, and the Air transport Industry.

5.

Undoubtedly there were some German businessmen who did not profit from the corpse industry or the slave labor program, or who did so only under duress and without pleasure. Undoubtedly there were German businessmen who did not put themselves out to further fascism either at home or abroad.

I do not want to ennoble the German worker beyond his due. But if our Military Government people *must* have prejudices—and who anywhere does not?—they might do well to apply them with more discrimination. After all, the only profit the average

German *worker* got out of the concentration camp and slave labor programs was that, because he had become replaceable, his Government could promote him from the factory bench to the front lines. That was small profit indeed.

Chapter XIV   SScience

1.

On May 15, 1941, according to the testimony at Nuremberg, Dr. Sigmund Rascher, an Air Corps physician attached to the Seventh District Air Command at Munich, wrote a beguiling little note to his friend Himmler:

"Dear Reichsfuehrer,

"My sincere thanks for your cordial wishes and flowers on the birth of my second son. This time, it is a strong boy, though he has come three weeks too early. I may send you a picture of both children. . . .

"For the time being, I have been assigned to a medical course, in which researches on high-altitude flight play a prominent part. Considerable regret was expressed at the fact that no tests with human material have yet been made available to us, as such experiments are very dangerous and nobody volunteers for them.

"I put, therefore, the serious question: can you make available two or three professional criminals for these experiments?

"With heartiest good wishes, I am with Heil Hitler your gratefully devoted

S. Rascher."

Two or three "professional criminals?" What a humble petition! Himmler had millions available. For was not every Slav, every Jew, every prisoner of war, every concentration camp inmate—man, woman, or child—a professional criminal to the Nazis? Rascher got his two or three. In a matter of days the two or three grew into hundreds; in a matter of months into thousands and tens of thousands and hundreds of thousands.

The great tradition of German science—the science of Koch, Hertz, Humboldt, Roentgen—degenerated into senseless and sadistic butchery. The Roentgen ray became a weapon for mass sterilization and the murder of innocent people; the discoveries of Koch were harnessed, not to the curing of disease, but to its deliberate propagation. Man became a guinea pig in the hands of blundering, bloodthirsty savage little men who called themselves scientists; and the study of anatomy was valued only as an adjunct to the application of torture.

Why not? Who was to stay the brutal scalpel, the poisoned bullet, the typhus-carrying needle? The human guinea pigs of the concentration camps were defenseless beyond all imagining; they had no law, no lawyer, no policeman, no court, no ethical code, no man of God to protect them. They were meat, not men; and these so-called scientists of the Nazi era carved and hacked and pounded the living flesh with less concern than a butcher working upon a piece of steak.

2.

The experiments in the concentration camps were directed largely by an SS institution known as the *Ahnenerbe*, translatable roughly as the Institute for Heredity. It was one of the many SS institutions which German industry helped to finance through its contributions to the Himmler Fund.

The singular Dr. Rascher, doting father and no doubt also a most loving husband, was one of the Institute's earliest and greatest luminaries. His experimental technique, first applied to the studies of atmosphere pressure at Dachau, and later to studies of temperature at Auschwitz, are models of the simple and direct approach to problems which must have appeared of enormous complexity to lesser scientists.

At Dachau, he simply put the subject of his experiment into a windowed airtight chamber and then, depending upon the direction of his curiosity at the moment, proceeded to pump air into or out of the chamber until his subject reacted in satisfactory fashion.

The nature of these reactions was described to the Tribunal in an affidavit prepared by one of Rascher's co-workers, Dr. Pacholegg:

"I have personally seen, through the observation window of a chamber, how a prisoner inside would stand in a vacuum until his lungs ruptured. Some experiments gave men such pressure in their heads that they would go mad and pull out their hair in an effort to relieve such pressure. They would tear their heads and faces with their fingernails . . . They would beat the walls with their hands and head and scream in an effort to relieve pressure on their eardrums.

"These cases of extremes of vacuums generally ended in the death of the subject."

The pressure experiments went on for some months—apparently until Dr. Rascher, a very careful scientist indeed, became absolutely convinced that when you subject a man to atmospheric pressure high enough or low enough, he is bound to die in incredible torture. And having made this revolutionary discovery on behalf of the *Waffen SS* and Goering's Air Force, he went on to study methods for resuscitating people frozen into unconsciousness.

I quote from the testimony of Dr. Franz Blaha, a Czech physician and inmate of Dachau who performed autopsies on thousands of persons killed one way or another at the camp:

"Rascher also conducted experiments on the effect of cold water on humans to find a way for reviving aviators who had fallen into the ocean. The subject was placed in ice cold water and kept there until he was unconscious. . . .

"When the men were removed from the ice water, attempts were made to revive them by artificial warmth, by hot water, by electro-therapy and by animal warmth.

"For this last experiment prostitutes were used and the body of the unconscious man was placed between the bodies of two women. Himmler was present at one such experiment. I could see him from one of the windows in the street between two blocks.

"About 300 persons were used in these experiments. The majority died. Of those who lived many were mentally deranged."

Thus Dr. Blaha. Dr. Rascher, as befitting the director of the experiments, was more explicit. In an *Intermediate Report on Intense Chilling Experiments*, he wrote:

"The experimental subjects were placed in the water dressed in complete flying uniform. Water temperatures varied from 36.5 to 51 degrees Fahrenheit. As soon as the temperature [of the subjects] reached 82 degrees Fahrenheit, they died invariably, despite all attempts at resuscitation."

Moreover, Dr. Rascher discovered that rewarming by women's bodies was not to be recommended; it was too slow.

From the problem of freezing through immersion, Dr. Rascher switched his inquiries into the problem of "dry cold," a change of interest dictated no doubt by the Wehrmacht's unhappy experiences with the Russian winter. He put thirty naked people out-of-doors on the grounds of Dachau in the winter of 1942-43, and succeeded in resuscitating them after their temperatures had dropped to as low as 80 degrees Fahrenheit (or so he reported). But the careful doctor was not yet satisfied; Dachau, after all, is in southern Germany, and the mid-winter climate is by no means extreme. So he wrote to his friend Himmler:

"Auschwitz [in Poland] is, in every respect, better suited than Dachau for such a series of experiments because it is much colder and less excitement would be caused due to the fact that the camp is so much larger. The experimental persons yell when freezing intensely!"

But unfortunately, by the time Dr. Rascher was ready to resume his work, this time at Auschwitz, the Red Army was drawing near, and again the good doctor decided that the climate was unsatisfactory.

3.

The manager of the *Ahnenerbe* was Wolfram Sievers, a black-bearded gentleman with roving eyes and an extraordinarily fallible memory. For two sessions at the trial the brilliant young British prosecutor, Elwyn Jones, led the unhappy witness back through the diversified activities of the Institute during the war.

Jones began with a seemingly innocent reference to the interest of a Professor Hirt, of the Department of Anatomy of Strassburg University, in the collection of skeletons for the University museum.

Q. "This was just a piece of academic research, was it?"

A. "Yes, indeed."

Q. "Where were you going to get the skeletons from?"

A. "Particulars were to be handled by Professor Hirt."

Q. "Now just answer my question, witness, because you know perfectly well the answer to it. Where were you going to get those skeletons?"

A. "They were to be put at our disposal from Auschwitz."

Then it came out. Slowly the prosecutor read into the record a report prepared by Hirt and forwarded by Sievers to Himmler's office. Here are Hirt's words:

"We have a nearly complete collection of skulls of all races and peoples at our disposal. Of the Jewish race, however, only very few specimens are available. The war in the East now presents us with the opportunity to overcome this deficiency.

"The best practical method for obtaining and collecting this skull material would be by directing the Wehrmacht to turn over alive all captured Jewish Bolshevist Commissars to the field police.

"Following the subsequently induced death of the Jew, whose head should not be damaged, a special delegate will separate the head from the body and will forward it to its proper destination in an hermetically sealed tin can filled with a preserving fluid. Having arrived at the laboratory, the comparison tests and anatomical research can proceed."

Jones laid aside the document and resumed his questioning:

Q. "How many human beings were killed to create this collection of skeletons?"

A. "Here we are concerned with the figure of a 150 people."

Q. "That was all you assisted in murdering, was it?"

A. "I had nothing to do with the murdering. I purely and simply carried through the function of a mail-man."

Q. "So you were a post-office, another of those distinguished Nazi post-offices, were you?"

But the prosecution did not need Sievers. The documents spoke with unfailing memory. At least 115 persons were killed for the benefit of Professor Hirt's skeleton collection—79 male Jews, 30 Jewesses, 2 Poles and 4 Asiatics. Moreover, before their heads were severed from their bodies and sent to Strassburg in tin cans they were, while still alive, deliberately infected with a communicable disease.

As with the defendant Frank, the hangman of Poland, the witness Sievers' weak memory proved in the end his undoing. Both he and Frank had forgotten to destroy their diaries. Out of Sievers' diary and out of documents dovetailing with its entries, the Tribunal learned how the butchers of the *Ahnenerbe* used camp inmates as guinea pigs for spotted fever and yellow jaundice, gave them bloody gunshot wounds to test the efficacy of new coagulating agents, and filled their bellies with salt water in pursuit of methods to make sea-water potable.

But most characteristic of *Ahnenerbe's* activities was its limitless preoccupation with the problem of sterilization, a most potent weapon for genocide. Its researchers cut with knives and burned with X-rays and in the end were on the threshold of a discovery which might have put future generations of the world at the mercy of a spoonful of medication.

I say that this type of research was most characteristic of the *Ahnenerbe* because it was the logical outcome of Nazi preoccupation with race. The Nazis were seeking domination of the world by what they fondly called the "Germanic peoples." But there was a limit, even under Hitler's multifarious inducements to parenthood—including the institutions founded for lusty SS youth and patriotic German girls for propagation out of wedlock—to the virility of the Germans of the Third Reich. The most patriotic fervor in the world cannot produce a healthy child in fewer than nine months.

But dominance can be achieved as well by destruction of one's rivals as by self-expansion. Fecundity and sterilization are equal and parallel weapons in the arsenal of fascism.

This thought was in the mind of Dr. Pokorny, German physician, who some time in 1943 or 1944 wrote to Himmler as follows:

"Prompted by the thought that the enemy must not only be conquered but exterminated, I feel obliged to submit the following to you. Dr. Madous is publishing the results of his research into sterilization by medication (I enclose both works). The thought alone that the three million Bolsheviks now in German captivity could be sterilized, so that they would be available for work but precluded from propagation, opens up the most far-reaching perspectives."

Madous' discovery was the juice of the plant *Caladium seguinum*, which he said caused lasting sterility when taken orally or by injection. Unfortunately *Caladium seguinum* is a tropical plant and Sievers scored his greatest victory on the stand when he was able to show that the sterilization of three million Bolsheviks never developed beyond the plan stage. *Caladium seguinum* could not be grown anywhere on European soil.

So the Germans were forced to continue the plodding methods offered by the scalpel and the X-ray. I quote from a report of the U.S.S.R. Extraordinary State Commission on Crimes at Auschwitz:

"Up to four hundred women prisoners were interned in Block 10 of the camp and on these women experiments in sterilization by X-ray, with subsequent removal of the ovaries, were carried out. There were also experiments in the inoculation of cancer of the uterus and in abortion. . . .

"In Block 21 mass experiments on the castration of men were carried out. Very often the testicles were removed after their subjection to X-ray treatment."

A Dutch physician named De Vint, an inmate of Auschwitz, submitted testimony before the Tribunal on the treatment given by the Nazi scientists to fifteen 'teen-age girls:

"The young girls were placed between slabs through which passed ultra shortwaves; one electrode was placed on their stomach and the other on their ovaries. One girl died after terrible suffering. A month later, two controlling operations were carried out —one long slit and one cross slit—after which the genital organs were removed for examination.

"Physically, the girls changed completely and as a result they looked like old women."

These were not, needless to say, German girls. They were Poles and Greeks.

4.

I have called this chapter SScience because the SS were the chief butchers in the bloody parody on medical research performed by the Third Reich.

But the guilt belonged not to the SS alone.

Rascher's pressure and temperature work was reported directly to General Milch, deputy commander of the Luftwaffe under Goering. Work on malaria and experiments with yellow jaundice and spotted fever unquestionably was known to the army medical corps. Representatives of both the German Navy and Air Force were involved in experiments with sea water, in which gypsies were used as guinea pigs.

All this was shown by evidence produced at the trial. *What was not shown, because it had no relevance to the cases of any of the defendants, was the culpability of the supposedly "pure" scientists of Germany, the "non-political" savants who, in the laboratories of the great German universities, had for years been building up their country's enviable scientific reputation.*

These men, too, dipped their hands in an inexhaustible sea of human blood.

The proof is in the staid reports of famous German medical journals which before the war appeared on the shelves of medical libraries all over the world, and which continued publication right through the war. It is the war years' issues which tell the story.

I quote from the *Journal for Microscopic and Anatomical Research,* 1944:

"The thyroid glands of 21 allegedly healthy persons ranging in age from 20 to 40 years, who had died a sudden death. . . . The persons in question, 19 men and two women, had been living for several months prior to their death under absolutely identical conditions, even so far as nourishment is concerned. The food intake towards the end consisted mostly of carbohydrates. . . .

"It must be mentioned that the persons whose thyroid glands had been examined had been suffering from severe emotional excitement."

Did or did not the professor who wrote that know where the 21 bodies had come from?

From the same journal, issue of a year earlier, I quote from a report by Professor W. Blotvogel on research carried on by the Anatomical Institute of the University of Breslau:

"Over a rather long period of time, experimental material was gathered from the livers of 24 adult healthy persons who died suddenly between five and six o'clock in the morning. Various large pieces of liver were obtained not later than one-half hour after death."

And in the same issue of the same journal, from a report by H. Stieve, internationally known director of the Anatomical Institute in Berlin:

"The results of my observations with regard to 123 healthy women, of whom only very few had been operated upon in the clinic, but of whom the overwhelming majority died suddenly through an accident or some other cause. . . ."

I would like to question Dr. Stieve on the subject of "death through accident or by some other cause." Did he, perhaps, in the course of his autopsies, find a little hole in the skulls, and at the bottom of the hole a round piece of lead? And did he by chance wonder by what accident this foreign body had found its way into the frontal lobe?

The same gentleman writes in the *Journal for Cytology,* 1942, on the interesting subject of "the influence of the nervous system on stricture and performance of the female sex organs":

"In the following report I am describing entirely healthy women who died a sudden death. . . .

"I always examined the ovaries between ten minutes to three hours—the latter in the case of five accidentally killed women—after their death. . . .

"There are only few women who are so insensitive that their sexual organs perform regularly and normally when they are subjected to changed environment, changed nourishment and severe emotional strain, particularly fear of death."

So only five of Dr. Stieve's subjects died by accident. And how did the others die, those others of whom the author knew that they had been living under "fear of death"? And how did the doctor manage to get the ovaries before the corpses were ten minutes old? Is it possible the women were killed on the august premises of the Berlin Anatomical Institute itself? Or did Dr. Stieve wait in the laboratories of the Sachsenhausen camp near Berlin for the bodies to be brought to him from the execution yard—and, while waiting, perhaps hear the shots that killed them?

The Anatomical Institute of the University of Koenigsberg reports in the *Journal for Cytology and Microscopic Anatomy,* Vol. 53, on studies of "eight brain lobes, prepared while still warm, of decapitated men aged 19 to 40." In the *Journal for Microscopic and Anatomical Research,* 1942, Professor Max Clara of the University of Munich reports the results of studies on subjects who "without exception, died a sudden death." And in the same journal, one Lothar Heckel of the Anatomical Institute of the University of Leipzig complains that certain experiments performed on kidneys taken from "executed persons" in 1934 were not conclusive because of insufficient material, and he urges that "a thorough examination of properly conserved material from executed human beings seems desirable."

In the hands of Major Marvin Linick, of New York, former Public Health Officer with Military Government in Munich, lies documentary proof that officials of that city's Municipal Prison regularly informed the Munich Medical School of contemplated executions so that the scientists could obtain the corpses while still warm.

Then there is the case of the great Kaiser Wilhelm Institute, Germany's equivalent of the Rockefeller Foundation (indeed, the Foundation helped finance the Institute at one time; and James Loeb, of the American banking firm of Kuhn Loeb & Co., was one of the many international philanthropists who continued donating funds to it even after Hitler came to power). For five years the Institute's laboratory technicians in Munich were examining microscopically brain smears from children who had died in the nearby Asylum for the Insane at Harr-Eglfing. The death certificates which accompanied the smears regularly gave cause of death as "pneumonia" or "circulatory disorders."

Actually these children had been murdered systematically with injections of luminal, iodine or evipan under the Nazi nationwide plan for destruction of "useless eaters."

One may legitimately ask whether the noted scientists of the Kaiser Wilhelm Institute were fools who for five years carried out research on the basis of false death diagnoses, or were knaves who knew the truth and thus connived at murder? Most Americans who investigated the story on the spot refused to believe that the scientists were fools.

5.

Did they profit? Let us suppose that out of the torture chambers of Dachau, the slaughterhouse of Auschwitz, the gleaming white butcher shops of the Kaiser Wilhelm Institute or the Anatomical Institute of Berlin, had come some great discovery—a specific for typhus, perhaps, or a cure for cancer, or a method for rejuvenating the aging heart. What then would have been the verdict of history on Nazi science?

History will have no such difficult decision to make. Nothing came of Nazi science; nothing could have come of it because it was not science. Science is the establishment of fact on the evidence. The Nazis were only interested in establishing the evidence to prove their assumed fact.

The assumed fact was the doctrine of race superiority. Under certain conditions, such an assumption could be a legitimate scientific hypothesis to be tested against the results of honest research. But not under fascist conditions. For to the Fascist the doctrine of race superiority was at the outset not a scientific principle but a political weapon for the achievement of his ambition: conquest of the world. And he called in his scientists not to find out the truth, but to prove the untrue.

The sole contribution of fascist science to the world was the addition of a certain amount of calcium, potash, nitrogen and phosphorus to the reeking soil of Europe.

Chapter XV   Twentieth-Century Calvary

1.

In the case of the Jews, the defendants proved their own best prosecutors. No other section of the indictment was so clearly, comprehensively, and consistently proven by the Nazis' own words and their own orders, and I propose to let the documents speak for themselves.

Yet this documentary history, complete as it is, fails us on two points of significance: it tells us what happened, but not why; and nowhere has there been unearthed any direct documentary evidence concerning the time, the place, and the personnel involved when the decision was made to exterminate European Jewry.

On the second point, we do have certain circumstantial evidence to help us. We know that in 1939, certain high Nazis met —undoubtedly including Himmler as head of the German police and Heydrich as his deputy, and probably Hitler and Goering as well as others—and that as a result of the meeting, an order was issued by the SD (Security Police of the SS) for the collection of Eastern Jews into ghettos as a preliminary step to the "ultimate goal."

In this document the ultimate goal is not defined; it is quite possible it had not yet been formulated. As the war ground on, and the enormous military problems involved took up more and more of Hitler's time, there was a tendency at the Reich Chancellery to delay final decision on the Jewish question until after victory had been won. It is clear, however, through the direct evidence of many witnesses, that the extermination program began in midsummer of 1941, after the onslaught on Russia. That is when the gas chambers were projected. It was when the so-called Special Task Forces of the SD were sent in with the Army to collect victims for the extermination camps or, where that was not convenient, to kill in the towns and villages, on the roads, in the fields and forests, that part of the civilian population which, for one reason or another, the Nazis no longer wanted to let live. Jews were killed because they were Jews; others were killed as partisans, as hostages or for reprisals.

The date of the decision to exterminate is important because it opens up the question as to whether or not the Allied nations, had they opened their doors early enough, could have saved millions of lives. Rudolf Kastner, who as representative of Hungarian Jewry remained in close contact with Nazi leaders all through the war, believes that the decision to exterminate was reached tentatively in 1939, but did not become effective until the summer of 1941. The years 1939-41 he calls a "period of hesitation" in which the Lublin reservation for Jewry was created, but the Nazis were apparently not yet certain what they would do with the Jews once they got them there.

Certainly there is no documentary proof, or even hint of proof, that Hitler was unwilling prior to '41 to let the Jews go, provided they did not take property with them. Transport, once war had started, might have been difficult. But some percentage, perhaps as high as fifty percent, could have been moved *had the rest of the world opened its doors.* But the doors remained closed, and seventy percent of European Jewry found its "ultimate goal" in the crematoria of Auschwitz and Treblinka, or the mass graves of Poland and Western Russia.

The why of the extermination program is less certain than the when; the facts are not documented at all. None of the defendants, during the course of the trial, had any light to shed;

indeed, if one were to believe their testimony, none knew *what* had happened, no less why. "The first time I learned about these terrible exterminations was right here in Nuremberg," said Goering. He set the tone for the defendants who followed. A straight-faced Jodl, in one of the really incredible moments of the trial, swore from the witness chair that he had never heard of Buchenwald concentration camp until early in 1945 and then he thought "it was a military training center." Streicher recalled having read "something about exterminations" in the Swiss press of 1944, but he insisted stoutly that he had not believed the reports, persisting in his stand even when he was reminded that his own newspaper, at the time, had republished these reports with his own comment: "Here, at last, is no Jewish lie!"

No, there was no help from the twenty-one innocents in the dock on this subject. At one point during the cross-examination of the defendant Speer, who in the closing war period was virtually Hitler's production chief, Chief Justice Lawrence asked from the bench, "But the destruction of all these people hurt war production, did it not?" And Speer answered, "Yes." And there followed a curious silence in the courtroom, a suspension of thought and feeling, as if the tiny word "Yes" had introduced us into a new and strange world where logic, as we know it, and human emotion, and all the familiar terms by which we describe the motivations of man, had no longer any meaning, and other motivations, inscrutable and terrible, had taken their place.

Or that other time when Ohlendorf, slim, gray-looking young man who spoke so softly one had to strain to hear him, took the stand and recited how, as chief of Special Task Force A of the SD, his group had killed 90,000 men, women and children in a single year. At one point the Soviet Justice, General Nikitchenko, intervened:

"In your testimony you said that the *Einsatz* Group had the object of annihilation of the Jews and the Commissars, is that correct?"

A. "Yes."

Q. "And in what group did you consider the children? For what reason were the children massacred?"

A. "The order was that the Jewish population should be liquidated in its entirety."

Q. "Including children?"

A. "Yes."

Q. "Were all children murdered?"

A. "Yes."

That kind of an answer sheds no light on the question, of course; it sheds light only on Ohlendorf.

However much the German people condoned, they certainly did not initiate or demand the extermination of Jewry. It is doubtful even whether many of the defendants would themselves have resorted to wholesale murder purely out of anti-Semitism (possible exceptions are the fanatic pseudo-philosopher Rosenberg, the gangsters Sauckel and Kaltenbrunner, the moronic Streicher). The defendants murdered and connived at murder for various reasons, all cynical, and likely having more to do with opportunism and greed for power and other things than with anti-Semitism.

It is true that the murder program began when Germany was struggling with a growing food problem. "The Jews," wrote Frank in his diary, "represent for us extraordinary malignant gluttons." But whatever the food problem, it did not outweigh the potential labor power represented by five to eight millions of people. Many Germans themselves realized that. Speer's testimony proved it. And there are many documents of corroborative nature showing how certain factions in the German Army, anxious to keep Jews alive for economic reasons, quarrelled with the SS, who wanted to kill them off.

Here again was that dualism of Nazi policy: mass murder vs. mass production. In the case of the Jews, mass murder won hands down. The Jews were the earliest, and remained the primary, victims of the Fascists' genocide program, and this despite the fact that in killing Jews, the Nazis were destroying neither a "nation" nor even an identifiable class, much less a "ruling" or "intellectual" class. The Nazis killed with equal abandon the Jewish artist of Vienna, the Jewish intellectual of Vilna and the nearly illiterate, poverty-stricken Jewish petty tradesman or artisan of Ruthenia and the bleak Polish hinterland.

We are left with only one explanation: The Jews were killed because a handful of Nazi leaders—Himmler, Bormann, Hitler himself, and that fabulous Inquisition character, the Eichmann who headed the Jewish Affairs section of the Gestapo—wanted it that way.

Given this pressure from above, the rest was easy. The ground had been prepared among the rank and file of Germans—particularly those in uniform—by ten years of propaganda. Men like Streicher and Rosenberg and Goebbels had made hundreds of thousands—perhaps millions—of Germans ready to kill on order. The food problem merely gave some semblance of logic to the acts of madmen—their madness exemplified by the fact that they killed more Jews than they ever imported of all nationalities into the Reich as slave labor.

I am not herewith seeking to add to the already overflowing literature on the why and wherefore of anti-Semitism. Its economic basis, the varied facets of its psychological appeal, its role in the "scape-goat" technique, are common knowledge to the modern sociologist. I am not trying to find out why the Nazis did not like Jews; I have sought to explain why they herded them into gas chambers, filled ditches with their bodies, smashed infants' heads against stone walls.

And if I have failed, as I fear I have, to furnish a satisfactory explanation, perhaps the fault is not entirely my own. Some things are simply extraordinarily difficult of explanation. In this category fall such matters as the life-giving element in protoplasm, the conception of a finite universe, and the testimony of Ohlendorf.

2.

What follows is a history of Jewry's fate under the Third Reich as revealed in documents, the bulk of them German in origin and many marked "top secret," introduced at Nuremberg.

The history divides naturally into three periods.

The first—from the Nazi rise to power in 1933 to the outbreak of war—was the period devoted to creating pressure for emigration. It was marked by passage of familiar legislation—so familiar there is no need to cite it again in this book—which relegated Jews to second-class citizenship, hemmed them in with humiliating racial restrictions, and pauperized them through taxation, "Aryanization" and their exclusion from the nation's economic life.

It was marked also by sporadic acts of violence, occasional mass arrests, and a steady stream of propaganda designed to inflame the German people against the Jew.

From *The Kaiserhof to the Reich Chancellery* by Joseph Goebbels
[U. S. A. Exhibit 262]

The boycott against the world atrocity propaganda has started in Berlin and the entire Reich. Today [April 1, 1933] the Jews had better give up Germany for good and not make so much fuss. For the more they talk the more acute the Jewish question will grow, and as soon as the world will begin to concern itself with it, then this problem will always be solved to the disadvantage of the Jews.

Report of U. S. Consul in Leipzig, April, 1933
[U. S. A. Exhibit 265]

In Dresden several weeks ago uniformed "Nazis" raided the Jewish Prayer House, interrupted the evening religious service, arrested 25 worshipers, and tore the holy insignia or emblems from their head coverings worn while praying.

Five of the Jews were compelled each to drink one-half liter of castor oil. Some had to submit to the shearing of their beards, or to the clipping of their hair in the shape of steps. One Polish Jew in Chemnitz had his hair torn out by the roots.

Franconian Daily Journal reports a Streicher speech
to Nuremberg children, December 22, 1936
[British Exhibit 179]

"Do you know who the Devil is?" he asked his breathlessly listening audience.

"The Jew! The Jew!" resounded from a thousand children's voices.

Franconian Daily Journal, 1938
[U. S. A. Exhibit 267]

In Nuremberg the synagogue is being demolished! Julius Streicher himself inaugurates the work by a speech lasting more than an hour and a half. By his order then—so to speak as a prelude to the demolition—the tremendous Star of David came off the cupola.

In the courtroom, the defendant Streicher swore that he had destroyed the synagogue not because he disliked Jews, but because he disliked "Oriental" architecture.

But the most dramatic revelations concerning this first period of Jewish persecutions had to do with the great pogrom of November 10-11, 1938, which followed by a few days the assassination of a German consular official in Paris by a refugee Polish Jew.

[U. S. A. Exhibit 240]

Secret

COPY OF TELETYPE FROM MUNICH, 10 NOV. 1938, 1:20 A. M. TO ALL HEADQUARTERS AND STATIONS OF THE STATE POLICE. TO ALL DISTRICTS AND SUB-DISTRICTS OF THE SECURITY POLICE. SUBMIT IMMEDIATELY TO THE CHIEF OR HIS DEPUTY. RE: MEASURES AGAINST JEWS TONIGHT.

Because of the attempts on the life of Secretary of Legation vom Rath in Paris, demonstrations against Jews are to be expected tonight, November 10, 1938, throughout the Reich. The following instructions are given on treating these events:

1. Chiefs of the State Police or their deputies must get in telephonic communication with political leaders who have jurisdiction in their districts and have to arrange a joint meeting with the appropriate inspector or commander of the *Ordnungspolizei* to discuss the organization of the demonstrations.

At these discussions, political leaders must be informed that the German police have received from the Reichsfuehrer of the SS and the Chief of the German Police the following instructions:

a. Only measures should be taken which do not involve danger to German life or property. (For instance, synagogues are to be burned down only when there is no danger of fire to the surroundings.)

b. Business and private apartments of Jews may be destroyed, but not looted.

c. On business streets, particular care is to be taken that non-Jewish business should be protected from damage.

2. . . . The police have only to supervise compliance with the instructions.

3. . . . In all districts as many Jews, especially rich ones, are to be arrested as can be accommodated in existing prisons. For the time being, only healthy men, not too old, are to be arrested. Upon their arrest appropriate concentration camps should be contacted immediately in order to confine them in these camps as fast as possible.

(Signed) Heydrich, SS Gruppenfuehrer.

From Voelkischer Beobachter, November 11, 1938
[U. S. A. Exhibit 331]

After it had become known that the German Diplomat VOM RATH, who had been struck down by the hand of a murderous coward, had died, spontaneous antisemitic demonstrations developed all over the Reich.

Stenographic Report
of the Meeting on "The Jewish Question"
under the Chairmanship of Field Marshall
Goering
in the Reich Air Force Ministry
(12 November 1938—11 O'clock.)
[U. S. A. Exhibit 261]

Goering: Today's meeting is of a decisive nature. I have received a letter written on the Fuehrer's orders by the Stabsleiter of the Fuehrer's deputy, Bormann, requesting that the Jewish question be now, once and for all, coordinated and solved one way or another.

Gentlemen, I have enough of these demonstrations! They don't harm the Jew but me, who is the last authority for coordinating the German Economy.

Because it's insane to clean out and burn a Jewish warehouse, then have a German insurance company make good the loss. And the goods which I need desperately, whole bales of clothing and what not, are being burned; and I miss them everywhere.

I should not want to leave any doubt, Gentlemen, as to the aim of today's meeting. The fundamental idea in this program of elimination of the Jew from German Economy is first, the Jew being ejected from the Economy transfers his property to the State. He will be compensated. The compensation is to be listed in the debit ledger and shall bring a certain percentage of interest. The Jew shall have to live out of this interest.

Goebbels: In almost all German cities synagogues are burned. I am of the opinion that this is our chance to dissolve the synagogues. All those not completely intact, shall be razed by the Jews. The Jews shall pay for it. We shall build parking lots in their places or new buildings.

I deem it necessary to issue a decree forbidding the Jews to enter German theatres, movie houses, and circuses. Furthermore, I advocate that the Jews be eliminated from all positions in public life in which they may prove to be provocative. It is still possible today that a Jew shares a compartment in a sleeping car with a German. Therefore, we need a decree by the Reich Ministry for Communications stating that separate compartments for Jews shall be available.

Goering: I'd give the Jews one coach or one compartment. And should the train be overcrowded, believe me, we won't need a law. We'll kick him out and he'll have to sit alone in the toilet all the way.

Goebbels: It'll also have to be considered if it might not become necessary to forbid the Jews to enter the German forests.

Goering: We shall give the Jews a certain part of the forests, and the forest police shall take care of it that various animals that look damned much like Jews—the Elk has such a crooked nose—get there also and become acclimated.

Goebbels: Jews should not be allowed to sit around in German parks. Furthermore, Jewish children are still allowed in German schools. That's impossible.

Goering: I suggest that Mr. Hilgard from the insurance company be called in; he is waiting outside.

Hilgard: As for the glass insurance which plays a very important part in this: The majority of victims, mostly the owners of the buildings, are Aryans. The Jew has usually rented the store.

Goering: It doesn't make sense, we have no raw materials. It is all glass imported from foreign countries and has to be paid for in foreign currency. One could go nuts.

Hilgard: In my estimation, the approximate money value to which these damages amount is 6,000,000 marks—that includes the broken glass, glass which we shall have to replace, mainly to Aryans.

Goering: You'll have to pay in any case because it is the Germans who suffered the damage. But there'll be a lawful order forbidding you to make any direct payments to the Jews. You shall also have to make payment for the damage the Jews have suffered, not to the Jews but to the Minister of Finance.

(*Hilgard*: Aha!)

What he does with the money is his business. I wished you had killed 200 Jews, and not destroyed such values.

Funk: I have prepared a law elaborating that, effective January 1, 1939, Jews shall be forbidden to operate retail stores and wholesale establishments as well as independent artisan shops. They shall be further prohibited from keeping employees or offering any ready products on the market.

Goering: One more question, gentlemen: What would you think the situation would be if I'd announce today that Jewry shall have to contribute one billion marks as a punishment?

Buerckel: The Viennese would agree to this wholeheartedly.

Goering: I shall close the wording this way; that German Jewry shall as punishment for their abominable crimes, etc., etc., have to make a contribution of one billion. That'll work. The pigs won't commit another murder. Incidentally, I'd like to say again that I would not like to be a Jew in Germany.

Even before this trial began, it was known that the Nazis used anti-Semitism as a Fifth Column device designed to divide and conquer. But much of our knowledge was of the theoretical kind based on inference and analysis. The following document, issued under the aegis of the defendant Ribbentrop as Foreign Minister, confirms with utmost candor everything we guessed. It should be read with extraordinary interest by all American anti-Semites and most particularly by Father Coughlin. Words printed in large type appeared that way in the original document.

[British Exhibit 158]
Ministry of Foreign Affairs
Berlin, January 25, 1938
To
All diplomatic and qualified
consular representatives abroad.

The final goal of German Jewish Policy is the emigration of all the Jews living in Reich Territory. GERMANY MUST REGARD THE FORMING OF A JEW-ISH STATE AS DANGEROUS, WHICH EVEN IN MINIA-TURE WOULD FORM JUST SUCH AN OPERATIONAL BASE AS THE VATICAN FOR POLITICAL CATHOLICISM. The realization that World Jewry will always be the irreconcilable enemy of the Third Reich, forces the decision to prevent any strengthening of the Jewish position.

Germany is very interested in maintaining the dispersal of Jewry. In North America, in South America, in France, in Holland, Scandinavia and Greece, wherever the flood of Jewish immigrants reaches, there is today already a visible increase in Anti-Semitism. A TASK OF GERMAN FOREIGN POLICY MUST BE TO FURTHER THIS WAVE OF ANTI-SEMITISM. THIS WILL BE ACHIEVED LESS BY GERMAN PROPAGANDA ABROAD, THAN BY THE PROPAGANDA WHICH THE JEW IS FORCED TO CIRCULATE IN HIS DEFENSE.

The press and official correspondents continually report anti-Semitic demonstrations by the population of North America. It is perhaps indicative of the domestic political development in the U. S. A., THAT THE LISTENING - AUDIENCE OF THE "RADIO PRIEST" COUGHLIN, WHO IS WELL KNOWN TO BE ANTI-JEWISH, HAS GROWN TO OVER 20 MILLIONS.

The second period—between 1939 and 1941—is what Kastner called the "period of hesitation." Perhaps the "period of preparation" would be the apter phrase. In any case, it opened and closed on ominous notes.

Hitler speech to Reichstag, January 30, 1939
[U. S. A. Exhibit 268]
If the international Jewish financiers within and without

Europe succeed in plunging the nations once more into a world war then the result will not be the Bolshevization of the world, and thereby the victory of Jewry, but the obliteration of the Jewish race in Europe.

[U. S. A. Doc. 3363 PS]

Berlin, September 21, 1939

To

The Chiefs of all Special Task Forces
(Einsatzgruppen) of the Security Police.
Concerning: The Jewish problem in the occupied zone.

I refer to the conference held in Berlin today, and again point out that the *planned joint measures* (i.e. the ultimate goal) are to be kept *strictly secret.*

Distinction must be made between

1. the ultimate goal (which requires a prolonged period of time) and
2. the sectors leading to fulfillment of the ultimate goal (each of which will be carried out in a short time.)

On principle, all Jewish communities *under 500* heads are to be dissolved and to be transferred to the nearest concentration center.

The reason to be given for the concentration of the Jews in the cities is that Jews have most decisively participated in sniper attacks and plundering. [*Note that the war had not yet begun when this was written—V. H. B.*]

(Signed:) Heydrich.

[U. S. A. Exhibit 303]

February 12, 1940.

Top Secret:

Meeting under the chairmanship of Minister President General Fieldmarshal Goering on questions concerning the East ...

On the other hand it will probably be necessary to transfer into the Eastern Districts 30,000 Germans from the Lublin area east of the Weichsel river, *which is to be reserved for Jews.*

Diary of defendant Frank, Governor General for Poland, October-December, 1940
[Soviet Exhibit 223]

Gentlemen, I must ask you to rid yourself of all feeling of

pity. We must annihilate the Jews, wherever we find them and wherever it is possible, in order to maintain there the structure of the Reich as a whole.

The Jews represent for us also extraordinarily malignant gluttons. We have now approximately 2,500,000 of them in the General Government, perhaps with the Jewish mixtures and everything that goes with it, 3,500,000 Jews. We cannot shoot or poison those 3,500,000 Jews, but we shall nevertheless be able to take measures, which will lead, somehow, to their annihilation, and this in connection with the gigantic measures to be determined in discussions from the Reich.

In July, 1941, the defendant Goering gave over into the hands of Hangman Heydrich, Himmler's deputy and chief of the dread Security Police, the fate of European Jewry. Shortly thereafter Heydrich was removed to Czechoslovakia (whence a Czech patriot removed him still further) and his job was taken over by the defendant Kaltenbrunner. In any case the complex SS murder machine now began operations with Adolf Eichmann, Hebrew-speaking chief of the Jewish Affairs Office of the Gestapo, apparently at the throttle. So began the third period of the Jewish tragedy: the period of annihilation.

[French Exhibit 1311]

Secret

Memorandum for the Fuehrer

April 15, 1941

I beg the FUEHRER to permit the seizure of all Jewish home furnishings of Jews in PARIS, who have fled, or will leave shortly, and that of Jews living in all parts of the occupied WEST, to relieve the shortage of furnishings in the administration in the EAST.

I suggest to the FUEHRER that, instead of executing 100 Frenchmen, we substitute 100 Jewish bankers, lawyers, etc. It is the Jews in LONDON and NEW YORK who incite the French communists to commit acts of violence, and it seems only fair that the members of this race should pay for this.

(Signed:) A. ROSENBERG

[U. S. A. Exhibit 825]

Riga, November 15, 1941

To

The Reich Minister for the
Occupied Eastern Territories, Berlin

I should like to be informed whether your inquiry of October
31 is to be regarded as a directive to liquidate all Jews in the
East. Shall this take place without regard to age and sex and
economic interests (of the Wehrmacht, for instance, with respect to specialists in the armament industry)?

(Signed:) Reich Commissioner
for the East

[U. S. A. Exhibit 826]

Berlin W35, 18 December 1941

Top Secret

To

The Reich Commissioner for the East, Riga

(Re: correspondence of November 15, 1941)

Clarification of the Jewish question has most likely been
achieved by now through verbal discussions. Economic considerations should fundamentally remain unconsidered in the
settlement of the problem.

(By order, signed:) BRAEUTIGAM

[U. S. A. Exhibit 410]

Top Secret

ACTIVITY AND SITUATION REPORT No. 6
OF THE TASK FORCES (EINSATZGRUPPEN)
OF THE SECURITY POLICE AND THE SD IN THE U. S. S. R.

(*Baltic Area*): *The male Jews over 16 were executed* with
the exception of doctors, and after completion of this action
there will remain only 500 Jewesses and children in the Eastern
Territory. . . .

(*Ukraine*): As a measure of retaliation for the arson at Kiev,
all Jews were arrested and altogether 33,771 Jews were executed
on the 29th and the 30th September. Money, valuables and
clothing were secured and put at the disposal of the National
Socialist League for Public Welfare (NSV) for the equipment

of the National Germans *(Volksdeutschen)* and partly put at
the disposal of the provisional city administration for distribution to the needy population.

[U. S. A. Exhibit 242]

Dr. Rudolf Kastner, being duly sworn, deposes and says:

In the fall of 1941—according to a statement of Wisliczeny
made to me in January, 1945, in Vienna—Kaltenbrunner commissioned SS Standartenfuehrer Blobl to work out the plan of
the gas chambers. In the opinion of Wisliczeny the initiative
came from Eichmann. Hitler approved of the plan at once. The
execution was entrusted to the Eichmann-Himmler-Kaltenbrun-
ner trio.

In December, 1941, the first tests were carried out in Belzecz.
According to a statement of Wisliczeny made to me in Vienna
in February, 1945, it was a complete success. Thereupon three
more death-camps were set up in Treblinka, Maidanek, and Auschwitz.

According to statements of Krumey and Wisliczeny in February or March, 1945, a conference of the officers of IV. B. *[Jew-
ish Affairs Office of Gestapo]* was called to Berlin by Eichmann
in the spring of 1942. He then informed them that the Government had decided in favor of the complete annihilation of the
European Jews and this would be carried out silently in the gas
chambers.

The entire machinery of the German State supported Section
IV. B. in this work. In occupied countries the Commanders of
the Wehrmacht and the Gauleiters (Seyss-Inquart, Frank, Heydrich, etc.); in countries allied to Germany the German diplomats (Killinger in Bucharest, Wesenmayer in Zagreb, later
in Budapest) supported the work.

The plan of operation was almost identical in all countries;
at first Jews were marked, then separated, divested of all property, deported and gassed.

Regarding Hungarian Jews, the following general ruling was
laid down in Auschwitz: children up to the age of 12 or 14,
older people above 50, as well as the sick, or people with criminal
records (who were transported in specially marked wagons)
were taken immediately on their arrival to the gas chambers.

The others passed before an SS doctor who, on sight, indicated who was fit for work, and who was not. Those unfit were sent to the gas chambers, while the others were distributed in various labor camps.

[U. S. A. Exhibit 483]

Secret

Sluzk, October 30, 1941

To

The Commissioner General, Minsk

On 27 October at about 8 A. M. a first lieutenant of Police Battalion No. 11 from Kaunas (Lithuania) appeared and introduced himself as the adjutant of the battalion commander of the Security Police. The lieutenant explained that the Police Battalion had received the assignment to effect the liquidation of all Jews here in the town of Sluzk, within two days.

I immediately protested violently, pointing out that a liquidation of Jews must not be allowed to take place in an arbitrary manner. At the end of our conference, I mentioned that all tradesmen and specialists, insofar as they were indispensable, had papers of identification and that these should not be pulled out of the factories. The commander did not in any way contradict my idea and I had therefore the firm belief that the action would be carried out accordingly. However, a few hours after the beginning of the action, I noticed that the commander had not at all abided by our agreement. All Jews without exception were taken out of the factories and shops and deported in spite of our agreement.

I got in touch with the deputy commander, a captain. The captain stated that he had received orders from the commander to clear the whole town of Jews without exception in the same manner as they had done in other towns.

For the rest I must point out to my deepest regret that the action bordered on sadism. The town itself offered a picture of horror during the action. With indescribable brutality on the part of both the German police officers and particularly the Lithuanian partisans, the Jewish people, but also among them White Ruthenians, were taken out of their dwellings and herded together. Everywhere in the town shots were to be heard and in different streets the corpses of shot Jews accumulated. The White Ruthenians were in greatest distress to free themselves from the encirclement. Regardless of the fact that the Jewish people, among whom were also tradesmen, were mistreated in a terribly barbarous way in the face of the White Ruthenian people, the White Ruthenians themselves were also worked over with rubber clubs and rifle butts.

I was not present at the shooting outside the town, therefore I cannot make a statement on its brutality. But it should suffice, if I point out that persons shot have worked themselves out of their graves some time after they had been covered.

In conclusion I find myself obliged to point out that the Police Battalion looted in an unheard of manner during the action, and that not only in Jewish houses but just the same in those of the White Ruthenians. Anything of use such as boots, leather, cloth, gold and other valuables, has been taken away.

(Signed:) CARL
Commissioner for
the Sluzk Territory

[U. S. A. Exhibit 290]

Secret

In the Field, 2 December 1941

To

General of the Infantry, Thomas
Chief of the Industrial Armament Department

There is no proof that Jewry as a whole or even to a greater part was implicated in acts of sabotage. Surely, there were some terrorists or saboteurs among them just as among the Ukrainians. But it can be said that the work of the Jews who, of course, were prompted by nothing but the feeling of fear, was satisfactory to the troops and the German administration.

The Jewish population remained temporarily unmolested shortly after the fighting. Only weeks, sometimes months later, specially detached formations of the police *(Ordnungspolizei)* executed a planned shooting of Jews. This action as a rule proceeded from east to west. It was done entirely in public with the use of the Ukrainian militia and unfortunately in many instances also with members of the Armed Forces taking part voluntarily. The way these actions, which included men and old men, women and children of all ages, were carried out was horrible. The great masses executed make this action more gigantic than any similar measure taken so far in the Soviet Union. So far about 150,000 to 200,000 Jews may have been executed in the part of the Ukraine belonging to the Reichskommissariat (RK); no consideration was given to the interests of economy.

Inspector of Armament in the Ukraine.

[U. S. A. Exhibit 276]
Action Group A

Secret matter of the Reich

31. 1. 1942
40 copies
copy No. 23

TASK FORCE A

(Comprehensive Report up to 15 October 1941)

It was the duty of the Security Police to set in motion self-cleansing movements to direct them into proper channels in order to accomplish the purpose of cleansing operations as quickly as possible. In Lithuania, this was achieved for the first time by partisan activities in Kovno [*Author's note:* The word "partisan" here refers to pro-Nazi Lithuanians who went underground against the Red Army during the Soviet occupation of Lithuania]. Klimatis, leader of the partisan unit, succeeded in starting a pogrom in such a way that no German order or German instigation was noticed from outside.

This self-cleansing action went smoothly because the Army authorities who had been informed showed understanding for this procedure.

A survey of executed persons—Lithuania: 80,311 Jews, 860 Communists, total 81,171; Latvia: 30,025 Jews, 1845 Communists, total 31,870; Esthonia: 474 Jews, 684 Communists, total 1158; White Ruthenia: 7620 Jews, no Communists.

[U. S. A. Exhibit 288]

Top Secret

Kiev, 16 May 1942

To

SS-Obersturmbannfuehrer Raaff, Berlin

The overhauling of vans by group D and C is finished. While the vans of the first series can also be put into action if the weather is not too bad, the vans of the second series (Saurer) *stop com-*

pletely in rainy weather. If it has rained for instance for only one half hour, the van cannot be used because it simply skids away.

The place of execution is usually 10-15 kilometers away from the highways and is difficult of access because of its location. In damp or wet weather it is not accessible at all. If the persons to be executed are driven or led to that place, then they realize immediately what is going on and get restless, which is to be avoided as far as possible. There is only one way left: to lead them to the collecting point and to drive them to the spot.

I ordered the vans of group D to be camouflaged as house-trailers by putting one set of window shutters on each side of the small van and two on each side of the larger vans, such as one often sees on farmhouses in the country. The vans became so well-known, that not only the authorities, but also the civilian population called the van "death van," as soon as one of these vehicles appeared. It is my opinion, the van cannot be kept secret for any length of time, not even camouflaged.

I should like to take this opportunity to bring the following to your attention: several commands have had the unloading after the application of gas done by their own men. I brought to the attention of the commanders of those concerned the immense psychological injuries and damages to their health which that work can have for those men, even if not immediately, at least later on. The men complained to me about headaches which appeared after each unloading. Nevertheless they don't want to change the orders, because they are afraid if prisoners were used for that work, they could use an opportune moment to flee.

The application of gas usually is not undertaken correctly. In order to come to an end as fast as possible, the driver presses the accelerator to the fullest extent. By doing that the persons to be executed suffer death from suffocation and not death by dozing off as was planned. My directions now have proved that by correct adjustment of the levers death comes faster and the prisoners fall asleep peacefully. Distorted faces and excretions, such as could be seen before, are no longer noticed.

Today I shall continue my journey to group B, where I can be reached with further news.

(Signed:) Dr. Becker
SS Untersturmfuehrer

[U. S. A. Exhibit 827]

Secret

Minsk, July 31, 1942

To

Reich Commissioner for the East

Naturally the SD and I would like it best to eliminate Jewry once and for all in the District General of White Ruthenia. For the time being, the necessary demands of the Armed Forces, the main employers of Jewry, are taken into consideration. Besides the fact of this unequivocal attitude toward Jewry, the SD in White Ruthenia has in addition the grave task of transferring continually new contingents of Jews from the Reich to their destiny.

This is an excessive strain on the physical and psychical strength of the men in the area of White Ruthenia proper.

Therefore, I would be grateful if the Reich Commissioner could possibly stop additional deportations of Jews to Minsk at least until the peril of the Partisan [*i.e.*, Soviet partisans] movement has been conclusively subdued.

I fully agree with the commander of the SD in White Ruthenia, that we shall liquidate every shipment of Jews, which is not ordered or announced by our superior offices, to prevent further disturbances in White Ruthenia.

The Commissioner General
for White Ruthenia
(Signed:) Kube.

[U. S. A. Exhibit 494]

I, Hermann Friedrich Graebe, declare under oath:

From September 1941 until ·January 1944 I was manager and engineer in charge of a branch in SDOLBUNOW, Ukraine, of the Solingen building firm of Josef Jung. On 5 October 1942, when I visited the building office at DUBNO (Ukraine) my foreman, Hubert MOENNIKES, told me that in the vicinity of the site, Jews from Dubno had been shot in three large pits, each about 30 meters long and 3 meters deep. About 1500 persons had been killed daily. All of the 5000 Jews who had still been living in Dubno before the pogrom were to be liquidated. As the shootings had taken place in his presence he was still much upset.

Thereupon I drove to the site, accompanied by MOENNIKES and saw near it great mounds of earth, about 30 meters long and 2 meters high. Several trucks stood in front of the mounds. Armed Ukrainian militia drove the people off the trucks under the supervision of an SS-man. The militia men acted as guards on the trucks and drove them to and from the pit. All these people had the regulation yellow patches on the front and back of their clothes, and thus could be recognized as Jews.

MOENNIKES and I went direct to the pits. Nobody bothered us. Now I heard rifle shots in quick succession, from behind one of the earth mounds. The people who had gotten off the trucks—men, women, and children of all ages—had to undress upon the orders of an SS-man, who carried a riding or dog whip. They had to put down their clothes in fixed places, sorted according to shoes, top clothing and underclothing. I saw a heap of shoes of about 800 to 1000 pairs, great piles of under-linen and clothing. Without screaming or weeping these people undressed, stood around in family groups, kissed each other, said farewells and waited for a sign from another SS-man, who stood near the pit, also with a whip in his hand. During the 15 minutes that I stood near the pit I heard no complaint or plea for mercy. I watched a family of about 8 persons, a man and woman, both about 50 with their children of about 20 to 24. An old woman with snow-white hair was holding a one-year old child in her arms and singing to it, and tickling it. The child was cooing with delight. The couple were looking on with tears in their eyes. The father was holding the hand of a boy about 10 years old and speaking to him softly; the boy was fighting his tears. The father pointed toward the sky, stroked his head, and seemed to explain something to him. At that moment the SS-man at the pit shouted something to his comrade. The latter counted off about 20 persons and instructed them to go behind the earth mound. Among them was the family, which I have mentioned. I well remember a girl, slim and with black hair, who as she passed close to me, pointed to herself and said, "23". I walked around the mound, and found myself confronted by a tremendous grave. People were closely wedged together and lying on top of each other so that only their heads were visible. Nearly all had blood running over their shoulders from their heads. Some of the people shot were still moving. Some were lifting their arms and turning their heads to show that they were still alive. The pit was already 2/3 full. I estimated that it already contained about 1000 people. I looked for the man who did the shooting. He was an SS-man, who sat at the edge of the narrow end of the pit, his feet dangling into the pit. He had a tommy gun on his knees and was smoking a cigarette. The people, completely naked, went down some steps which were cut in the clay well of the pit and clambered over the heads of the people lying there, to the place to which the SS-man directed them. They lay down in front of the dead or injured people; some caressed those who were still alive and spoke to them in a low voice. Then I heard a series of shots. I looked into the pit and saw that the bodies were twitching or the heads lying already motionless on top of the bodies that lay under them.

The following is from the official report of the SS officer who commanded the unit which crushed the 1943 uprising in the Warsaw Ghetto.

[U. S. A. Exhibit 275]
THERE IS NO JEWISH GHETTO IN WARSAW ANYMORE
(Dated May 16, 1943)

The resistance put up by the Jews and bandits could be broken only by relentlessly using all our force and energy by day and night. *On 23 April 1943 the Reichsfuehrer SS issued through the Higher SS and Police Fuehrer East at Cracow his order to complete the combing out of the Warsaw Ghetto with the greatest severity and relentless tenacity.* I therefore decided to destroy the entire Jewish residential area by setting every block on fire. The Jews then emerged from their hiding places and dug-outs in almost every case. Not infrequently, the Jews stayed in the burning buildings until, because of the heat and the fear of being burned alive, they preferred to jump down from the upper stories after having thrown mattresses and other upholstered articles into the street from the burning buildings. With their bones broken, they still tried to crawl across the street into blocks of buildings which had not yet been set on fire or were only partly in flames.

Considering that the greater part of the men of the *Waffen-SS* had only been trained for three to four weeks before being assigned to this action, high credit should be given for the pluck, courage, and devotion to duty which they showed. It must be stated that the Wehrmacht Engineers, too, executed the blowing up of dugouts, sewers, and concrete buildings with indefatigability and great devotion to duty. Officers and men of the Police, a large part of whom had already been at the front, again excelled by their dashing spirit.

Only through the continuous and untiring work of all involved did we succeed in catching a total of 56,065 Jews whose extermination can be proven. To this should be added the number of Jews who lost their lives in explosions or fires but whose numbers could not be ascertained.

Finally there was an end to the slaughter. Although the exact date is uncertain, it came barely before there was an end to the Jews. It is amazing how, in the blackest heart, there are revealed measureless depths of mercy and compassion, once the other fellow has the gun.

[U. S. A. Exhibit 242]

Dr. Rudolf Kastner, being duly sworn, deposes and says:

In the first half of November, 1944, about 20,000 Jews were taken from Theresienstadt to Auschwitz and were gassed, on instructions from Eichmann. As far as I could ascertain, this was the last gassing process.

According to Becher, Himmler issued instructions on November 25, 1944, to dynamite all gas-chambers and crematoria in Auschwitz. He also issued a ban on further murdering of Jews.

After the fall of 1944, Himmler granted several concessions. Thus he permitted the departure for Switzerland of 1700 Hungarian Jews deported to Bergen-Belsen camp and also agreed to suspend the annihilation of the Jews of the Budapest Ghetto. He permitted the handing over to the Allies of the Jews of Bergen-Belsen and Theresienstadt without a shot being fired, which in his eyes and the eyes of his colleagues was such a generous and colossal concession that he certainly hoped for some political concession in return.

In the hope of establishing contact with the Allies, Himmler made some concessions even without expecting economic returns.

To this desire of Himmler may be ascribed the general prohibition, dated November 25, 1944, concerning the further killing of Jews. On November 27, 1944, Becher showed me a copy of Himmler's order on this subject. Eichmann at first did not obey this order.

*Interrogation of Oswald Pohl, chief of the SS Main Office
Economics and Administration*

Q. What was done following Himmler's order in the fall of 1944? Were any of the gas chambers destroyed that were for the extermination of Jews?

A. Well, the order concerning the banning of all extermination of Jews was given by Himmler in March, 1945. That is when he said no more Jews were to be exterminated and that the Camp Commandant would be responsible in case a single one of them disappeared.

Q. How do you reconcile that statement with the statement of Hoess that the mass killing had ceased late in 1944 on order of Himmler?

A. About that I don't know. This is the first time I have heard about it, that Himmler gave the order in the fall of 1944, to stop all such measures.

[U. S. A. Exhibit 296]
*Affidavit of Dr. Wilhelm Hoettl
26 November 1945*

I, Wilhelm Hoettl, state herewith under oath:

My occupation until the German collapse was that of a reporter and deputy Group Leader in Office VI of the Reich Main Security Office.

At the end of August 1944 I was talking to *SS-Obersturmbannfuehrer* Adolf Eichmann, whom I had known since 1938. The conversation took place in my house in Budapest.

According to my knowledge Eichmann was, at that time, Section Chief of Office IV (the Gestapo) of the Reich Security Main Office and in addition to that he had been ordered by Himmler to get hold of the Jews in all the European countries and to transport them to Germany. He expressed his conviction that Germany had now lost the war and that he, personally, had no further chance. He knew that he would be considered one of the main war criminals by the United Nations since he had millions of Jewish lives on his conscience. I asked him how many that was, to which he answered that although the number was a great Reich secret, he would tell me since I, as a historian, would be interested and that he would probably not return anyhow from his command in Rumania. He had, shortly before that, made a report to Himmler, as the latter wanted to know the exact number of Jews who had been killed. On the basis of his information he had obtained the following result:

Approximately four million Jews had been killed in the various extermination camps while an additional two million met death in other ways, the major part of whom were shot by operational squads of the Security Police during the campaign against Russia.

Himmler was not satisfied with the report since, in his opinion, the number of Jews, who had been killed, must have been more than six million.

3.

The ignorance of the defendants continued unassailable.

Sir David Maxwell-Fyfe, of the British prosecution, cross-examined Goering:

Q. "Hoettl says approximately four million Jews have been killed. . . . Assume these figures are only fifty per cent correct, are you telling this Tribunal that a Minister with your power in the Reich could remain ignorant of what was going on?"

A. "That is what I am stating, particularly because it is true. These things were kept secret from me. I am even of the opinion the Fuehrer did not know approximately what was going on."

Goering's voice was petulant. He was always petulant when questioned about murder. Once he exclaimed to an interrogator, "Why do you keep asking me about this business of annihilation camps?" When, in the course of certain standard psychological tests given the defendants, he was handed a white card with small red splotches on it, his reaction was to try to flick the spots off with a pudgy fingertip.

The defendants not only disclaimed knowledge; they laid claim to good will. They loved Jews. Ribbentrop's attorney spoke of his client's desire for a "chivalrous solution" of the Jewish question. Another lawyer spoke of Frank's "noble anti-Semitism," good for the Jew as well as for the non-Jew. The defendant Funk explained that he signed, as Economics Minister, the "Aryanization" decrees in order to "safeguard Jewish property from looting." The defendant Frick said he signed, as Minister of the Interior, the decree compelling Jews to wear the Star of David to save them from "Aryan rage." Streicher insisted he was a Zionist.

Nevertheless, the Jewish section of the indictment succeeded, where other sections failed, in eliciting a show, at least, of repentance on the part of certain of the defendants.

It began with Robert Ley, the drink-sodden Nazi labor boss who robbed justice by hanging himself in his prison cell before the trial opened. He left a note:

"God led me in whatever I did, he led me up and now he lets me fall. I am torturing myself to find the reason for the downfall, and this is the result of my contemplations:

"We have forsaken God, and therefore we were forsaken by God. In anti-Semitism we violated a basic commandment of his creation.

"Anti-Semitism destroyed our outlook and we made grave errors. It is hard to admit mistakes, but the whole existence of our people is in question: we Nazis must have the courage to rid ourselves of anti-Semitism.

"God shows you the way. Learn from your downfall. Reconcile yourself with the Jew. Invite him to make his home with you."

The defendant Funk felt guilt, too, or so he said. Lieutenant Bernard Meltzer, U. S. N., of the United States prosecution, introduced into the record an interrogation of the former Economics Minister:

Q. "All the decrees excluding the Jews from industry were yours, were they not?"

A. "So far as my participation in this Jewish affair is concerned, that was my responsibility, and I regretted later that I ever did participate."

Q. "You know that the looting and all that was done at the instigation of the Party, don't you?"

(The defendant weeps)

A. "Yes, most certainly. That is when I should have left—in 1938. Of that I am guilty. I am guilty. I admit that I am a guilty party there."

And there was Frank, the doughty Governor General of Poland, who in 1941 said that "We must annihilate the Jews. wherever we find them." In the course of the trial, he re-embraced religion and repentance. His lawyer asked him:

"Have you ever participated in the destruction of Jewry?"

And Frank answered:

"I myself have never installed an extermination camp for Jews or demanded that they should be installed, but if Adolf Hitler personally has turned that dreadful responsibility over to these people of his, then it must be mine, too.

"We have fought against Jewry . . . and we have allowed ourselves to make utterances—and my own diary has become a witness against me—utterances which are terrible. It is my duty —my only duty—therefore to answer your question with Yes. A thousand years will pass and this guilt of Germany will still not be erased."

Frank liked the role he played in the witness stand, and a few days later he wrote to his wife about it. I obtained a copy of the letter, which read in part:

"On Thursday before Easter I passed the great test of my life before the Justices by simply confessing the truth as I saw it in a clear and firm manner—for why should they not know what God knows anyway and what humanity has a right to know? Don't be sad, for in taking the guilt upon myself, I at least demonstrated that our great suffering people is innocent of these terrible happenings. One, at least, had to confess, since these defendants who preceded me all protested their innocence. . . ."

The heroic note was a little strident. Actually, Frank hadn't confessed half as much as he pretended to his wife. He had denied outright, or evaded, or squirmed around, every specific charge brought against him by the prosecution.

Most dramatic of the repenters was Schirach, Hitler's Youth Leader. A few days before the trial opened, he wrote to his family:

"Today I am certain that the root of the world disaster which Hitler conjured up was his *racial policy*. . . . His movement was the carrier of this racial policy and I was one of the representatives of this movement; that is a fact."

Later, in the courtroom, he elaborated this line under questioning by defense counsel:

Q. "You have heard the testimony of Hoess, a commander at Auschwitz concentration camp, who reported to us that in that camp alone, I believe, 2,500,000 to three million people, primarily Jews, had been executed. What does the name Auschwitz mean to you today?"

A. "That is the greatest and most devilish mass murder of history. It is a crime which is shameful to every German. German youth has no part in it, and no guilt. It was anti-Semitic, but it did not want the extermination of Jews. . . .

"I have educated that generation in faith to Hitler and loyalty to him. It was my guilt, which I will have to carry before God and the German nation, that I raised that youth for a man who committed murders million fold. But that guilt is my own, my personal guilt; I alone carry the guilt for that youth.

"If on the basis of racial politics and anti-Semitism an Auschwitz becomes possible, then Auschwitz must become the end of racial politics and anti-Semitism."

Was this sincere repentance? Was Frank's, Funk's? It is impossible to tell. Certainly the confessions served a purpose for the German people, who read the texts in the German press and were impressed, particularly by Schirach's. But the confessions may also have been designed for another purpose. There were a few Jewish members in all four prosecution delegations, and I have no doubt the defendants were convinced there were more than there actually were. (German listeners to Gaston Oulman, who broadcast the trials on the German radio, wrote him that Jackson's real name was Jacobson, and Sir David Maxwell-Fyfe in real life was

David Funfer). Under such circumstances, the confessions could take on another meaning.

For myself, I prefer the confession of Ley. He had nothing to gain from his except that short-lived peace of soul which may have come to him between the time he lay down his pen and the moment he jumped off the toilet seat with the edge of the towel around his neck.

But then, some of the other defendants insisted, when they learned of the suicide note, that Ley's brains had gone soft from too much alcohol.

Chapter XVI   6,000,000 Slaves

1.

On V-E Day there were more than 6,000,000 foreign slaves on German soil. Four million of these were Slavs or workers from the East—Russians, Ukrainians, Poles, Balts, Czechs and Yugoslavs.

The Nazi slave labor program was the most grandiose scheme of its kind in history. Nuremberg showed that, in the end, it was a grandiose flop. Its failure was inherent in the fascist mentality which gave it birth.

The Nazis knew it was failing as early as March, 1943. I quote from the official report of a conference held on that date in Goebbels' Ministry of Propaganda:

"The hitherto prevailing treatment of Eastern workers has led not only to *diminished production* but has *most disadvantageously influenced the political orientation* of the people in conquered Eastern territories and *has resulted in the well-known difficulties for our troops.*" (My italics—V. H. B.)

The "well-known difficulties" was a reference to increased partisan warfare behind the German lines.

Two months later Himmler's Reich Security Main Office and Goebbels' Propaganda Ministry embodied the decisions of this meeting in a joint memorandum to the national party leadership:

"Foreign workers employed within the Reich are to be treated so that their reliability is retained and expedited and a rise in production ensues. Everyone, even the primitive man, has a fine perception of justice! Consequently every unjust treatment must have a very bad effect. Injustices, insults, trickery, mistreatment, etc., must be *discontinued*. Punishment by beating is forbidden.

"Winning someone to active cooperation is impossible if his self-esteem is wounded at the same time. From people who are described as beasts and sub-humans, no great accomplishments can be expected."

The memorandum went on to prescribe better food, housing and working conditions for foreign labor.

But all this was too little and too late.

It was too little because this same memorandum, which spoke so touchingly of the sense of justice inherent in every man—even the primitive!—reaffirmed the doctrine of race and warned all Germans that they were liable to "severest penalties" if they failed to adhere to the "fundamental principles of the National Socialist conception of blood." The memorandum left the foreign worker what he had been from the beginning, a social outlaw, an inferior being; and it was a notion that could enter only the thick skull of the arrogant Fascist that a man's "fine perception of justice" would be satisfied by the kind of treatment the careful owner gives to his valuable dray-horse or dog.

It was too late because, by the spring of 1943, the behavior patterns of both the Germans and their slaves were fixed too firmly to be changed by mere decree. The Nazis could no more discard their whip than the slaves their hate. The concept of "beast" and "sub-human," as applied to the enemy, was by now deeply rooted in millions of German minds, and the early doctrine of genocide, never really abandoned, had taught too well the lesson that mass murder was not only a patriotic necessity, but a racial virtue.

So, despite war production needs, the work-to-death order that prevailed legally within the concentration camp system, prevailed psychologically even outside. And there can be little doubt that, on V-E Day, the Allied armies not only liberated 6,000,000 people

from mass slavery, but saved most of them from ultimate mass
graves.

2.

The Nazis launched their slave labor program with reckless
optimism. They were going to get their slaves by a volunteer system.

Civilian administrations in the various occupied areas would en-
list the volunteers. The army would provide transportation into the
Reich. Government and Industry would place its demands for
labor through a special department of Goering's Four-Year-Plan
organization, which would allocate the incoming transports.

Pay rates were carefully formulated: Polish agricultural workers
were to receive "in principle" less than the German worker; the
Eastern (Russian) worker "may receive a little pocket money.
. . . All financial measures undertaken must be based on the
Fuehrer's categorical order that payment of minimum possible
wages in the East is a prerequisite to Germany's being able to meet
its debts after the war."

It did not take the Nazis long to discover that the lure of lovely
Germany, and of lower wages, were not profitable products for
export. Less than eight months after the conquest of Poland, and
less than six months after the attack on Russia, the "recruiting"
system was backed by decrees legalizing compulsory labor drafts.

It was not until March, 1942, however, that the slave labor program was put on an efficient, businesslike basis. A Plenipotentiary
General for Labor Mobilization was created and Sauckel, a lively
and vicious Gauleiter from old Nazi days, was given the job. He
entered into it with zest:

"All prisoners of war from the West as well as from the East,
must be completely incorporated into the German armament and
nutrition industries. Apart from PW's, we must requisition from
Soviet territory male and female labor beginning at the age of 15.

"In order to relieve the German housewife, especially the mother with many children, and also the busy farm wife, the Fuehrer
has also charged me with the procurement of 400,000-500,000

selected healthy and strong girls from the Eastern territories for Germany.

"All workers must be fed, sheltered and treated in such a way as to exploit them to the highest possible extent at the lowest possible cost. It must be remembered, however, that even the work of a machine is conditioned by the amount of care given to it. How much more must conditions be considered in the case of men, even of a low kind and race!

"The principles of German cleanliness, order, and hygiene must therefore also be carefully applied to Russian camps."

I don't know whom Sauckel was trying to impress with his prattle of German cleanliness and order; the realities were quite different. In any case, he soon forgot his preoccupation with the treatment of workers under the necessity of gathering them. For the next two years we see him panting all over Europe, burning down houses, blowing up villages, killing old men, women, and children in a desperate attempt to force into the Reich the millions needed to keep the German war machine going.

In October, 1942, Sauckel ordered the Occupied Eastern Territories to supply a half-million workers within six months. He knew it was a tough job, but noted his conviction that "with the ruthless commitment of all resources, the execution of the new demands can be accomplished."

Let's see how he did accomplish it.

Three months after the order was issued Rosenberg, who as Reich Minister for the Occupied Eastern Territories was supposed to cooperate in its fulfillment, was gently remonstrating:

"It must be avoided that lines in front of theaters be arrested bodily and be brought from there directly to Germany."

And a few days later Rosenberg complained again, directly to Sauckel:

"You and I have, with regard to the solution of the labor problem in the East, represented the same viewpoint from the beginning. Nevertheless, I find it necessary to point out methods applied by your agencies and collaborators.

"In order to secure the required number for the labor transport, men and women including youngsters from 15 years on up, are allegedly picked up on the street, from the market places and village festivals, and carried off. After public beatings during the month of October, so letters state, came the burning down of homesteads and of whole villages as retribution for failure to comply with the demand for labor."

And some less restrained language in a report prepared by the Political Department in Rosenberg's ministry:

"We now experience the grotesque picture of having to recruit millions of laborers from the Occupied Eastern Territories, after prisoners of war have died like flies from hunger, in order to fill the gaps that have formed within Germany.

"In the prevailing limitless abuse of Slavic humanity, recruiting methods are used which probably have their origin in the blackest periods of the Slave Trade. Without consideration of health or age, the people were shipped to Germany, where it turned out immediately that far more than 100,000 had to be sent back because of serious illness."

And a vivid report, prepared in the Nazi Central Office for Eastern Nationals, Berlin, on the conditions under which the sick were returned:

"There are dead in the train of returnees. Women gave birth and the new-born babies were thrown out of the windows during the journey. Persons with tuberculosis and with venereal diseases rode in the same cars. Dying persons lay in freight cars without straw, and finally one of the dead rolled off and landed on the railway embankment. . . ."

Through 1942, the labor draft weighed relatively lightly on the French. Sauckel had indicated, on taking office, that at least two-thirds of the foreign manpower he wanted would have to come from the East, and only a third from the West. And from March, 1942, until January, 1943, Sauckel worked with some moderate success through the Petain regime to fill the French quota.

But at the opening of the new year, Speer, the new German Armaments Minister, prevailed upon Hitler to decree that "it was no longer necessary to give special consideration to the French. . . . recruiting can proceed with sharpened measures." Speer's most pressing need was for skilled workers, especially smelters, and at a meeting of the Central Planning Board—roughly the equivalent of the American War Production Board—the Armaments Minister suggested an excellent scheme for getting them:

"Through industry we could deceive the French by telling them that we would release for their use all prisoners of war who are rolling-mill workers and smelters, if they would only give us the names. They give the names and then we have them! Do that!"

The year 1943 was difficult for Sauckel. Quotas kept rising: 200,000 from the West, hundreds of thousands from the East. The army helped by rounding up labor for him wherever it could, but it was a retreating army now, and the area it was now traversing backwards had already been combed. Moreover, as we shall see, the Plenipotentiary for the Mobilization of Labor was beginning to meet competition from other labor-hungry Nazi agencies.

The big blow fell on Sauckel in March, 1944. Hitler had ordered him to procure four million new workers for that year. He reported, tearfully, to the Central Planning Board, that he wasn't at all sure he could fill that tremendous quota. He complained that no one would play ball with him: Speer had created a series of "protected" armament factories in France from which workers could not be taken; army commanders, in the East, insisted on saving many workers for themselves; and the enemy civilians of working age, who in the past had so obligingly let themselves be picked up in front of theaters and churches and at village fiestas, were now hiding in the woods and becoming partisans.

The French situation bothered Sauckel particularly:

"In a discussion lasting five or six hours, I got from M. Laval the concession that the death penalty will be threatened for officials who try to sabotage the flow of labor. Believe me, this was very difficult, but I succeeded and now in France the Germans ought to take very severe measures.

"The most abominable point made by my adversaries is their claim that no executive had been provided to recruit in a sensible manner the French and Belgian quotas. Thereupon I even proceeded to employ and train a whole batch of French and female agents, who for good pay went hunting for men and liquored

them up—in the old days it would have been called 'shanghaiing'
—in order to dispatch them to Germany."

And Sauckel added bitterly:

"Out of the five million foreign workers who arrived in Germany, not even 200,000 came voluntarily!"

(Personally, I think Sauckel was boasting a little. It may be that
as many as 500,000 came voluntarily. I base this on talks I had
during 1945-46 with inmates of DP camps in the American zone
of Germany who had refused repatriation. Particularly among the
Balts and Polish Ukrainians did I find many who admitted they
had come to Germany voluntarily out of fear of the Russians, or
because they were beguiled by promises of good wages, or because
they were frankly pro-Nazi.

By 1945-46, of course, they had learned to hate the Germans,
but they had also come to be very fond of UNRRA rations, so
they preferred to stay on German soil in UNRRA care rather than
return home.)

In June, 1944, German Army Group Center made a small contribution towards the solution of Sauckel's problem—a plan for
the drafting of 40,000 to 50,000 Eastern boys ten to fourteen
years of age. "It is intended," the Army Group plan explained,
"to allot these juveniles primarily to German trades as apprentices
for use as skilled workers after two years' training. . . . This action
is not only aimed at preventing a direct reinforcement of the
enemy's military strength, but also at a reduction of his biological
potentialities as viewed from the perspective of the future."

Army Group Center never did get time to complete the execution of its remarkably logical scheme; and very soon Sauckel's wor-
ries became academic, too. For in a very few months there was
practically no occupied country from which Germany could gather
workers, juvenile or adult, procreative or non-procreative. There
was only the menacing pincers of the Allied armies closing inexorably upon Berlin; and from his bunker beneath the Reich Chancellery a mad Hitler, determined to pull down all Germany with
himself, was frantically sending out orders that the factories for
which he shortly before had been trying so desperately to find
workers, should be blasted to the skies.

Speer, the only defendant at Nuremberg who apparently had the courage to buck Hitler openly at any time, intervened in the closing weeks of the war and saved whatever still stands today of German factories, highways, and bridges. For this he must be given credit.

3.

Aside from Kaltenbrunner, Sauckel was the most persistent and least accomplished liar in the dock. Despite the fearful documentary evidence piled up against him, he steadfastly insisted he had never had anything but the health and welfare of the foreign worker at heart. He achieved, quite early in the trial, a persecution complex; and to the very day of his death, complained to his official cell visitors that the Tribunal was doing him a terrible injustice.

It may be that he believed his own lies. Certainly he displayed, in his career as Nazi labor boss, examples of such extravagant disregard for truth, of such colossal intellectual arrogance, that he might be deemed a victim of self-hypnosis. "I myself report to you," he once wrote to Hitler, ". . . that never before in the world were foreign workers treated as correctly as they are now being treated, in this hardest of all wars, by the German people." And in a really remarkable display of brazenness, even for Sauckel, he once expressed indignation because foreigners didn't like to work for the Germans:

"These occupied territories are indeed not able to exist unless they produce the things which Europe wants from them, and since the planning of production for the whole of Europe is done exclusively and solely by Germany, all these nations are indebted to Germany alone and to nobody else for the fact that they have bread and work."

So Sauckel's defense against the slave labor evidence was studiously to ignore the documents; Rosenberg's, to study the documents with an intensive sense of selectivity. The fact that those documents which best served Rosenberg's defense were precisely those which were most damning to Sauckel, did not stop the former boss of the Eastern Occupied Territories, who referred the Tribunal again and again to the complaints he had registered against the "excesses" committed in the East by Sauckel's subordinates.

In this connection I want to quote a letter written, not by one of Sauckel's subordinates, but by one of Rosenberg's. The writer was Paul Raab, an official in the German civil administration of the Soviet Ukraine, who had been charged by certain German military authorities with burning down houses in two villages in an attempt to enforce the labor draft. It is not clear whether the military, in preferring charges, was motivated by outraged conscience or a personal grudge. In any case, Raab admitted the charge and went on to explain:

"1. Strict measures, such as the burning down of houses, were used in only a few cases. Such measures assured that the recruiting of workers did not tie down too many police forces, which because of other duties could not be used for that purpose all the time.

"2. I was entitled to use such measures by the secret Labor Directive for the Labor Commitment Staff in the District of Kiev. [That would be Sauckel's staff.—V. H. B.]

"3. The delivery of 31,000 workers to the Reich is definitely important to the war effort. Stern measures are definitely justified to prevent failure of the program.

"4. My measures were thought to be just by the biggest part of the population. They only caused displeasure to Germans who had only small tasks to perform in the Ukraine and therefore had too much time for philosophy."

This letter was addressed to Rosenberg as the Reich Minister for the Occupied Eastern Territories. And to it, one of Rosenberg's lieutenants appended the official verdict of the Ministry:

"I don't see any reason for taking measures of any kind against Raab."

Chapter XVII   Larceny Unltd.

1.

The Nazis never broke a law if they could help it. They simply changed the law or proved, by a triumph of rationalization, that what looked like a law or a treaty or an agreement was merely a passing phenomenon which had to do with the past or the future, but never with the present.

In this fashion, the Nazis laid the "legal" groundwork for their unlimited international larceny. Evidence produced at the trial showed that they stole everything they could lay their hands upon. They stole banks and trolley cars and gold teeth and alarm clocks and armament factories. They stole old clothes and coal mines, pigs and Dürer etchings, locomotives and spectacle frames. They stole whole countries, incorporating the victims' economy into their own, leaving a Europe bankrupt and economically anarchic, where no one knows who owns what and most of the legitimate owners are dead.

This free-booting was made "legal" by German juristic genius through two simple rulings. We have already seen that in the East, the Hague Rules of Land Warfare, limiting wartime looting to the actual needs of the occupying forces, were declared not to be applicable because the U. S. S. R. was "dissolved as a State." In the West, the approach was a little more subtle.

"The formulation of the Hague Rules of Land Warfare," ruled the Chief of German Military Administration in Belgium and Northern France, "were adopted to the circumstances of the year 1907, a time in which war operations were limited in space. The modern war, however, in its extension to 'total' war, is no longer limited in space but has become a struggle of nations and of economic spheres.

"Therefore, an appropriate interpretation of the principles of the Rules of Land Warfare requires that requisitions are not only permissible for the needs of the occupying forces in a narrow sense of space, *but for the overall interests of the German waging of war.*" (My italics—V. H. B.)

I don't know what gold teeth, spectacle frames and Gobelin tapestries have to do with the "overall interests" of German warmaking, but aside from that, the document puts new meaning into the phrase *Armed Forces.* Under the Nazi definition, an army is not an army any more; it is a very large and especially well-equipped gangster mob sent over into the next country to steal everything in sight.

And we will see that the German Army, proud bearer of the tradition of Prussian discipline and courage and honor, was exactly this; and neither Keitel nor Jodl nor either of the navy men in the defendants' box could deny that the war machine which they led was up to its neck in thievery from the beginning to what I hope, but am still not certain, is its end.

2.

The representative of the OKW (Armed Forces High Command) attached to the Armament Procurement Office, prepared the following memorandum on November 30, 1941, while the Wehrmacht was still marching unstopped through western Russia:

"The general principles of economic policy in the newly occupied Eastern areas are stated in the following:

"The highest possible production surplus for the supply of the Reich and of other European countries is to be attained by cheap production based on the maintenance of low living standards for the native population.

"Besides covering thereby the European needs for food and raw materials, this measure is intended to create a source of income for the Reich which will make it possible to liquidate, in a few decades and with utmost consideration for the German taxpayer, an essential part of the debts incurred in the financing of the war."

It is most unusual for an army to be raising money for the taxpayer; generally it is the other way around. And this planned theft by the Fascists of a whole civilization—for what else is a modern civilization than a standard of living?—epitomizes the difference between the Axis and the Allies. Germany planned to squeeze a conquered Poland and Russia dry for all eternity, robbing countless future generations of their birthright; we today are sending food into a conquered Germany.

We have already seen, in connection with Case Barbarossa, how Germany was prepared deliberately to impose famine upon millions of Soviet citizens in order to make Russian economy complement her own. The German Army anticipated this plan in full awareness of its consequences:

"The war can only be continued if all Armed Forces are fed by Russia in the third year of the war," runs an Army Operations memorandum of May 2, 1941 (seven weeks before the attack on Russia). "There is no doubt that as a result many millions of people will starve to death if we take out of the U.S.S.R. the things necessary for us."

Two years later, in a directive in which the OKW again emphasizes that the Hague Rules of Land Warfare do not apply because the "U. S. S. R. is considered dissolved" as a nation, the order was given to "bring into, and utilize for the German war economy, all available quantities of non-ferrous metals."

The quest for metal was an old story in the Third Reich. Those of us who were in Germany in 1938 remember the iron fences pulled down from Jewish burial grounds, later from Jewish property generally, and finally from "Aryan" property as well. By January, 1943, the Nazis were climbing church steeples to get bronze, stripping Belgium of her church bells. The catholicity of

Germany's thefts generally is revealed in the secret minutes of a series of conferences held by the Fuehrer at his headquarters in 1942 and 1943, at many of which the defendant Speer was present:

"Rolling stock is to be taken away from occupied territories without any consideration. I [*Hitler*] am told by Goering that four express trains run daily between Brussels and Paris. German interests must come first in this case!

"It is to be investigated—without attracting particular attention—how much copper could be obtained in France by ruthlessly removing church bells and monuments. . . .

"The Fuehrer draws special attention to the fact that shortages in the Reich must be remedied at the expense of occupied territories. When, for instance, armament workers are short of bicycles, one must, to begin with, fall back on bicycles from Holland, Belgium, Denmark, etc., . . . He notes my [*i.e., Speer's*] misgivings that the military commanders will not be sufficiently ruthless in the execution, but he rules that this attitude must be neutralized by corresponding orders by himself.

"Trolley cars are urgently needed for bomb damaged towns in the Reich. . . . One could take away some trolley cars, for instance, from Warsaw, where they look very well. After all, the trolley traffic in Warsaw is not as important as in Germany. One could also take some trolley cars from France. . . .

"The shifting of ingots from the Donets area must be speeded up. The Fuehrer emphasizes that the area must continue to remain in our possession, but that everything that is not absolutely essential must disappear from there in order not to provide the enemy with valuable assistance should circumstances oblige us to evacuate."

And while Speer was helping himself to bicycles and trolley cars, Himmler's Commissariat for the Consolidation of German Nationhood was busy stealing real estate from Polish farmers and giving it to Germans. This was done by a Himmler decree which stated that "conditions permitting seizure are always present if the property belongs to a Pole, for Polish real estate will be needed without exception for this Consolidation of German Nationhood." Naturally, the same decree subjected the property of Jews and other Stateless persons to equally facile confiscation.

Compensation? Yes, quite typical compensation: "The former owners of Polish farms together with their families will be transferred to the Old Reich by the employment agencies for work as farm laborers." On some of the confiscated land the annihilation camp of Auschwitz was built; and some of the former owners became Auschwitz inmates.

By May 21, 1943, the Nazis had confiscated outright 676,000 acres of Polish land and seized—preparatory to confiscation—more than fifteen million acres additionally.

3.

The Nazis plundered brutally both in the East and in the West, although the methods differed. Whatever the Wehrmacht conquered in the East was either to become incorporated into the Reich or to be treated as a colonial possession. Under such circumstances, there was no need to fool around with occupation costs or to indulge in any of the more respectable forms of swindling in order to obtain possession of property. One just took by decree, or better still, by the taking.

But Hitler never planned to make a colony of France, at least not in the accepted sense of the word. He had a much more easily realizable idea. He would buy France out with phony money printed on French presses at French expense, and at the end of the war he would own France bodily, and all a Frenchman would have that he could call his own would be a tri-colored rag to fly over the offices of another puppet Petain who would rule in France's name for the glory and profit of the Third Reich.

The French prosecution spent three weeks describing in minute detail to the Tribunal the various ways in which the Nazis milked not only France, but the Lowlands, Denmark, and Norway. Indeed, the French case was in effect an itemized bill for reparations of staggering dimensions. The Nazis swindled in every fashion known to modern finance and invented a few ways of their own. They watered stock, levied occupation costs, fixed prices at gun's point and invented something called "clearing" by which Reich importers received goods and all the French sellers got was paper money printed at their own expense as French taxpayers.

Occupation costs alone cost France four hundred million francs daily and were later increased to half a billion. The head of Germany's own Armistice Commission protested to the Nazi Ministry of Foreign Affairs that "these considerable payments would enable Germany to buy the whole of France, including its foreign interests and investments, and would mean the ruin of France." Moreover, the Nazi Supreme Command openly admitted that, in violation of the Hague Rules of Land Warfare, the bill France was forced to pay was far in excess of actual occupation costs:

"To the extent to which the amounts paid and marked in France are not utilized by the troops in France, the Supreme Command of the Army reserves for itself the right to dispose later of the currency. . . . The remainder shall be at the disposal of the Supreme Command for important ends of the Four Year Plan."

The "clearing" system was a barter arrangement, invented by Schacht, which sounds extraordinarily reasonable on paper and only becomes unreasonable when it ends up in paper money. Through it, by the end of the war, France had sold to Germany 221 billion francs worth of goods, and Germany had sold to France exactly five hundred million francs worth of goods. The difference —220.5 billion francs—had been paid out to the French exporters by the French clearing banks, all of it in paper money with nothing behind it except the Nazi pistol point.

Such dealings were not only carried on in France, but everywhere in western Europe and in the Balkans. Through them the Reich got its resources for waging war, and German industrialists and bankers reaped enormous profits immediately and laid the groundwork for what quite literally would have become their future ownership of the continent had not the Allied armies smashed up both their hopes and many of their factories.

4.

The German industrialists were vultures soaring and dipping on the carrion left by battle. In their greed they quarrelled among themselves, sometimes even with the Reich Government. But their pet hate was the genial Hermann, master plunderer, whose Hermann Goering Works grew almost as fast as the Wehrmacht advanced, and who always managed to reach the booty first.

The industrialists' swindle began very early, when the war was only a few days old. They were busy, then, camouflaging their properties abroad as "independent" foreign enterprises and at the same time working out means for transfer of profits to Germany. This was, of course, not particularly a Nazi trick; it is a characteristic technique of industry in all countries.

The story of the international looting by Nazi industrialists during the war was scarcely touched upon during the trial because no industrialist was in the dock, but I have seen many of the relevant documents.

The war was barely a month old when six of Germany's major steel companies—including Krupp, Flick, Mannesmann and United Steel Works—proposed to the defendant Funk, then Economics Minister, that they should be given first choice in the annexation of smelting plants in the Western Occupied Territories. Funk asked them to be patient for a little while, undoubtedly reminding them that such a thing as the Western Occupied Territories did not yet exist.

Out in the newly acquired Upper Silesian section of Poland, however, booty was already available, and here the quarrels broke out. United Steel Works objected because it had not been consulted in certain early allocations of plants, but presumably did not press its claim when it was informed that Hitler had personally ordered that Krupp be given a "reserve" plant. A few months later Roechling, Krupp, and others of the Iron and Steel Group made a personal inspection of Upper Silesia, escorted by some people from Funk's ministry, and put in their claims.

"Concern is expressed," reads a summarized report of this trip, "that the Hermann Goering Works have acquired the profitable enterprises, namely the coal mines, thus endangering the smelting plants which depend on the coal. Willuhn recommends that the Reich Minister of Economics be informed about this."

No doubt Funk was informed, but Goering was a bigger man than the Economics Minister in more ways than one. He had already disposed of one Economics Minister (Schacht); he was not going to kowtow to this lesser fellow. And in the scramble for loot all through the war, he was consistently ahead of both Funk and the industrialists, and consistently was able to hold what he got.

In September of 1940, with the Western Occupied Territories now an indisputable fact, the rivalry broke out anew. The following is from the summarized report of a conference attended by members of the Reich Group Industry and the Reich Chamber of Commerce:

"A number of concerns, particularly the Hermann Goering Works, have been sending agents to Holland and Belgium to negotiate with firms there with the object of taking them over. These agents have intimidated Dutch and Belgian economic circles to such an extent that the impression prevails there that the Belgian and Dutch firms face immediate expropriation by the Hermann Goering Works."

The next big fight grew out of Arbed, Luxembourg coal and iron combine, of which Goering wanted a "controlling minority" of stock. Gustav Simon, the Gauleiter of Luxembourg, preferred Arbed to remain independent, for reasons not difficult to guess. In the course of the debate, one of Goering's hirelings pointed out defensively, "In the distribution of smelting plants in the West, the United Steel Works got the *Huette Differdingen*, one of the most modern plants, while the Goering works is asking for only 25 percent of Arbed."

This time the case had to go all the way up to Hitler before Goering won.

It must not be thought, however, that Goering got everything. Twelve firms (including Goering's) shared in the division of smelting plants in Luxembourg and Lorraine alone. The plants were handed over to the industrialists by the Reich Government "for exploitation and management in the name of the Reich but for their own account" and with a specific pledge of option for outright ownership "as soon as conditions permit."

Indeed, the division of spoils in the West was satisfactory enough all around so that, one month after the attack on Russia, Poensgen of the United Steel Works was asking for a division along similar lines in the East. But General von Henneken, chief of the iron and coal section in Funk's Economics Ministry, told Poensgen that Hitler preferred to acquire the Eastern properties through creation of a new corporation in which the government would own a majority of shares.

"However," reads a summarized report of the discussion, "Henneken considers the creation of such a corporation to be only a war measure and consoles Poensgen (who would rather see private firms take over) by stating that after the war, all the conquered plants in the East would be turned over to private German enterprise. He adds that this will surely also be the case with Reich-owned corporations within the Reich itself."

I have here discussed only the looting activities of Germany's heavy industry. I. G. Farben, giant of the chemical world, was just as active, acquiring new possessions all over the continent. Clothing manufacturers did not lag, either. In 1944 the Reich Group Industry sponsored a German press tour to Lodz, in Poland, and a summarized report of the trip closes with the words, *"In the Ghetto, where nine-year-old children have been recruited for labor, the clothing industries are well developed."*

5.

I come now to the icons and altar cloths, the Gobelins and antiques, the Rubenses and Rembrandts and rare books and Torahs which, by the legerdemain of German law, were declared legitimate booty presumably as contributing to "the overall interests of the German waging of war." The theft by the Nazis of *objets d'art* from all over Europe formed one of the most incredible chapters of the trial. A huge proportion of the art went to swell the personal fortunes of Nazi chieftains, particularly the postcard painter Hitler and the swashbuckling Goering, addicted to morphine, medals, and Old Masters. By the time the war ended, the art possessions of these two men alone could be counted in trainloads and their wealth may well have rivaled that of the fabulous rajahs.

The thieving began for presumably "educational" reasons. Late in 1939, Hitler planned the postwar creation of a *Hohe Schule*—Institute for Advanced Learning—which was to become the "center for national socialist ideological and educational research" and Rosenberg was authorized to form a Special Purpose Staff to gather the material. His function was soon broadened to include the right to seize and transport to Germany all "cultural goods which appear valuable to him and to safeguard them there; the Fuehrer has reserved for himself the decision as to their use."

Rosenberg was a good man to direct the job. By 1941 he was able to report to Hitler on progress in the West:

"I report the arrival of the principal shipment of ownerless Jewish 'cultural property' in the salvage depot located at Neuschwanstein. The special train, arranged for by Reichsmarshal Hermann Goering, comprised 25 express baggage-cars filled with the most valuable paintings, furniture, Gobelins, works of artistic craftsmanship and ornaments . . . consisting chiefly of the most important parts of the collections of Rothschild, Seligmann, Bernheim-Jeune, Halphen, Kann, Weil-Picard, Wildenstein, David-Weill, Levy-Benzion.

"Besides this special train, the masterpieces selected by the Reichsmarshal, mainly from the Rothschild collection, have been forwarded some time ago to Munich in two special cars; they have been deposited there in the air raid shelters of the Fuehrer building."

The work was not without difficulties, however. Competition among various German agencies to get possession of these treasures was keen, and Rosenberg's Special Staff had to fight off the greed of its competitors.

"The SS Reich Security Main Office," Rosenberg complained in a letter to Hitler's deputy, Bormann, "has claimed the following from the library of a monastery: *The Catholic Handbook*, Albertus Magnus; *Edition of the Church Fathers*; *History of the Papacy* by L. v. Pastor and other works. That means historical sources and works are already being claimed from the monastery libraries which should remain uniquely reserved for the national leadership of the Party."

A little later the General Commissar for White Ruthenia, in a letter to Rosenberg in the latter's capacity as Reich Minister for the Occupied Eastern Territories, complained not only about the SS but also about thieving and vandalism by the army:

"Minsk had a large and in part very valuable collection of art treasures and paintings which were removed almost in their entirety. On order of SS Reich Leader Himmler, most of the paintings were packed by the SS and shipped to the Reich. They are worth several millions of marks.

"According to the report made by a Major of the 707th Division, the SS left the rest of the paintings and art objects to the Wehrmacht for further pillaging. . . . General Stubenrauch has taken a valuable part of art treasures from Minsk with him up to the front."

But in these difficulties Goering, at least so far as he had a vested interest in Rosenberg's work—and that was quite often—staunchly supported the Special Purpose Staff. A member of the Nazi Military Government in Paris wrote to his Berlin chief:

"During this confidential conversation [*with Goering*] I again called the Reich Marshal's attention to the fact that a note of protest had been received from the French Government against the activity of the Rosenberg Special Purpose Staff, with reference to the Hague Rules on Land Warfare. Thereupon the Reich Marshal said the following: 'My orders are decisive. You will act directly according to my orders.' The art objects collected in the Jeu de Paume are to be loaded into a special train immediately and taken to Germany, on orders of the Reich Marshal. Those art objects which are to go into the Fuehrer's possession and those art objects which the Reich Marshal claims for himself will be loaded into two railroad cars [*and*] will be taken to Berlin.

"When I made the objection that the jurists would probably be of a different opinion and that protests would most likely be made by the military commander in France, the Reich Marshal answered, saying verbatim as follows: 'Dear Bunjes, let me worry about that, I am the highest jurist in the State.' "

In July, 1944, the pictorial art section of the Special Purpose Staff reported on its acquisitions to date in the western occupied areas alone. The figures are a little staggering, and I think that the Tribunal, too, was staggered when the prosecution handed up thirty volumes of art catalogues as representing a mere fraction of what the Nazis had stolen.

"During the period from March, 1941, to July, 1944," said the report, "the Special Staff for Pictorial Art brought into the Reich 29 large shipments including 137 freight cars with 4174 cases of art works. Up to July 15, 1944, the following had been scientifically inventoried:

"5281 paintings, pastels, water colors, drawings.

"684 miniatures, glass and enamel paintings, books and manuscripts.

"2477 articles of furniture of value to art history.

"5825 hand made art works.

"1286 East Asiatic art works. . . . (etc.)

"These figures will be increased, since seizures in the West are not yet completed. The extraordinary artistic and material value of the seized art works cannot be expressed in figures. Included therein are absolutely authenticated signed works of Rembrandt van Rijn, Rubens, Frans Hals, Vermeer van Delft, Velasquez, Murillo, Goya, del Piombo, Palma Becchio, etc. . . .''

But perhaps the most charming of the documents presented in connection with this part of the case was the letter Rosenberg wrote to Hitler on April 16, 1943:

"My Fuehrer!

"In my desire to give you, my Fuehrer, some joy for your birthday I take the liberty to present to you a folder containing photos of some of the most valuable paintings which my Special Purpose Staff secured from ownerless Jewish art collections in the Occupied Western Territories. These photos represent an addition to the collection of 53 of the most valuable objects of art delivered some time ago to your collection. . . .

"I shall take the liberty during the requested audience to give you, my Fuehrer, another 20 folders of pictures, with the hope that this short occupation with the beautiful things of art which are nearest to your heart will send a ray of beauty and joy into your revered life.

"Heil, my Fuehrer

(Signed:) Alfred Rosenberg"

It was about this time that, from the annihilation camps to the vaults of the Reichsbank in Berlin, the flow of gold dentures and marriage rings and alarm clocks and bits of old jewelry and lensless spectacle frames was reaching its peak. Much of those beautiful things of art which were to send beauty and joy into Hitler's revered life were now indeed ownerless.

Chapter XVIII   The Honorable Profession
of Arms

1.

Informed that Keitel and Jodl had been condemned to death
by hanging, General Eisenhower briefly told newspapermen:

"I was surprised that they found it so easy to convict a military
man. I thought the military would provide a special problem for
the Tribunal."

Here is the voice of the international military caste speaking in
defense of the honorable profession of arms. It is also the voice of
a popular hero who apparently had not had the time to read the
Nuremberg evidence.

What *is* the honorable profession of arms? What are its goals,
its rules? What is its relation to modern war—that phenomenon
of totality in which, unhappily, the professional soldier can no
longer claim a monopoly of interest?

"War . . . serves the survival of the race and State *or the assurance of its historical future.*

"This high moral purpose gives war its total character and its
ethical justification.

"A declaration of war is no longer necessarily the first step at
the start of a war.

"The normal rules of war towards neutral nations may be considered to apply only on the basis of whether the operation of

these rules will create greater advantages or disadvantages for the
warring nations."

Is *this* the honorable profession of arms? Or is it, perhaps, quite
another kind of profession—a profession of faith in war itself
as the highest instrument of State policy, a profession of faith
in the law of the jungle?

I don't think General Eisenhower subscribes to any such profession.

What I quoted is from a top-secret memorandum on *The Direction of War as a Problem of Organization* originated and written
by the High Command of the German Armed Forces, of which
Keitel was Chief of Staff and Jodl was then a member as commander of the National Defense Section.

I have used word "originated" purposefully. No one told the
High Command what to write. There can be no plea here of Superior Order. The document itself bears on its face the legend that
it is the "considered opinion of the High Command."

The date of the document is April 19, 1938—sixteen months
before the outbreak of war.

2.

Keitel remained Chief of Staff of the High Command throughout the war. Jodl was his Chief of Operations.

Both were involved in the initiation and execution of every
phase of Nazi aggression. Keitel's or Jodl's initials were appended
to the attack orders—every one of them issued in violation of existing treaties—on Poland, on the western neutrals, on Norway and
Denmark, on Yugoslavia, Greece and the U. S. S. R.

But these men not only started an illegal war; they *waged* it in
illegal fashion. There's hardly a provision of the laws of war,
whether set down in formal international agreements such as the
Hague and Geneva Conventions or established by common usage,
that the Germans did not violate *under deliberate orders of the
High Command.*

Such violations of the laws were listed in the indictment

under Count 3 as War Crimes, as distinguished from Crimes against Humanity listed under Count 4. But more often than not the crimes overlapped; War Crimes were committed on so vast a scale that they became Crimes against Humanity.

And the honorable profession of German arms committed crimes against Humanity on so vast a scale as to contribute vitally to the uniquely German fascist crime of genocide.

The Wehrmacht's treatment of prisoners of war, particularly though not exclusively Soviet prisoners, is a case in point.

You will recall that the war on the U. S. S. R. was barely a month old when Heydrich, as Himmler's deputy, placed special details in PW camps to weed out and kill all political "undesirables." These murders were made possible through a specific agreement between Heydrich and *Keitel's High Command.*

In September, 1941, General Reinecke, Chief of the Prisoner of War Department of the High Command, issued regulations for the treatment of Soviet War Prisoners. I quote from the document:

"The Bolshevist soldier has therefore lost all claim to treatment as an honorable opponent in accordance with the Geneva Convention. The order for ruthless and energetic action must be given at the slightest indication of insubordination, especially in the case of Bolshevist fanatics.

"Insubordination, active or passive resistance, must be broken immediately by force of arms (bayonets, butts, and firearms). Anyone carrying out the order who does not use his weapons or does so with insufficient energy is punishable.

"Prisoners of war attempting to escape are to be fired upon without previous challenge. No warning shot must ever be fired. The use of arms against prisoners of war is, as a rule, legal."

The regulations provide for the segregation of PW's on political, as well as racial and national grounds, and reaffirm the authority of the Heydrich special details to screen prisoners for political "undesirables."

The prosecution at Nuremberg revealed that one week after these regulations were issued, Admiral Canaris, Chief of Foreign

Military Intelligence, protested both their legality and wisdom in a memorandum addressed to Keitel:

". . . Principles of general international law, since the eighteenth century, have gradually been established along the lines that war captivity is neither revenge nor punishment, but solely protective custody of which the only purpose is to prevent the prisoners from further participation in the war.

"This principle was developed in accordance with the view held by all armies that it is contrary to military tradition to kill or injure helpless people.

"The decrees for the treatment of Soviet prisoners of war are based on a fundamentally different viewpoint."

But Keitel dismissed Canaris' complaints with a brief notation penciled in purple on the face of the memorandum:

"The objections arise from the military concept of chivalrous warfare. This is the destruction of an ideology. Therefore I approve and back the measures."

Keitel never changed his mind about chivalrous warfare. I skip three years and turn to another top secret document introduced at the trial, this one an order issued by District Commanders of the Security Police and SD to all branch offices:

"On March 2, 1944, the Chief of the Secret Police and SD, Berlin, forwarded the following *High Command* order:

"1. On recapture, every escaped officer among PW's, with the exception of British and American, is to be handed over to the Chief of the Security Police and SD.

"2. The fact that PW's are being thus handed over must under no circumstances become known to outsiders. The recaptured persons have 'escaped and not been recaptured.' The same information should be given in reply to inquiries by the Protecting Power, International Red Cross and other similar institutions.

"3. Should escaped British and American officers be recaptured . . . decision as to whether or not they should be handed over to the Chief of the Security Police and SD is to be requested immediately from the Chief of the Prisoner of War Department of the High Command.

"In this connection, the Chief of the Security Police and the SD has issued the following instructions:

"1. The Gestapo will take over from the Camp Commandants the recaptured officers and take them . . . to the Mauthausen Concentration Camp. The Camp Commandant of Mauthausen is to be informed that the prisoners are being handed over under 'Operation Bullet' (Aktion Kugel)."

Operation Bullet meant execution by shooting in the neck.

Three weeks after this decree was issued, there was a mass break of 76 RAF officers from one of Goering's Luftwaffe PW camps. Fifty were turned over to the Gestapo and shot after recapture. Keitel's direct guilt in this was fixed by the testimony at Nuremberg of Major General Westhoff of the High Command's Prisoner of War Department:

"Keitel sent for me. I went with General von Graevenitz. When we entered, Keitel was very excited and nervous and said, 'Gentlemen, this is a bad business. This morning Goering reproached me in the presence of Himmler for having let some more PW's escape. It was unheard of.

" 'Gentlemen, these escapes must stop. We shall take very severe measures. I can only tell you that the men who have escaped will be shot; probably the majority of them are dead already.'

"General von Graevenitz intervened at once and said, 'But, sir, that is out of the question. Escape isn't a dishonorable offense. That is especially laid down in the Convention.'

"Whereupon Keitel said, 'I don't give a damn. We discussed it in the Fuehrer's presence and it cannot be altered.' "

In the meantime—and it is almost anti-climactic to say this— the High Command was collaborating with Sauckel in an illegal labor program of vast dimensions for war prisoners, who by international law are supposedly protected from any work in munitions or related industries. By 1944, the Central Planning Commission was officially informed, 40 percent of all armaments for the Reich was being produced by prisoners of war.

3.

The honorable profession of German arms deliberately fought a persistent and bloodthirsty war against unarmed men, women, and children.

The *Einsatzkommandos* were part of this war. You will remember these Special Task Forces: the witness Ohlendorf, who told the Tribunal he had killed 90,000 civilian Jews in a year, was chief of one on the South Ukraine front. *Ohlendorf could do what he did because the Quartermaster-General of the German Army* (the United States Army equivalent is the Commanding General, G-1) *entered an official agreement with Heydrich in May, 1941, assuring the* Einsatzkommandos *all necessary Wehrmacht cooperation during the Russian campaign.*

A-Day for Case Barbarossa was more than a month off when this agreement was signed. It was still a month off when a top-secret decree was issued from Hitler's headquarters on the "application of military jurisdiction" in the Barbarossa area:

"Until further notice, Military Courts and Courts Martial will not be competent for crimes committed by enemy civilians.

"Persons suspected of criminal action will be brought at once before an officer. This officer will decide whether they are to be shot.

"Collective despotic measures will be taken without delay against *localities* from which cunning or malicious attacks are made on the Armed Forces.

"With regard to *offenses* committed *against enemy civilians* by *members of the Wehrmacht* and its employees, *prosecution is not obligatory* even where the deed is at the same time a military crime or offense." [Italics in original.]

Thus, on the one hand, the power of life or death over all civilians was given into the hands of any second lieutenant for spot decision, and the principle of Lidice—a whole community for an attack on a single German soldier—was enacted into German military law. And on the other hand, the German soldier was virtually given *carte blanche* to steal, rape, and murder to his heart's content.

Even this decree, signed by Keitel, apparently wasn't enough. Barbarossa was less than a month old when the Chief of the High Command signed a supplementary decree, drawn up by Jodl, laying down a fundamental principle:

"In view of the vast size of the occupied areas in the East, the forces available for establishing security will be sufficient only if all resistance is punished not by legal prosecution of the guilty, but by the spreading of such terror by the occupying forces as is alone appropriate to eradicate every inclination to resist among the population."

Terror dawned red in the East, and moved with the sun. By September, 1941, resistance movements were springing up everywhere in the West, to a great extent sparked by Communists whose frustrations had been released by the attack on the U. S. S. R. With the Communists worked patriots of every political shade in every occupied country. But the German High Command, as sensitive to propaganda values as to problems of security, insisted that the facts should be drowned in communist blood:

"It should be inferred in every case of resistance, no matter what the individual circumstances, that it is of Communist origin.

"In this connection, it should be remembered that a human life in unsettled countries frequently counts for nothing. The death penalty for 50-100 Communists should generally be regarded in these cases as suitable atonement for one German soldier's life.

"It should be born in mind and so represented in propaganda, that stern measures also rid the inhabitants of the Communist criminals, and are thus to their own advantage."

This decree was distributed to commanding generals in every occupied land from Crete to Norway, from the Atlantic coast to the Russian front. It was signed by Keitel.

The move was not as shrewd as the High Command had hoped, not even from the propaganda point of view. Peasants and noblemen closed ranks with workers and intellectuals in the resistance movements; and I can imagine that the Germans had certain difficulty convincing the French villager that *le baron*, who owned half the land for miles around, was a Communist. So on October 1, 1941, the Germans put the system of hostages and reprisals on a scientific basis:

"It is advisable that Military Commanders always have at their disposal a number of hostages of different political tendencies, namely: Nationalist, Democratic-Bourgeois, Communist. Depending upon the membership of the culprit, hostages of the corresponding group are to be shot in case of attacks."

This decree, too, was signed by Keitel.

Then, on December 7, 1941, came the infamous decree which German officialdom itself, with ghoulish humor, called *Nacht und Nebel*. Night and Fog! One day, I am sure, a movie, a book, a play, will be written with that title; one can only hope the author will be equal to his subject.

The decree was simple enough. Civilians in occupied territories who were charged with crimes against the German State or occupying power were to be tried on the spot only if there was assurance that sentence would be passed within eight days *and that the sentence would be death*. Otherwise the prisoners were to be *secretly* transferred to the Reich for *secret* determination of their fate.

"Efficient and enduring intimidation," explained a covering memorandum, "can only be achieved either by capital punishment or by measures by which neither the relatives of the criminal, nor the population, know his fate."

This fate is no longer a secret. Night and Fog prisoners were turned over to the Gestapo. What the Gestapo did with them is made clear in an order issued by Pohl's SS-Main-Office Economics and Administration:

"Re: Night and Fog Decree.

"To: Commanders of Concentration Camps.

"The corpses of executed or otherwise deceased 'Night and Fog' prisoners are to be handed over to the State Police for burial. Attention is drawn to the instructions for secrecy. In this connection it is necessary to take special care that the graves of N.F. prisoners should not be marked with the names of the deceased."

Two years after *Nacht und Nebel* was issued, the French Delegation with the German Armistice Commission complained the

FINAL JUDGMENT

decree was being used not only against persons actually charged
with crime, but also against persons whom the Germans suspected
might commit a crime. And in 1944 the German Foreign Office,
itself apparently in receipt of complaints from neutral capitals,
pointed out respectfully to the High Command and to the SS that
"members of neutral countries also had been 'turned into fog' by
mistake."

Nacht und Nebel was issued over Hitler's signature, but Keitel
wrote several covering memoranda and interpretations. Indeed, the
name of the Chief of the High Command was so closely identified
with the order that it was sometimes referred to as the "Keitel
Decree."

4.

I have been writing of directives, decrees, and memoranda issued at highest level. They tell only half the story. They tell not
what happened, but only what was *planned* to happen by secluded
field marshals and generals who could order the shedding of
blood with great equinamity, knowing that they would never have
to see that blood—and not dreaming that one day they might have
to taste their own.

So I turn now to other documents produced at Nuremberg for
revelation in part—in minutely small part—of what happened at
the lower end of the chain of command in the Wehrmacht.

*I think, for instance, of the Jodl-Keitel order for the use of ter-
ror as a pacification weapon in the East.*

"The fight against [partisan] bands," wrote the Reich Commissar for the Eastland to his superiors in Berlin, "is taking on
forms which are highly questionable if pacification and exploitation are the aims of our policy. It should be possible to avoid
atrocities and to bury those who have been liquidated. To lock
men, women, and children into barns and to set fire to them does
not appear to be a suitable method of combatting bands, even if
it is desired to exterminate the population."

Burning alive was by no means the only method the Germans
had for spreading terror.

"At the beginning of 1943," testified Joseph Ivanovitch Vas-
ilevick to Soviet authorities of the city of Stanislav, "we buried
the people right near the cemetery. There were many occasions on
which children and women were thrown into the grave alive. One
woman asked the officer not to shoot her, and he said, 'I give you
my word that you will not be shot.' When the shooting of the
other people was over, the officer himself took her into his arms
and threw her into the grave, and thus she was buried."

*I think of the early Keitel order for "collective despotic meas-
ures" against localities:*
"Telegram: 10.10.41
"To Army Hq. Staff 12 Athens
"Daily Report. 1) The villages of Ano-Kerzilion and Kato-
Kerzilion proved to be the base of a rather large guerilla band in
this area. They were razed to the ground on October 7 by troops
of the Division. The male inhabitants between 16 and 60 years
of age, totaling 207 persons, were shot. Women and children
evacuated.
"2) No other special incident.
"164th Inf. Div. 1."

Letter from Terboven, Reich Commissioner for the Occupied
Northern Territories, to Goering, dated May 1, 1942:
"Several days ago we flushed out a Norwegian sabotage unit.
On the same day, and at the same hour, nineteen Norwegians who
had been captured some time previously attempting to reach
England illegally, were shot on my order.
"Also on the same day the entire community, which had granted
a hiding place to the sabotage unit, was burned down and the pop-
ulation deported. All males were sent to a Concentration Camp in
Germany without notification to their families; the women were
sent to a female forced labor camp in Norway, and the children
who were not capable of working were sent to a children's home."

*I think of Reinecke's special regulations for the treatment of
Soviet prisoners of war:*

"The camp for Russian prisoners of war is separated from our camp by a double row of barbed wire," wrote Philippe de Poix, French war prisoner in Germany, in his diary. "The sentries walk up and down between the two rows.

" I have a small piece of bread as big as a hen's egg, close to my breast, under my shirt. The sentry turned his back. Quickly I pull out my little piece of bread and throw it over into the Russian prisoners' camp.

"Thirty prisoners threw themselves upon the small piece of bread, but the sentry turned around, aimed, and shouted 'Forbidden!'

"The men step back with clenched fists. One of them, with the eyes of a madman, did not move and stared as if bewitched at the forbidden piece of bread. His nerves give way; he throws himself upon the piece of bread.

"The sentry fires. The Russian falls to the ground with the piece of bread in his mouth, with feverishly clenched fists. A stream of blood runs from his temple down over his beard and his mouth and dyes the piece of bread red."

That is de Poix's diary entry for May 20, 1942. On May 28, he wrote:

"A large number of Russian prisoners of war die daily. The corpses lie amongst their living comrades for about two days, as there are too many dead to be taken away immediately.

"Today, during soup distribution, two Russians who are standing in line in front of the kitchen, hold up one of their comrades who has died during the night. They have pulled his cap down over his eyes. One of them carried two bowls, his and that of the dead man. The living will get an additional portion of soup which they will share between them.

"Every second day the dead and dying were loaded into a truck. Trenches were dug about one kilometer away. The dead and dying were thrown together into the trenches and covered with earth.

"Occasionally a German non-commissioned officer finished off the dying with a pistol shot. But in most cases the trenches were covered over without waste of ammunition, even though 'the dying wriggle like worms,' as a German declared, smirking."

5.

It is very difficult to debate with your own signature. The representatives of the honorable profession of German arms in the dock did not try. In their own defense, they said only: "I signed that because Hitler told me to, and soldiers must obey." Or sometimes they said, "I signed that because the kind of war the Allies were fighting made no other course possible."

The Tribunal lent very attentive ear to the second argument. Up to a point, the Justices found it sound, and undoubtedly it saved the lives of Doenitz and Raeder, the navy men. Both pointed out the U-boat policy of torpedoing without warning was (*a*) also followed by the United States Navy in the Pacific, as testified to by our own Admiral Nimitz in an affidavit; and (*b*) made necessary because cargo ships were armed and because each cargo ship, through its radio, functioned as part of the Allied anti-submarine intelligence network.

On the whole, Doenitz was sentenced to ten years, and Raeder to twenty, less because of war crimes (though both were convicted on that count, chiefly in connection with the sinking of neutral vessels) than because of the crime of aggressive war. Raeder, as Naval Commander-in-Chief, rebuilt the German Navy in violation of Versailles; cooperated with Hitler during the pre-1939 war planning and was the key figure in the planning and execution of the attack on Norway. Doenitz, as commander of U-boats and later Raeder's successor as Naval Commander-in-Chief, was among Hitler's inner circle of advisers; and, as Hitler's successor in the closing days of the war, urged Germany to continue the fight in as pretty a Nazi oration as Hitler ever made.

The "necessity" defense served the High Command defendants less well. The stony-faced Keitel and the vivacious Jodl, infinitely more intelligent than his superior, both tried to make the Tribunal understand that partisan warfare was the most dangerous of all kinds of warfare, and the most difficult to combat; that no army, under any circumstances, could countenance unrest, sabotage and active resistance in its rear. But the Tribunal also understood that the German Army would have had no such difficulties had it not insisted on exposing its rear in places where the impulse to kick it was irresistible.

And the Tribunal, undoubtedly, understood something else. It was aware that the policy of terror in the East could hardly be defended as a necessary reaction to partisan warfare. The policy *preceded* the warfare; it preceded the attack on Russia itself. The decision encouraging destruction of a whole community for any attack on a single German soldier was made more than a month before Barbarossa. So was the decision to slaughter Soviet leaders. So was the decision to help Ohlendorf go out and kill Jews and Communists. All the criminal decrees which followed Barbarossa were designed merely to sharpen the original measures; they were the whetting of a sword already forged.

All this, of course, was perfectly consistent with the philosophy to which the German High Command had committed itself a year before the attack on Poland. What can one expect of men who said quite frankly that, as a matter of policy, the laws of war should be obeyed only when such obedience is advantageous to Germany? What can one expect of men who saw the ethical justification of war in that it "serves the survival of the race and State or the assurance of its historical future?" (Note that it is *or*, not *and*; the phrase "historical future" therefore means something other than mere survival. Actually, even the most casual student of Nazi rhetoric knows that the phrase envisages German hegemony over Europe and ultimately over the world.)

The defendants' other line of argument, that of Superior Order —"You can't blame *me;* as a soldier, I had to obey orders"—was happily hamstrung from the outset. Major legal decisions everywhere—including those in German courts—are quite clear on the point: a soldier is not required to obey an order which he knows to be illegal. Therefore the Charter creating the Tribunal outlawed Superior Order as an absolute defense, although permitting its use as a possible mitigating circumstance.

In the course of the trial neither Keitel nor Jodl even attempted to deny that they had issued decrees in full knowledge of their illegality. And while it is true that many of these decrees were issued at Hitler's order, it was difficult to accept the fact as a mitigating circumstance. After all, Hitler was simply ordering them to put into practice what they had already, in the High Command's memorandum of 1938, approved in principle.

The fact is that the military defense lacked not only legal validity; it lacked sincerity. Keitel insisted he disapproved of the Commando order by which Allied Commandos *in uniform or not* were to be "slaughtered to the last man" when captured. But this insistence lacks conviction, coming from a man with Keitel's attitude towards "chivalrous warfare." Jodl said that he, too, at heart disapproved of many High Command decrees; but he approved, at the time, the Commando decree and he was directly responsible for the destruction of thousands of Norwegian homes in the closing days of the war.

And Goering, Chief of the Luftwaffe, not only vehemently denied complicity in the shooting of the fifty RAF officers who had escaped from one of his prison camps, but insisted that he always wanted enemy fliers treated with utmost chivalry. Yet Goering approved (as did Jodl in principle) the Keitel-signed decree legalizing the lynching or execution without trial of downed Allied fliers.

They lied and lied and lied on the stand, did these representatives of the honorable profession of German arms. And I wondered, watching them, how many women and children they had killed in their attempt to crush the fighting spirit of the populations whose lands they had overrun, whose houses they had burned down, whose young manhood they had slain on the battlefield. No one knows the number; crematories tell no tales, nor do ashes spread over the fields of Europe.

But no matter what the number, it was not enough for a fascist victory.

Chapter XIX   Collective Guilt

1.

Ignorance has become a national virtue in Germany. "I didn't know!" cried the defendants. "I didn't know!" cried the man in the street. It was a mighty invisible force, emanating from an invisible source, that had plucked millions of people out of Europe, dropped them on Mars, and there smote them down with invisible death rays. . . .

These Germans lie. Every German knew something, a few knew everything, *millions knew more than they will today admit.* The proof is implicit in scores of documents introduced at Nuremberg. The prosecution did not introduce these documents as evidence against the German people, for the German people were not on trial at Nuremberg. But the evidence is there, nonetheless—evidence the more convincing for the very reason that it was not part of the prosecution's case, but grew almost accidentally, as it were, out of the facts themselves.

This evidence showed that knowledge of atrocities, extending far beyond those persons directly implicated, penetrated into wide Nazi party circles, into the ranks of the Wehrmacht, into business and industrial groups and into whole communities that were at times literally blanketed with the stench of death.

Mass killings began in Germany during the winter of 1939-40.

246

They were not of Jews or Slavs or Frenchmen, but of Germans—the German "insane." I put the word in quotations because no one knows how many perfectly normal people, or how many merely mentally retarded, were also destroyed in this systematic series of so-called mercy killings.

Knowledge of this was widespread in Germany.

In December, 1940, 370 patients were removed by bus from an insane asylum at Erlangen, next door to Nuremberg. Soon afterwards relatives began to receive notices that the patients had died of pneumonia or some "infectious disease" and that the bodies had been cremated. A Nazi official, reporting to his superior, commented on the result:

"The population is terribly disturbed. They connect it with the cases of death which are becoming known in rapid succession. They are speaking partly openly, partly secretly, about the illegal elimination of patients."

The people knew that the patients were being eliminated; they did not know it was being done "legally" under a secret order issued by Hitler and Himmler.

Here is an official report on the situation at Ansbach, west of Nuremberg:

"The removal of patients of sanatoria and nursing homes to other districts naturally could not remain hidden from the public. It also appears that the Commissions work in too great haste and many mistakes occurred. One family received two urns."

Here is an official report on the situation in the little town of Absberg, west of Munich, whence buses had just removed some dozens of patients from a local asylum:

"These people were taken away in the most conspicuous manner imaginable. The vehicles were stationed outside the asylum in the middle of the market place. The inmates who were to be removed and were accordingly excited had to be taken to the vehicles singly and by force. The whole population of Absberg watched the incident, crying loudly."

The party district leader in the town of Lauf, east of Nuremberg, quoting a local physician, put the whole matter succinctly:

"Families are refusing to send their sick to institutions, as they do not know whether they will ever get them back alive."

And now I quote from a letter written by the Bishop of Limburg, near Frankfurt, to the Reich Minister of Justice about happenings in the neighboring small town of Hadamar:

"Several times a week buses arrive in Hadamar with a considerable number of such victims. School children of the vicinity know this vehicle and say: 'There comes the murder box again.' After the arrival of the vehicle, the citizens of Hadamar watch the smoke rise out of the chimney and are tortured with the ever-present thought of the miserable victims, especially when repulsive odors annoy them, depending on the direction of the wind.

"The effect: Children call each other names and say, 'You're crazy, you'll be sent to the baking oven in Hadamar.' Those who do not want to marry say, 'Marry? Never! Bring children into the world so they can be put into the bottling machine?' You hear old folks say, 'Don't send me off to a state hospital. After the feeble-minded have been finished off, the next useless eaters whose turn will come are the old people.' "

These documents relate to conditions in two German areas alone: Bavaria and Greater Hesse. But from Wuerttemberg, Bishop Wurm complained to the Reich Minister of Justice that "the systematic extermination of lunatics, weak and frail compatriots . . . is reaching the proportions of a great danger and a scandal." And there were hundreds of asylums all over Germany whence inmates were removed and dozens of crematories where they were turned into ashes. The methods followed were exactly the same; and if people knew what was happening under their noses in Bavaria, Hesse, Wuerttemberg, then they also knew in Westphalia and Brandenburg and Hanover and Pomerania.

2.

The German Army was the soul of honor. "There were two wars going on," testified a general at the trial. "One was ideological, the other military. We soldiers fought the military war; the ideological war was kept separate."

Yes? The following is from a report of a simple soldier of the honorable German Army. It was published during the winter of 1945-46 in a German magazine, *Die Wandlung,* in Heidelberg.

Before the troops marched against the East, wrote Paul Herzog, they knew that "houses would be blasted, cities burned down, prisoners would be herded into a camp and left to die like cattle." He adds:

"Every recruit felt it, every member of the older age groups who had been recruited for this new Hitler war, knew it.

"And where they didn't know, somebody told them, an officer would imply it in his weekly lectures, and secret reports were relayed through divisions down as far as company staffs.

"What kind of a people is this, in which every soldier swaggers through the PW camp with a stick fashioned by the prisoners themselves? All these men were destined to die. For a long time we could not really comprehend this, even though it had been told to me by our training officer."

Paul Herzog and thousands of his colleagues were guilty only of knowing without doing. Others of his fellow soldiers bear greater guilt. I quote again from a report of a field inspector to his superior, General Thomas, chief of the Wehrmacht Industrial Armaments Office:

"Detached formations of the police executed a planned shooting of Jews. *It was done entirely in public* with the use of the Ukrainian militia and unfortunately in many instances *also with members of the Armed Forces taking part voluntarily."* (My italics— V. H. B.)

The whole Waffen SS knew about atrocities, several hundreds of thousands of them who served in the East. "The SS ranks knew very well about the bloody deeds which were committed by the SS in Poland," testified David Wasnapel, a concentration camp survivor, at the trial. "In particular they told me personally about mass murders of Jews in Maidenek (in November, 1943). This fact was no secret. It was common knowledge among the civil population as well as among the lowest ranking SS men."

Knowledge of atrocities spread through all ranks and all sections of the Wehrmacht. It spread like cancer. We know already

the direct complicity of higher army ranks, many of whom worked
hand in hand with the SD to commit the atrocities. Army courts
knew, for in certain instances they tried soldiers for atrocities;
military police knew, for they sometimes arrested the culprits.

There is a case on record of two German soldiers locking fifty
Jews in a synagogue and shooting them dead—apparently purely
for diversion. The men were sentenced first to nine years, then
to three years in prison by courts martial, *and then were released
on demand of army headquarters*, which pointed out that one of
the culprits "as an SS man, particularly sensitive to the sight of
Jews, acted quite thoughtlessly, in a youthful spirit of adventure."

How long could a thing like that be kept secret from gossiping
soldiers? Unless, of course, it was so usual an occurrence that it was
not worth recounting.

The Wehrmacht was on Russian soil for nearly four years, on
Polish soil for nearly six. The longer it stayed, the more it learned.
Ohlendorf said he killed 90,000 Jews in his Southern Front area
in a single year. How long could this have been kept a secret from
the occupation troops, *especially when many of the killings were
held in public?*

And with respect to gas vans, one recalls the letter of Dr.
Becker:

"The vans became so well known, that not only the authorities
but also the civilian population called the van the 'death van'. . . .
It is my opinion the van cannot be kept secret for any length of
time."

This was in Kiev, under command then of a German military
government, garrisoned by German troops, patrolled by German
military police. But I dare say there is not a German today who was
then in Kiev who would admit that he knew anything about gas
vans.

And the innocent Wehrmacht was involved up to its neck not
only on occupied soil, but on German soil. You will remember
the order from the OKW that, among Russian war prisoners, all
Jews, Communists and other politically or industrially important
people were to be shot. The following is a report by the commandant of the Gross Rosen concentration camp in Silesia, one

of the camps at which the executions were carried out:

"The commandants of the concentration camps are complaining that five to ten per cent of the Soviet Russians destined for execution are arriving in the camps dead or half dead. Therefore the impression has arisen that the PW camps [run at that time by the Wehrmacht, not by Himmler] are getting rid of prisoners in this way.

"It was particularly noted that, when marching for example from the railroad station to the camp, a rather large number of PW's collapsed on the way from exhaustion, either dead or half dead, and had to be picked up by a truck following the convoy.

"*It cannot be prevented that the German people take notice of these occurrences.*

"*Even if the transportation to the camps is generally taken care of by the Wehrmacht,* the population will still attribute this situation to the SS." (My italics—V. H. B.)

This is really a precious document. The camp commandant is complaining that the Russians are dying before he has a chance to kill them. And he is worried lest the German people be misled into laying the sins of the Wehrmacht at the door of the pure, the noble, the generous SS.

3.

That the German people knew enough about concentration camps to want desperately to keep out of them is obvious. But they knew more than that—oh, ever so much more!

I want first to quote from an interrogation of Oswald Pohl, SS Economics Director:

Q. "But Kaltenbrunner had told the Tribunal that there were only a handful of people in the RSHA [Reich Security Main Office] who had any control and knew anything about concentration camps."

A. "Well, that is complete nonsense. I described to you how these were handled in the RSHA. As, for instance, in the case of the use of textiles and the turning in of valuables, and also from Gluecks and Loerner right on down to the last little clerk, they all must have known what went on in the concentration camps, and it is complete nonsense for him to speak of just a handful of men."

Down to the last little clerk. Did none of these little clerks ever tell his family? Or his friends? Not even over a glass of beer? These things were going on, it must be remembered, not just for a few weeks, but for four or five years.

All right, the little clerks as well as the big clerks, the subordinates as well as the bosses, proved utterly, unbelievably, inhumanly secretive, and never, never, not even during the coziest domestic evening with their wives, or in their drunkest moments with their friends, divulged a single word about what they were doing, what the SS was doing, why for six days a week in the course of four years they left their homes every morning at nine and didn't come home until six or later.

Many, many, many Germans didn't have to be told. *They knew.*

"We were required to carry out these exterminations in secrecy," testified Rudolf Hoess, commandant of the extermination camp at Auschwitz. "But, of course, the foul and nauseating stench from the continued burning of bodies permeated the entire area and all of the people living in the surrounding communities knew that exterminations were going on at Auschwitz."

But Auschwitz, you say, was Poland, not Germany. Still, Hoess was talking about the period 1941-45. These were years, if I remember correctly, that the Polish Government General was being run by Germans, occupied by Germans, exploited by Germans. The Governor General was a German named Frank; his subordinates were all trusted Germans, the occupation troops were German; the commanders were German; the police were ruled by Germans; the principal industries and businesses were taken over by Germans.

Did none of these people ever hear about Auschwitz, see the flames from its chimney at night, smell its stench? Did they never write home about it, or more likely speak about it when they got home on furlough or on vacation or on business?

All Poland knew about Auschwitz. The few Jews remaining in Germany—mostly Jews and half-Jews married to Christians—knew about Auschwitz and extermination camps. *They knew that de-*

portation meant death. And if they, themselves, strictly obeyed the law of the land and never spoke of their fears to their "Aryan" neighbors, what about their Christian spouses? Did *they* never speak the dread word "extermination" to their friends?

Yet the German people today maintain they knew nothing about exterminations; they knew only that the Jews were being deported for work. Apparently even the following order, issued by the defendant Sauckel on November 26, 1942, and which reached employment offices and Chambers of Commerce and eventually every sizeable employer of labor in the land, made no one suspicious.

"In agreement with the Chief of the Security Police and the SD," says the order, "Jews who are still in employment are, from now on, to be evacuated from the territory of the Reich and are to be replaced by Poles who are being deported from the General Government."

The whole world learned of the extermination program long before the end of the war. The defendant Streicher swears he first learned of it from the Swiss press. Did everyone know about it except the Germans, under whose nose the whole thing was operating? Is this really credible?

I quote briefly from the cross-examination of Mme. Vaillant-Couturier, a prosecution witness and concentration camp graduate, by defense counsel for Streicher:

Q. "You said before that the German people knew of what went on in Auschwitz. What are your grounds for this statement?"

A. "I base it, on the one hand, on the fact that when we left, the Lorraine soldiers of the Wehrmacht, who transported us to Auschwitz, told us, 'If you knew where you were going, you would not be in a hurry to get there.'

"And I base it on the fact that in all the factories where the prisoners worked, they were in contact with German civilians, as well as with the overseers. They had relations with their families and friends, and often would tell what they had seen."

Yes, the prisoners in Poland and in Russia often worked in factories—factories run by Germans. There was the evidence of Herr Graebe, manager of a factory in the Ukraine taken over by the firm of Josef Jung of Solingen, Germany. He told, you will recall, of his Jewish workers having been taken out of his factory and vividly described the ghastly scene at the death pits—the victims stripped and shot in rows as they stood at the edge of the mass grave. *He* knew. And there were hundreds of German businessmen in the conquered territories in the East in those days.

You remember the testimony of Reich Commissioner Carl of the Sluzk territory, the man who complained of a German police battalion taking all the Jews out of his town — including those who were working in factories for the benefit of the German Army —and shooting them. The commander of the battalion was surprised at Carl's objections. His orders, said the commander, were to clear the town of Jews in two days; *and in this, he explained, Sluzk was just like all other towns.*

All the towns were made *Juden-Frei*, one after the other, and to clear them of Jews it was necessary to take the Jews out of the work shops and factories and stores, many of them run by Germans.

Is it really credible that the Germans back home didn't know about these things that were happening in the East?

It isn't necessary to guess the answer. The Germans themselves furnish it. I quote from a confidential information bulletin issued from the Nazi Party Chancellery on October 9, 1942, addressed to lower party ranks:

"While the final solution of the Jewish question is being worked out, discussions are lately going on among the population of various parts of the Reich concerning 'very severe' measures against the Jews, particularly in the Eastern territories. Investigations have shown that such statements, mostly in distorted or exaggerated form, were passed on by men on leave from various units employed in the East who personally had the opportunity to observe such measures."

So the Germans back home were not only learning about what was happening in the East from eyewitnesses, but they were actually getting exaggerated accounts. To many it would seem very difficult indeed to exaggerate the actuality in this instance, but then perhaps the Germans have more imagination than most.

We turn away from the Eastern territories now and look at

German soil. The story of Gross Rosen, in Silesia, is clear enough: "It cannot be prevented that the German people take notice of these occurrences," wrote the camp commandant about the collapse of Russian PW's marching from the railroad station to the camp.

Silesia is in the far southeast corner of Germany. Buchenwald is near Weimar, in central Germany.

"At the time when our convoys arrived," testified Victor du Pont, a survivor of Buchenwald, "the prisoners were naked, and others were half-clad, and the spectators who were at the station where they arrived were quite numerous, and they saw these convoys.

"Then there were work groups who worked outside the camp. There were work commandos who went to Weimar, some to Erfurt, and some others to Vena; they left in the morning and came back in the evening. During the day they were in places where this civilian population was present in the factories with the prisoners. . . . During all day long the supervisors made the prisoners work in the same factory where there were civilian workers.

"The feeding in the camps was carried out and the food supply was insured by the civilian service. I have seen civilian trucks come into the camp. And those in charge of the railroads were forced to know about these things. The numerous trains which came every day and brought prisoners from one camp to another, and from France to Germany. . . . In Buchenwald there was the regular railroad service which ended at the station of Buchenwald. This was the end of the line; those in charge of the railroad had the opportunity to be informed about these convoys."

Do the bodies of Communists, Jews, anti-Fascists, smell less or differently when burned than the bodies of the German insane? Were the crematories of Dachau, near Munich in South Germany, any different than those in Hadamar in West Germany, which the Bishop of Limburg said stank so frightfully? Or the crematories of Buchenwald in Central Germany or of Gross Rosen in Southeast Germany or of Oranienburg, near Berlin, in the heart of Prussia—were these different?

There is a special story about Oranienburg which was not told at the trial because the Tribunal ruled it inadmissible on technical grounds. It has to do with a letter written to the Mayor of Oranienburg by counsel for Kaltenbrunner, Hangman Heydrich's successor as right-hand man to Himmler. In this letter the counsel, Kauffmann, poses three principal questions:

"1. Was the population of Oranienburg aware of any details of the atrocities committed in the local concentration camp?

"2. Did the population of Oranienburg know if, and how many, other concentration camps had been set up?

"3. Are there any inmates of the local concentration camp available who are perhaps prepared to declare on oath that during their stay in the camp, atrocities were not, or were hardly ever, committed, or that they personally did not experience such atrocities?"

This letter was written on February 15, 1946. Mayor Kausmann of Oranienburg answered on March 8. I give the answer textually:

"*To point 1.* The population of Oranienburg knew from the time the concentration camp started about the ill-treatment and the atrocities. Owing to the fact that many citizens of Oranienburg were themselves inmates, and owing to their living so close together, it was not possible to keep the catastrophic conditions secret. After the construction of the gas ovens, a sort of pestilential stink spread over the town for weeks. . . .

"*To point 2.* The exact number of concentration camps was not known, but through the camp of Ravensbrueck, which was situated in the vicinity, and owing to the number of people who were continually brought in to the local camp and sent out of it, the population knew that there were many similar camps in Germany.

"*To point 3.* There are still 91 prisoners from the local concentration camp available. Unfortunately none of them can satisfy your wish and state on oath that no atrocities took place; on the contrary, every single one of them is prepared to swear that they not only saw these things but experienced them on their own bodies.

"We can therefore not contribute to the exoneration of the people responsible for these things who are being defended by you in Nuremberg."

This was not, of course, exactly the kind of answer Kauffmann had anticipated. He put it in his files and tried to forget about it. Not so the prosecution, who were in receipt of a copy and tried to introduce it as evidence. But the Tribunal ruled adversely. This letter, said the Tribunal in effect, was the private property of defense counsel and could not be introduced without defense counsel's consent.

Defense counsel, needless to say, did not oblige.

4.

A German girl is typing this chapter in my office in Nuremberg. I have sometimes found her crying over its pages. This was no compliment to my literary style; she was crying over the documents, crying out of pity for the dead and shame for the living—herself and her people, who let such things be. She is a good Catholic girl in her middle twenties, who during the war worked in a small armaments factory in a small town in the South German mountains. She was never a party member, had no politics except her Church. She knew a little of what was going on, half-knew more, probably suspected still more, but had not the courage to cry out. No one had extended to her the hand that gives courage, the hand of fellowship, the hand that brings one out of loneliness into a common cause and gives the strength to fight. Not from her fellow workers had she gotten this hand, nor from her own people, nor from her family, nor from her Church.

And even as there are millions of Germans who are lying today, lying about the past and the present and the future, there are also millions like her who are trying to be honest with themselves and with others, who only half-understand what has happened to them and why, who have no political direction or conviction, and who for the moment have nothing to give to the world they shattered but tears of contrition.

And then there are a few Germans today, some themselves out of concentration camps, who see and understand what has happened, and speak out with terrible earnestness to their own people.

The Communist Ernst Wiechert, who is also a writer, told German youth at a meeting held in Munich last summer:

"It had become clear to the Supermen that they had nothing to fear from this German people. More burned up in the Reichstag fire than a heap of stone and wood. Rights, law, and truth disappeared, and no Phoenix rose from its ashes, but the blond beast preparing to jump at his own brother. The cries of those who were tortured and beaten to death were heard in the streets. With the first barbed wire around the first concentration camp, sentence was pronounced over an entire nation, a nation which had recognized the evil but hid in palaces and huts not to hear the cries. . . . A nation which pressed its hands against its eyes in order not to see the stream of blood which slowly, slowly, but growing wider and redder, flooded the German soil.

"A nation looked aside, cowardly, when it saw the tears of the women and children—an ocean of tears, not shed in a thousand years, shed only for the greater glory of the Fatherland. . . . In these twelve years almost an entire people was spoiled and poisoned."

I quote briefly from an editorial in *Der Simpl*, a German magazine, issue of June, 1946. The writer is discussing the attitude of the defendants at Nuremberg:

"Whence do these former leaders take the courage to say, *I didn't know*. Governing leaders! *Every tenth member of the German community knew what was happening.* Can there really be such infamy?

"And worst of all, most incomprehensible, is that after all these inhuman revelations at the trial, the whole people did not cry out in revulsion, that it listened to the reports as one listens to instructions in the use of a washing machine.

"How we must have deteriorated—and not only externally!"

But these cries are rare in Germany today, and one hears them only against the low mass mutterings of the querulous and the self-righteous, the hypocritical and the outright impenitent. Nor is the United States, as an occupying power, doing much to dispel this self-deception which holds the German people as in a vice. The Germans who govern in the American zone today are the holy Know-Nothings, the blessed innocents who, because they never joined the party, must therefore have been deprived, for twelve years, of their eyes, their ears—and their noses.

And most tragic is the American failure to see that the disunity of the left in Germany which in 1933 lost democracy, today stands in the way of the regaining of democracy. I am not overselling the German Left. It was the Communists who, in those last catastrophic months which led to the Nazi triumph, on many occasions turned more savagely upon the Social Democrats than they did upon the Brownshirts. It was the Social Democrats who turned a deaf ear to the communist plea for a general strike. . . . They have much to atone for, these workers of Germany.

But among these workers are a few who see the sins of the past. Their voices must be heard. There is no other hope for Germany.

Chapter XX   Final Judgment

The newspapermen worked late on the last day. Pity, too, because much of the work was wasted. Somebody picked this day to put spots on the sun, garbling radio communication. Parts of *Newsweek* copy—or was it *Time?*—ended up in the Baltimore *Sun*, my own copy got through hours late and some New York *Times* copy never did get through.

I left the courthouse for the last time and waited in the parking lot for a Press Camp car. A German policeman was squatting gingerly on the slack chains that fenced the lot. He regarded my correspondent's patch quietly for a moment and then nodded towards the courthouse.

"Hanging them all?" he asked.

"Eleven," I said. "Twelve with Bormann. Three went free."

"No!" He seemed genuinely shocked and stared at me out of very small, very bright blue eyes. He was pale and pudgy, with a flattish nose that seemed to be rather more man's work than nature's. He spoke an educated German.

"Please tell me," he asked, "who are the innocent angels?"

"Schacht, Papen, Fritzsche."

He began to laugh, showing very few teeth, all of them bad. "Excuse me," he spluttered, "I would laugh just the same for any other three." He rocked gently. "Who will hang, then?"

I told him.

260

"Hmmm. And why do our three friends go free?"

I thought there might be a good interview here for me, and anyway I was full of the story, so I explained:

"The charge against Schacht and Papen was that they conspired with Hitler and others to make war. The Tribunal ruled that while Schacht and Papen had helped the Nazis in certain ways, there was not enough evidence to show that this help was given *with knowledge* that the Nazis were planning war."

"Helped the Nazis! *Mein Gott!* They brought them to power! And Schacht invented all that funny money so Hitler could have guns. And Papen in Austria—"

I interrupted. "But you don't understand; you aren't a lawyer. Take the word *conspiracy*. It can be interpreted broadly or narrowly, as you like; the Tribunal preferred to interpret it narrowly. It said, 'the conspiracy must not be too far removed from the time of decision and of action.' And it decided that the Nazi conspiracy to wage aggressive war didn't begin until the fall of 1937, or thereabouts.

"So what Schacht and Papen did in 1932 and 1933 cuts no ice.

"As for Schacht's rearming of Germany, the Tribunal decided that, under the Charter, rearmament itself was not criminal. To be a crime under the Charter, the Tribunal said, it must be shown that Schacht carried out this rearmament as part of the Nazi plans to wage aggressive war.

"But Schacht said in court he didn't build guns for war, but only to help Germany become strong so her foreign policy would be respected abroad. Apparently the Tribunal believed him."

The policeman rose, his eyes shining. "A poem," he said unexpectedly. "I remember a poem. Wait. Wait. How did it go?" He scowled ferociously, struggling with memory. Finally he uttered the lines, hesitantly at first, then with increasing confidence:

"And when we go to war at last,
Just fight and die—you duffer!
For win or lose, the war once past,
Be sure *Herr Schacht* won't suffer!"

"So till it comes—that battle day
You'll toil and starve and hope and pray . . .
When beaten, sore, with crumbling wall,
The wretched Germans flee,
Behind it all, behind it all
Herr Schacht will hide—you'll see!"

I stared at him. "When was that written?"

"Ah," said the policeman triumphantly. "That's the whole point! It was written in 1931. One-nine-three-one." He struck fist into palm to emphasize each number. He was showing his blackened teeth again in a broad, delighted grin. "You don't believe me? Look up the file of *Simplicissimus* for that year. Poet was a fellow named Kindt, Karl Kindt. I've given you only a small part of the poem. But its all about Schacht, every stanza."

I knew the magazine *Simplicissimus* by reputation; during the Republic, it was one of the best of the continental humorous publications, witty, satiric, sophisticated. It could very well have published that poem (I checked later: It did).

"Too bad more people didn't take Kindt seriously," I said. "Usually, people mistake wit for wisdom; with Kindt, it seems to have been the other way around."

"Ah!" said the policeman, relapsing into glumness.

"As for Papen," I went on, returning to my disquisition on law, "the Tribunal admitted that his prime purpose as Minister to Austria was to bring about Anschluss and that for this purpose he used politically immoral methods. But the Tribunal pointed out that political immorality is not a crime under the Charter.

"Indeed, the Tribunal ruled that, under the Charter, it could find no one guilty of anything—*not even genocide*—except in connection with aggressive war. And if the mass murder of minorities, whether on a national or racial or any other basis, is not an international crime, I don't know what is.

"Anyway, while the Tribunal agreed that Anschluss was carried out 'by the methods of an aggressor,' it also insisted that the act in itself did not constitute aggressive war. After all, you know, there was no shooting."

"But there was no shooting in Denmark either," the policeman broke in, "or very little—"

"As for Fritzsche," I continued remorselessly, "the Tribunal simply didn't think he was important enough to be convicted, despite his jobs as Chief of Radio in the Propaganda Ministry and as Plenipotentiary for the Political Organization of the Greater German Radio. What names you Germans give things!

"The Tribunal pointed out that there was always someone over Fritzsche. The Tribunal admitted he broadcast many lies for Goebbels, but said it wasn't proven he *knew* they were lies when he broadcast them; it admitted he broadcast anti-Semitic speeches, but said he never urged persecution or extermination of Jews."

"But in his very last broadcast—"

"He urged German civilians to join the Werewolves and go underground against the Allies. Yes, I know. But in the Tribunal's opinion, Fritzsche was just a patriot trying to arouse popular sentiment in support of Hitler and the German war effort."

The policeman took a few paces. "Very complicated," he muttered. "For such complicated reasoning, eleven months were not too much."

"You seem very bitter," I said.

"Why not? My name is No. 537214." He rolled up the dark blue of his re-dyed uniform and showed me the tatooed number on his forearm, the mark of the KZ. "Eight years."

I noticed that his right hand had no fingertips.

"Political?" I asked.

"Vice-President of the Toymakers Union. A few of us worked overtime to make dolls of Hitler and Streicher. The Gestapo didn't like them." He grinned suddenly. "They were very comical dolls. The tongues moved."

"If it makes you feel any better," I said, "the Soviet Justice has put in a dissenting opinion. He believes the three should have been found guilty, and also the Reich Cabinet and High Command, which the Tribunal acquitted."

If he did feel better, he didn't let on.

"But then," I continued, "the Russians probably approach these things with a different attitude. Anglo-Saxon law highly treasures certain institutions: free speech, free enterprise, a free market place for political forces." (At this point certain reservations came to my mind.) "I speak in general terms, of course.

"Anyway, our courts are slow to make any decision which might restrict these freedoms. Very, very slow. The case has to be air-tight, watertight, sealed, nailed, and pasted with precedent and statute. Evidently this case had a crack."

"A crack? What crack?"

"The crack that Schacht, Papen, and Fritzsche crawled through —Schacht with his freedom to make armaments, Papen with his freedom to make immoral politics, Fritzsche with his freedom to make lying propaganda."

The Press Camp car had come and left without me. The police-man and I began to stroll up the Fuerherstrasse, along the length of the sprawling Palace of Justice.

"Like most newspapermen," I said, "I talk too much and don't listen enough. Tell me, you think the Nuremberg trial was a flop, don't you?"

"Not at all." He spoke slowly and with great emphasis. "To think so would be a terrible blunder.

"You spoke of certain freedoms. One freedom the Tribunal has decided against. That is the freedom of one nation to attack an-other. That was a very great decision. It was never made before, not by a great legal court. You will see: the decision will become greater and greater in time. One day there will be an international police force just to see that this decision is obeyed."

He paused for a moment and turned to me.

"I was very angry when you told me about the three. There is eight years' worth of anger burning in me. It is a frightful burn-ing. But anger is blind. I must not let my personal hurt hide from me the big work the Tribunal has done, even if it wrongly acquit-ted three. Of all the unbelievable crimes we Germans have com-mitted in these last years, the greatest was that we made war. For in the crime of war are all other crimes.

"And on this question the Tribunal made the right decision. On this question there was no dissent. The powers that today rule the world agreed on this."

We resumed our walk.

"There is another thing," the policeman said. "Let us for a moment forget the defendants. After all, what matters 21 criminals when there are millions? Let us forget the Tribunal and the Judgment, for is there not a greater Tribunal and a greater Judgment?

"I am thinking of the people, the ordinary workers everywhere, here in Germany, in your country, in China. Do we need black gowns and a high bench to become a Tribunal? No. All we need is the evidence. And this the Nuremberg trial gave us. Not all the evidence, not by any means all; but for us Germans, perhaps too much, and for the rest of the world, enough for a very good start. The world can learn many, many lessons from Nuremberg."

"Do you think the Germans are learning lessons?"

"*I* am," he said grimly. "But then, I suppose I am not the average German."

"No," I said. "I don't suppose you are."

He looked at me a long moment and said quietly, "You don't like the Germans, do you?"

"I prefer to put it another way. I don't like the people who permitted the Nazis to come to power, who gloried in Nazi Germany so long as it was victorious, who sang *Wir Fahren Gegen England* through their noses to keep out the stench of the crematory ovens.

"In short, I don't like people who didn't fight against the Fascists."

"Yes," said No. 537214. "I can understand that. But isn't it one of the lessons of Nuremberg that it took your people, too, a long time to begin to fight the Fascists?"

The question stayed with me as I said good-bye to him and returned to the courthouse, thinking to file a story on the interview. But the hardworking RCA boys were up to their necks in copy and the sun spots were still messing up transmission, so I decided I wouldn't file.

Anyway, it wasn't the kind of story that called for much hurry, particularly with the lead I was planning to write for it: "The people will write the Final Judgment."

Nuremberg and New York, 1946

Appendix

EXTRACTS FROM THE INDICTMENT
Count One—The Common Plan or Conspiracy

All the defendants, with divers other persons, during a period of years preceding 8th May, 1945, participated as leaders, organizers, instigators or accomplices in the formulation or execution of a common plan or conspiracy to commit, or which involved the commission of, Crimes against Peace, War Crimes, and Crimes against Humanity, as defined in the Charter of this Tribunal, and, in accordance with the provisions of the Charter, are individually responsible for their own acts and for all acts committed by any persons in the execution of such plan or conspiracy.

Count Two—Crimes Against Peace

All the defendants with divers other persons, during a period of years preceding 8th May, 1945, participated in the planning, preparation, initiation and waging of wars of aggression, which were also wars in violation of international treaties, agreements and assurances.

Count Three—War Crimes

All the defendants committed War Crimes between 1st September, 1939, and 8th May, 1945, in Germany and in all those countries and territories occupied by the German armed forces since 1st September, 1939, and in Austria, Czechoslovakia, and Italy, and on the High Seas . . . All the defendants, acting in concert with others, formulated and executed a common plan or conspiracy to commit War Crimes as defined in Article 6 (b) of the Charter.

The said War Crimes . . . constituted violations of international conventions, of internal penal laws and of the general principles of criminal law as derived from the criminal law of all civilized nations, and were involved in and part of a systematic course of conduct.

Count Four—Crimes Against Humanity

All the defendants committed Crimes against Humanity during a period of years preceding 8th May, 1945, in Germany and all those countries and territories occupied by the German armed forces since 1st September, 1939, and in Austria, Czechoslovakia, and Italy, and on the High Seas.

All the defendants, acting in concert with others, formulated and executed a common plan or conspiracy to commit Crimes against Humanity as defined in Article 6 (c) of the Charter. This plan involved, among other things, the murder and persecution of all who were suspected of being hostile to the Nazi Party and all who were or who were suspected of being opposed to the common plan alleged in Count One.

The said Crimes against Humanity . . . constituted violations of international conventions, of internal penal laws, of the general principles of criminal law as derived from the criminal law of all civilized nations and were involved in and part of a systematic course of conduct.

Extract from the Charter

Article 6:

The Tribunal established by the Agreement referred to in Article 1 hereof for the trial and punishment of the major war criminals of the European Axis countries shall have the power to try and punish persons who, acting in the interests of the European Axis countries, whether as individuals or as members of organizations, committed any of the following crimes. . . .

(b) WAR CRIMES: Namely, violations of the laws or customs of war. Such violations shall include, but not be limited to, murder, illtreatment or deportation to slave labor or for any other purpose of civilian population of or in occupied territory, murder or ill-treatment of prisoners of war or persons on the seas, killing of hostages, plunder of public or private property, wanton destruction of cities, towns or villages, or devastation not justified by military necessity;

(c) CRIMES AGAINST HUMANITY: namely, murder, extermination, enslavement, deportation, and other inhumane acts committed against any civilian population, before or during the war, or persecutions on political, racial or religious grounds in execution of or in connection with any crime within the jurisdiction of the Tribunal, whether or not in violation of the domestic law of the country where perpetrated.

INDIVIDUALS INDICTED AND THE FINAL JUDGMENT AGAINST EACH

Hermann Goering

President of the Reichstag, Reich Minister for Air, Commander-in-Chief of the Air Force, President of the Council of Ministers for the Defense of the Reich, General in the SS, at one time Successor Designate to Hitler.

Indicted on: Counts 1, 2, 3, 4.
Verdict: Guilty on all counts.
Sentence: Death by hanging.

Rudolph Hess

Up to 1941 Deputy to the Fuehrer, Reich Minister Without Portfolio, member of the Reichstag, member of the Council of Ministers for the Defence of the Reich, General in the SS, Successor Designate to the Fuehrer after Goering.

Indicted on: Counts 1, 2, 3, 4.
Verdict: Guilty on Counts 1, 2.
Sentence: Life imprisonment.

Joachim von Ribbentrop

Reich Minister for Foreign Affairs, Organizer and Director of Special Office Ribbentrop, member of Hitler's Political Staff at General Headquarters, General in the SS.

Indicted on: Counts 1, 2, 3, 4.
Verdict: Guilty on all counts.
Sentence: Death by hanging.

Wilhelm Keitel

Chief of the High Command of the German Armed Forces, member of the Council of Ministers for the Defence of the Reich, and Field Marshal.
Indicted on: Counts 1, 2, 3, 4.
Verdict: Guilty on all counts.
Sentence: Death by hanging.

Ernst Kaltenbrunner

Member of the Reichstag, General in the SS, at one time State Secretary for Security in Austria in charge of the Austrian Police, Head of the Reich Main Security Office and Chief of the Reich Security Police and Security Service.
Indicted on: Counts 1, 3, 4.
Verdict: Guilty on Counts 3, 4.
Sentence: Death by hanging.

Alfred Rosenberg

Member of the Reichstag, Reich Leader in the Nazi Party for Ideology and Foreign Policy, Editor of the *Voelkischer Beobachter,* head of the Foreign Political Office of the Nazi Party, Special Delegate for the Spiritual and Ideological Training of the Nazi Party, Reich Minister for the Eastern Occupied Territories, organizer of *Einsatzstab Rosenberg.*
Indicted on: Counts 1, 2, 3, 4.
Verdict: Guilty on all counts.
Sentence: Death by hanging.

Hans Frank

Member of the Reichstag, Reich Minister Without Portfolio, Reich Commissar for the Coordination of Justice, President of the International Chamber of Law and Academy of German Law, Governor General of the Occupied Polish Territories.
Indicted on: Counts 1, 3. 4.
Verdict: Guilty on Counts 3, 4.
Sentence: Death by hanging.

Wilhelm Frick

Member of the Reichstag, Reich Minister of the Interior, General Plenipotentiary for the Administration of the Reich, head of the Central Office for the Incorporation of Sudetenland, Memel, Danzig,

the Eastern Incorporated Territories, Director of the Central Office for all Occupied Territories and Reich Protector for Bohemia and Moravia.
Indicted on: Counts 1, 2, 3, 4.
Verdict: Guilty on Counts 2, 3, 4.
Sentence: Death by hanging.

Julius Streicher

Member of the Reichstag, General in the SA, Gauleiter of Franconia, Editor-in-Chief of the anti-Semitic newspaper *Der Stuermer.*
Indicted on: Counts 1, 4.
Verdict: Guilty on Count 4.
Sentence: Death by hanging.

Walter Funk

Member of the Reichstag, Press Chief of the Reich Government and later Reich Minister of Economics, President of the German Reichsbank, Plenipotentiary for War Economy and member of the Council of Ministers for the Defence of the Reich.
Indicted on: Counts 1, 2, 3, 4.
Verdict: Guilty on Counts 2, 3, 4.
Sentence: Life imprisonment.

Hjalmar Schacht

Member of the Reichstag, Reich Minister of Economics, Plenipotentiary for War Economy, President of the Reichsbank, Reich Minister Without Portfolio.
Indicted on: Counts 1, 2.
Verdict: Acquitted.

Karl Doenitz

Commander-in-Chief of the U-boat Arm of the German Navy, advisor to Hitler, later *Grossadmiral* and Commander-in-Chief of the German Navy and Successor to Hitler as head of the German Government in the closing days of the war.
Indicted on: Counts 1, 2, 3.
Verdict: Guilty on Counts 2, 3.
Sentence: Ten years' imprisonment.

Erich Raeder

Commander-in-Chief of the Germany Navy and later *Admiralinspekteur.*
Indicted on: Counts 1, 2, 3.
Verdict: Guilty on all counts.
Sentence: Life imprisonment.

Baldur von Schirach

Member of the Reichstag, Reich Youth Leader on the Staff of the SA
Supreme Command, Leader of Youth of the German Reich, Reich
Governor and Gauleiter of Vienna.
Indicted on: Counts 1, 4.
Verdict: Guilty on Count 4.
Sentence: Twenty years' imprisonment.

Fritz Sauckel

Gauleiter and Reich Governor of Thuringia, member of the Reichstag,
later General Plenipotentiary for the Employment of Labor, General in
the SS.
Indicted on: Counts 1, 2, 3, 4.
Verdict: Guilty on Counts 3, 4.
Sentence: Death by hanging.

Alfred Jodl

Chief of Operations in the Supreme Command of the German Armed
Forces, Chief of Staff to Keitel with rank of Colonel-General.
Indicted on: Counts 1, 2, 3, 4.
Verdict: Guilty on all counts.
Sentence: Death by hanging.

Martin Bormann (in absentia)

Member of the Reichstag, Chief of Staff in the Office of the Fuehrer's
Deputy, successor to Hess as head of the Party Chancellery, Secretary of
the Fuehrer, organizer and head of the *Volksturm,* General in the SS.
Indicted on: Counts 1, 3, 4.
Verdict: Guilty on Counts 3, 4.
Sentence: Death by hanging.

Franz von Papen

Reich Chancellor, Vice-Chancellor under Hitler, Ambassador in Vienna and Ambassador in Turkey.
Indicted on: Counts 1, 2.
Verdict: Acquitted.

Arthur Seyss-Inquart

Austrian Minister of the Interior and of Security, Chancellor of Austria, later Reich Minister Without Portfolio, Deputy Governor-General of the Polish Occupied Territory and finally Reich Commissar for the Occupied Netherlands.
Indicted on: Counts 1, 2, 3, 4.
Verdict: Guilty on Counts 2, 3, 4.
Sentence: Death by hanging.

Albert Speer

Member of the Reichstag, Chief of the Organization Todt, Reich Minister for Armament and Munitions, General Plenipotentiary for Armaments, Chairman of the Armaments Council.
Indicted on: Counts 1, 2, 3. 4.
Verdict: Guilty on Counts 3, 4.
Sentence: Twenty years' imprisonment.

Constantin von Neurath

Predecessor to Ribbentrop as Reich Minister for Foreign Affairs, Reich Protector for Bohemia and Moravia, member of the Reichstag.
Indicted on: Counts 1, 2, 3, 4.
Verdict: Guilty on all counts.
Sentence: Fifteen years' imprisonment.

Hans Fritzsche

Head of official German news agency DNB and of Home Press Division of Reich Ministry of Propaganda, later Ministerial Director of the Reich Ministry of Propaganda as Chief of the Radio Division and Plenipotentiary for the Political Organization of the Greater German Radio.
Indicted on: Counts 1, 3, 4.
Verdict: Acquitted.

ORGANIZATIONS INDICTED AND THE FINAL JUDGMENT AGAINST EACH

Reich Cabinet
Indicted on: Counts 1, 2, 3, 4.
Verdict: Acquitted.

Leadership Corps of the Nazi Party
Indicted on: Counts 1, 2, 3, 4.
Verdict: Guilty (with exception of certain lower ranks of officials).

SS and SD
Indicted on: Counts 1, 2, 3, 4.
Verdict: Guilty (certain minor groups excepted).

Gestapo
Indicted on: Counts 1, 2, 3, 4.
Verdict: Guilty (certain minor groups excepted).

SA
Indicted on: Counts 1, 2, 3, 4.
Verdict: Acquitted.

General Staff and High Command of the German Armed Forces
Indicted on: Counts 1, 2, 3, 4.
Verdict: Acquitted.

NOTE. The Soviet Justice handed down a dissenting opinion calling for a death sentence for Hess and arguing against the acquittal of Schacht, Papen, Fritzsche, the Reich Cabinet and the General Staff and High Command.

Document Index

All quotations from transcript and documents used in this book generally follow the official translations as introduced into the trial record or Courthouse document files. On occasion I have changed wording slightly where the official translations—which were almost always made under severe pressure of time—left the meaning unclear. I have also frequently condensed quotations by omitting sentences which, for my purposes, were irrelevant or of lesser importance. In no instance, however, has editing altered the sense of any quotation.

Transcript page references refer to the original multigraphed transcript as produced from day to day during the course of the trial. The full, official translations of most of the documents indexed below will be found, identified by Document Number, in the 8-volume NAZI CONSPIRACY AND AGGRESSION published by the United States Government Printing Office. Documents quoted in Chapter XV on the Jews are identified by *Exhibit* Numbers rather than *Document* Numbers; a cross-index, available at Nuremberg, correlates these different numerical listings.—V. H. B.

Index